TALES OF A
CURLING HACK

TALES OF A
CURLING HACK

DOUG MAXWELL

whitecap

WHITECAP BOOKS

EDITED BY KATHY EVANS
PROOFREAD BY MARILYN BITTMAN
COVER ILLUSTRATION AND DESIGN BY FIVE SEVENTEEN
INTERIOR DESIGN BY DIANE YEE

PRINTED AND BOUND IN CANADA

LIBRARY AND ARCHIVES CANADA CATALOGUING IN PUBLICATION

MAXWELL, DOUGLAS
    TALES OF A CURLING HACK / DOUG MAXWELL.

ISBN 1-55285-801-4
ISBN 978-1-55285-801-1

    1. CURLING 2. CURLING—HISTORY. 3. CURLING—CANADA.
4. MAXWELL, DOUGLAS. I. TITLE.

GV845.M393 2006   796.964   C2006-900706-3

The publisher acknowledges the financial support of the Government of Canada through the Book Publishing Industry Development Program for our publishing activities. We also acknowledge the financial support of the Province of British Columbia through the Book Publishing Tax Credit.

CONTENTS

FOREWORD

THERE AREN'T MANY WRITERS WHO CAN LOOK AT THE PAST HALF-CENTURY of curling in Canada, from local events, to the Brier, World or Olympics, and weave details from all of them into compelling stories about the game. Doug Maxwell is such a writer. Thanks to his remarkable memory and insider's knowledge he shares many of those curling stories with us in this book.

Doug Maxwell is an institution in curling. He's been, most recently, a curling historian. He began as a broadcaster for radio and TV; then went on to be a writer, editor and publisher; a curling official, developer, promoter and innovator; an association administrator. Over 50 years ago, when he went to work as a CBC announcer in Montreal, one of his first assignments was to cover the inaugural Canadian Schoolboy Curling Championship in Quebec City, 1950.

Doug threw his first rock in 1949 at the Heather Curling Club in Montreal. His first Canadian championship was the Lakehead Brier in 1960, where he did CBC radio reports with another curling legend, Bill Good Sr. In Kitchener, 1962, he was the voice for the first live Brier telecast, the playoff between Ernie Richardson and Hector Gervais. It wasn't long before he became involved in a made-for-TV series called "CBC Championship Curling," first with Don Chevrier and later Don Duguid. About the same time he and three friends were instrumental in founding the 16-sheet Humber Highland Curling Club in Toronto.

A total curling enthusiast, Doug served for over 20 years as executive director of the world curling championship, then known as the Air Canada Silver Broom.

Jim Waite

Doug tells me we first met in 1968, when I played in, and he covered, the Kelowna Brier. I don't recall that moment, but I do remember the 1986 World Curling Championship in Toronto when I first became aware of Doug's memory mastery. At Roy Thomson Hall, before a packed-house opening party, Doug rattled off the names of over 60 competing players and coaches with perfect pronunciation and inflection...and did it all without notes. He brings to this book that same memory of behind-the-scenes-stories, little-known-but-interesting-facts, never-before-revealed Olympic details, and sparks them to life with humour and his personal touch. You will travel back through some of the great competitions, meet wildly interesting characters, captivating personalities, and I guarantee you will learn things about curling people and events you've never heard about, till now. The stories are all real. They are true and accurate accounts of the events and people that have shaped modern curling history.

I well recall when the Trillium Curling Camp was established in 1992. Doug, then executive director of the Ontario Curling Federation, was able to convince Hamilton officials to invest a part of their 1991 Brier profits in a junior curling camp, and Doug asked me to run the camp. It is still in operation.

Doug Maxwell is credited with inventing curling's Skins Game. He found an ally in Jim Thompson of TSN, and between the two of them, the Skins Game as we know it today, was born in 1986. He has other "firsts" to his name too. Want to find out about the origin of time clocks in curling? It's here, in this book. The Free Guard Zone rule?

Maxwell tells how the FGZ was established (as the Howard rule) and used for the first time in the Moncton 100, the $250,000 cashspiel that served as the kick-off to Moncton's centennial year. It is still curling's richest-ever bonspiel, organized by, you guessed it, Doug Maxwell.

In 1980, Doug became publisher and editor of the *Canadian Curling News*, Canada's oldest curling publication, which he recently sold. He continues to write a column for the *Curling News*, and also pens a column for the *Scottish Curler*. Doug is the author of *Canada Curls*, the only book that covers the history of curling all across the country. It recently passed the "bestseller" mark of 10,000 copies sold.

Tales of a Curling Hack is at times a rollicking account of some of the humorous things that have happened at events where Doug was present and at other times provides details that will give you insight into the history of the game.

JIM WAITE
Canada's National Olympic Men's Coach

PREFACE

BEING, ON OCCASION, A MODEST SORT OF CHAP, I NEVER THOUGHT MUCH about my place in the world of curling. Oh, I knew that my commentator's countenance on television, first with the CBC's "Cross Canada Curling," Brier telecasts, and a variety of curling shows in the sixties and seventies, and later with TSN (The Sports Network), gave me some sort of recognition. But I didn't think it was anything other than the kind of notoriety that goes with boob tube familiarity. I knew, too, that my 18-year stint as executive director of the Air Canada Silver Broom World Curling Championship had given me a certain profile among some of the elite players of the game, but I dismissed that as more face recognition than peer respect. After all, they were the stars of the show, and I was mainly the plumber, the promoter, the public presence of the event.

Then, following the publication of my 2002 book *Canada Curls: The Illustrated History of Curling in Canada*, I began to get letters asking questions or suggesting theories that the correspondents felt I could address. People seemed to think I might have a secret source of curling information, and, on the odd occasion, I realized maybe they were right. I had to admit that, yes, I might be the only one still alive who had some arcane detail or piece of curling trivia stuck in a recess of my mind.

I read in Bill Bryson's fascinating book *A Short History of Nearly Everything* that when the British astronomer Sir Arthur Eddington was asked "Is it true you are one of only three people in the world who actually understands Einstein's Theory of Relativity?" the famous Brit was silent for a minute and then replied, "I'm trying to think who the other two might be."

Once or twice, over the past few years, I have felt like Sir Arthur E.—not about Einstein's theory, of course—but perhaps, maybe, curling? Without being too immodest, I think I bring a variety of credentials to the challenge of this book. At one time or another, I have been a broadcaster, reporter, official, umpire, statistician, organizer, promoter, innovator, sponsor and, most recently, a historian of the game. So occasionally, just like Eddington, I've tried to think who the other know-it-alls might be. And then, as I came up with their names, I recruited them to add some of their comments to mine. The result, I hope, will be fun for all of us.

About the title of this tome, namely, *Tales of a Curling Hack*—until I looked it up in the Canadian Oxford Dictionary, I didn't know there were such a variety of definitions for "hack." There are, count 'em, three major definitions, with seven variations.

There's the hack that is a cough, and the hack that is a "chopping cut." Perhaps you're thinking of a hack that is the act, by an editor, of cutting short a written item. Don't forget the hack meaning the action of the blankety-blank who invades your email, steals your identity and shuts down your computer. There's more, says the dictionary. How about "hack" as the informal name for a cab driver, or a horse, or perhaps the rack that holds fodder for cattle?

And there is, says the dictionary, finally getting around to our topic of interest, the hack that is used to steady the foot when delivering a stone in curling. But the definition that best touches the vicinity inhabited by this book is the one that says a hack is "a writer of mediocre literary or journalistic work."

While there are a number of factual bits in the following pages—perhaps ones you never knew about before—there are also some bits of drollery that I hope will bring a contemplative chuckle.

The fact that I served as executive director of the Air Canada Silver Broom from its inception in 1968 to Air Canada's departure as sponsor in 1985, and then continued as a partner in Hexagon Curling International, followed by a stint as consultant to several world championship host cities, gives me an insider's vantage point from which to view the growth of the game, in Canada and around the world. While the Silver Broom looms large in my memory, there were many years prior to the Broom when I was involved in the game.

In 1949 I had just arrived in Montreal as a CBC staff announcer, and promptly joined the Heather Curling Club. It was probably that association that prompted the CBC to send me to Quebec City the following spring to cover the inaugural Canadian School Curling Championship. It was there I first met the legendary three-time Brier winner, Ken Watson of Winnipeg, who was deeply involved in the development of school curling and who proved to be a wonderful friend to a rookie reporter.

When I returned to Toronto in the fifties, I began a three-a-week radio show centred on curling, the first of its kind, so I was told, in Canada. The jump from radio's "Curling with Doug Maxwell" (how's that for an inspired program title?) to some of the first televised coverage of the sport was easy and swift. Sometime in the fifties, I recall waiting for the ice to freeze at the old Tam O'Shanter Curling Club in suburban Toronto so we could continue to film some of the earliest televised curling. "Waiting for the ice to freeze," you say? "Why, wasn't it frozen before you started filming?" Well, yes, it was. But the ceiling above the ice was fairly low, and in the early days of television, we were using heavy klieg lights that were brutally hot and, well, the ice got pretty soft and mushy. So we'd stop the game, turn off the lights, wait for the ice to freeze again, turn on the lights, and get another two or three ends of play in before we'd be in the soup again.

I know there are fans today who still insist that television lights exert a warming influence on the ice, but trust me— 'tain't so. Today's television lights produce "cool" light, and if there's anything that causes the ice to sweat these days, it is more likely to be the fans in the stands.

By 1960 I was tagged by CBC Radio to head to Thunder Bay (except it was called Fort William then) to work with Bill Good, the famed "Breathless" Bill, on the daily coverage of the Lakehead Brier.

The Richardson family team from Regina had burst onto the Brier scene the previous winter in Quebec City and had surprised most observers by winning the '59 Macdonald Brier Canadian Championship. It was the last time the Richardsons would surprise anyone with their prowess or charisma. By 1960 they were on the champions' pedestal and over the next four years would become the most famous names in all of curling, then or now. If you were going to be a curling journalist or broadcaster, how much luckier could you be than to be around when the Richardsons were in their prime? But I digress.

To this radio and television brew, mix in a later 20-year stint of happy times as publisher and editor of the *Canadian Curling News* (the country's first national curling publication started in 1957 by Ted Thonger of Calgary) and I guess you could say I've enjoyed an insider's seat to much of the growth of the game over the past half century. (In the interest of accuracy, I should add that after I sold the CCN a few years ago, it now operates as The Curling News, under the guidance of George Karrys.) Throw in my role in organizing the first two Canadian Mixed Curling Championships (after running the Toronto Mixed Bonspiel for a number of years), and the Tournament of Champions at Maple Leaf Gardens, plus coverage of some of the country's other big title-shoots and, well, you get the idea.

Let's face it: Curling is not a major sport on the world scene. When any nation, including Canada, wins a world curling championship, or Olympic curling title, traffic, in even the most rabid of curling centres, is not stopped by joyous fans spilling out onto the streets. It may be difficult for curlers to accept, but there are many people who do not see curling as a sport that sets the synapses jangling. There are many precincts where a description of the sport elicits only a yawn. Or a giggle. But if you know anything about the game, you probably know that curlers, and curling fans, can be just as loyal to their game as any soccer, hockey or jai alai buff. And they are quite willing—if you let them—to tell of the latest bit of fun from their idiosyncratic game.

To be a curling reporter I couldn't have picked a better time than an era whose boundaries include Ken Watson, Matt Baldwin, Ernie Richardson, Joyce McKee, Chuck Hay and teams of that time at one edge; and Brad Gushue, Randy Ferbey, Sandra Schmirler, Russ Howard, Colleen Jones, Ed Werenich and Kevin Martin at the other edge. And that includes such other giants in between as Hec Gervais, Ron Northcott, Vera Pezer, Don Duguid, Pat Ryan, Linda Moore, Ed Lukowich, Rick Folk and Shannon Kleibrink. And those are just a few of the Canadian names!

If you've read this far, I hope you'll agree to continue as I try to explain what it is that has made curling so special—and so much fun—not only for me but also for thousands upon thousands of others.

ACKNOWLEDGMENTS

BECAUSE THE REMINISCENCES THAT SPAWNED THIS BOOK COME FROM my sometimes errant memory, I asked a few knowledgeable friends to check my facts and recollections and let me know if I had strayed. In that regard, I particularly want to express my gratitude to (alphabetically) **Laurie Artiss, Hal Cameron, the Earl of Elgin, Chuck Hay, Tony Schoen, Kay Sugahara, Ray Turnbull**, and **Keith Wendorf.**

There are three chapters provided by two fellow scribes and a coordinator friend. The scribes appeared on the Brier scene about the same time I did, and I'm happy to give them special kudos. **Larry Wood** contributed "Curling Beats Fun" (Chapter 12) and helped with some of the details about the 1988 Olympics in Calgary for Chapter 31. **Bob Picken** recounts two items from his memory bank: the Uniroyal World Junior Championships in "The Backyard Approach," (Chapter 33), plus a sequel to the famous incident described in Chapter 16, "LaBonte's Boot." **Robin Wilson**, the most experienced and co-operative curling event coordinator in the world, sent along Chapter 8, entitled, appropriately enough, "Dream Job."

There are others to thank. **Jack Matheson**, famed former sports editor of the late, lamented *Winnipeg Tribune*, cast his eye over much of the early manuscript and made suggestions that were unerringly helpful. I am indebted also to **Jim Waite**, Canada's outstanding national Olympic coach and team leader. Not only did he contribute some fancy words in the foreword—for which I am exceedingly grateful—but, whenever asked, also helped with inside information on a wide array of curling matters. **Pat B. Reid** was an outstanding curler when I first met her and from there moved effortlessly and impressively to become a top coach and organizer. I'm happy to nominate her as one of the best-ever Canadian Curling Association presidents (1996–97), and when she became curling's voice as Canada's first Olympic "A" director, she helped smooth the rough edges of my Olympic cynicism.

There was a whole range of other friends who helped in a variety of ways. They are: **Laura Argue, Detlev Bandi, Gerald (Soupy) Campbell, Don Canning, Reg Caughie (a.k.a. Brier Bear), John Chaput, Bob Cowan, Gordon Craig, Scoop Fredstrom, Bud Gerth, Don Goodwin, Warren Hansen, Neil Houston, Russ Howard, Al Hutchinson, Danny Lamoureux, Gerry Peckham, June Perry, Alex Roberts, Håkan Sundstrom** and **Jim Ursel**.

I should also add a few words of appreciation for my wife, **Anne,** who read each chapter (in various drafts) and expressed herself unequivocally on each one. While she did not have veto power (hah!), her suggestions inevitably were sound, and I bowed to her observations more often than not. The other woman in my life (surrounding this book) was Kathy Evans, the same **Kathy Evans** who edited my earlier Whitecap book, *Canada Curls,* and whose knowledge and unfailing good humour saved me on the many occasions when she patiently pointed out errors of syntax or other writing booboos.

And, of course, if you think you have found an error or two in the book, I'll take the blame; just don't expect a subsequent book to correct those mistakes. If there are screw-ups, you'll just have to live with them.

Chapter One

PIERRE, VINCE AND PINEROLO

WHEN YOU'RE A PRINT MEDIA GUY/PERSON/CHAP, YOU CAN GET A CERTAIN sense of satisfaction from the printed word that stares back at you. The words can be easily filed, if you want to look at them some time later, in your dotage. It's not the same with radio or TV. Oh, I suppose you could develop a collection of audio or videotapes, but that's easier said than done. If you're working close to home, it's easy to file 'em away each day. But if you're half a world away from home, and you only have a certain number of cassettes with your tape recorder, sometimes you simply record over an old tape, so the subsequent filing is lost. And getting a videotape or a DVD of a certain occasion can entail battling a maze of red tape, so in most cases you forget it. All of this explains why my curling library is heavy on print, but light on recordings.

There's another factor that occasionally gets involved—the phantom interview. For example, the interview I recorded for use the day President John F. Kennedy was assassinated never did make it to air, and today I can't remember who I talked to, what we talked about or what happened to the tape.

Sometimes the interview you would like to do is simply impossible to arrange. Take the imaginary sound bite I dreamt of using at the 2006 Olympic Winter Games, covering the curling action in Pinerolo, some 35 kilometres outside Torino. It's a short interview that goes something like this.

Canada's bronze medal team from Calgary. Back row: national Olympic coach Elaine Dagg-Jackson and coach Daryl Nixon. Front row: (l–r) Sandra Jenkins, Christine Keshen, Glenys Bakker, Amy Nixon and Shannon Kleibrink. Photo courtesy of Jim Waite

ME: [*Here is my service message to the studio back home, with the interview intro.*] What follows is a chat with two of the giants from the world of sport. On my left here in the Elysian Fields is Baron Pierre de Coubertin, founder of the Modern Olympics and, on my right, coach Vince Lombardi of the Green Bay Packers. We'll be chatting about curling and the Winter Games. It comes your way in 5–4–3–2–(pause).

ME: First of all, gentlemen, thank you for sparing time from a very busy schedule to chat today. Baron, now that curling is an official medal sport at the Winter Olympics, what would you say to those curlers who dream of making it to the podium in Pinerolo?

PIERRE DE COUBERTIN: The most important thing in the Olympic Games is not to win but to take part, just as the most important thing in life is not the triumph but the struggle. The essential thing is not to have conquered but to have fought well. I first enunciated that thought about a hundred years ago, and I believe it is known today as the Olympic Creed.
ME: In essence then, if I may paraphrase, winning isn't everything.
P DE C: Oui, certainement ... exactly.
ME: Mr. Lombardi, your comments?
VINCE LOMBARDI: That may have been okay for the first Winter Games in 1928, but not in today's world. Me? I say winning isn't everything; it's the *only* thing.
ME: Thank you Baron Pierre de Coubertin and coach Vince Lombardi.

It wasn't until 2006 that Canadian curling moved to the Lombardi side of the discussion. Before that, de Courbertin's edict was the inferred, if not the preferred, message. After Canada experienced a disappointing showing in 2002, in Salt Lake City (17 medals), the Canadian Olympic Committee turned tough. In essence, they said they weren't going to clutter up the Canadian Winter Games contingent with athletes who didn't stand a reasonable chance of a strong— meaning a medal or top ten—showing. That philosophy found expression in a program with a fancy name: Own the Podium (OTP), aimed primarily at producing 25 medals in 2006 and an unheard-of target of 35 medals in the 2010 Winter Games in Vancouver/Whistler.

In curling, the Canadian Curling Association had already introduced, with little fanfare, its own OTP-complementary programs, La Releve Elite and La Releve Core. La Releve? Rough translation: the next generation, the lads and lasses (mostly under age 30) on whom the CCA would lavish attention, coaching and dollars. La Releve Elite targets the top-rated young curlers; La Releve Core targets the up-and-comers. Like the OTP effort, the La Releve target is gold in 2010. The fact that the program produced gold and bronze in 2006 was considered a wonderful bonus. In one sense, the curling gold medal for Brad Gushue's team, and the bronze for Shannon Kleibrink's, proved that both Lombardi and de Coubertin were right.

The golden huzzahs for twenty-somethings Jamie Korab, Mike Adam, Mark Nichols, Brad Gushue from Newfoundland and Labrador, and late addition Russ Howard from Moncton, New Brunswick (who celebrated his fiftieth birthday in Pinerolo), would undoubtedly have caused Lombardi to say "I told you so." But the longtime efforts of Shannon Kleibrink would surely have moved de Coubertin to salute the struggle of the Calgary shotmaker.

Canada had already won gold with its women curlers in 1988, when Linda Moore's foursome won the women's demonstration event in Calgary. Ten years later, at the 1998 Winter Olympics in Nagano, Japan, after curling had been named an official medal sport, Sandra Schmirler, with Marcia Gudereit, Joan McCusker, Jan Betker and Atina Ford, grabbed gold in Karuizawa, the Nagano curling site. And when the country cheered Sandra in '98, they also recalled that, at the 1997 Olympic Trials, it was Kleibrink who looked to have the trip to Nagano in her pocket, until a Schmirler shot of Olympian proportions sent Shannon to the sidelines. Most curlers would have cried a little and then shelved their dreams, but not Kleibrink. She continued her quest for glory and with a new team of Christine Keshen, Glenys Bakker, Amy Nixon and Sandra Jenkins fought her way through the 2005 Canadian Olympic Trials. Then the Calgary crew battled their way to a bronze

There were two medal ceremonies at the 2006 Winter Olympics. In the Pinerolo Palaghiaccio curling hall following the gold medal game, the three medal-winning teams received floral tributes. Here the Canadian gold medallists show off their flowers. From left to right: Brad Gushue, Mark Nichols, Russ Howard, Jamie Korab, Mike Adam. Photo courtesy of Jim Waite

medal in Pinerolo. De Coubertin would have been both proud and moved by that effort. The struggle that led to triumph was indeed worth the effort.

The Kleibrink squad would be the first to salute their Torino teammates from Newfoundland and Labrador as curling's headline-grabbing story of 2006. In 2001, Brad Gushue, Mark Nichols, Mike Adam and Brent Hamilton had garnered men's gold at the world junior curling championships. But they dreamed of more. They confided in their St. John's curling club manager, Reg Caughie, and sports psychologist Bas Kavanagh, who had worked with them from their junior days, that they had set themselves a more formidable target: a Brier title, a world crown and an Olympic medal. By 2003 Gushue was at the Brier, where he finished with a respectable 6–5 record. He recorded the same 6–5 mark in 2005, and sandwiched those years with a 2004 appearance, where he moved to an 8–4 mark. He was still short of his Brier target, but then he qualified for the 2005 Halifax Olympic Trials by winning the 2004 Canada Cup East series.

In prepping for the trials, the Gushue quartet realized they needed something extra if they were to earn the Torino trip. Although they had been early recruits to La Releve, working with many of the CCA's top coaches, they sensed the need for some added heft, if they were to get past the favoured teams of Randy Ferbey, Kevin Martin, Jeff Stoughton and Glenn Howard. That concern prompted the team, through coach Toby MacDonald, to contact the veteran Russ Howard in Moncton. Gushue had warmed to Howard at the 2003 Brier when the New Brunswick skip had encouraged him, following a tough loss, to keep working, telling him his day would come. When asked if he would consider signing on as fifth man for the Gushue hopefuls, Howard, with 13 Brier appearances (and more wins than any other Brier skip in history), with two Canadian and world titles, said he'd be honoured. He only hoped he might be able make a contribution.

To make room for Howard, second Mike Adam volunteered to switch roles with the veteran. He would become fifth man, and Russ could settle into Mike's second stone position, call the strategy in the rings, and leave Gushue to concentrate on throwing final stones. A measure of how well the switch worked could be seen in the team's 2005 cashspiel winnings. BR (Before Russ) the team earned a little under $3,000 in four events. AR (After Russ) they won close to $11,000 in three events. Then, at the Olympic Trials in Halifax, riding a crest of nine victories (with only two losses), the new combination finished atop the preliminary standings, and then triumphed over the favourites in the playoffs.

Pinerolo was another matter, however. The combination of fast ice, with little or no curl to it, and new stones that had not yet been fully "seasoned," created problems for all 10 teams entered. Defending Olympic champion Pål Trulsen of Norway could only manage a 5–4 won-lost mark. Three-time world winner Peja Lindholm of Sweden finished in a humiliating tie for eighth place, with a 3–6 record. The Howard–Gushue combo wound up with a 6–3 mark, tied for second place with the USA (Pete Fenson) and Great Britain (David Murdoch), but were awarded second rank in the standings, having beaten both of them in their earlier games. Finland's Markku Uusipaavalniemi (or U-15 as a BBC commentator tagged him) finished in first place at 7–2. That established the playoff pairings as Finland vs Great Britain, and Canada vs USA.

The change that followed the preliminary games rescued the Pinerolo party. In the playoffs, each team, rather than using assigned stones, could choose the granites it wished to use, and it was here that the veteran Howard advanced the Gushue cause.

The polite way of putting it is that Russ's expertise in identifying rock characteristics is extensive and legendary. The impolite way? There are those who insist that any game that Howard has lost over the years was (according to Russ) primarily due to stones that would grind, glide or galumph in ways never intended. The more accurate way of describing Russ and curling rocks, is that he is the most precise, most persnickety of players when it comes to identifying granite characteristics. So when it came time to select the Canadian stones for the playoffs, Russ Howard's opinions, along with Mike Adam's notes, were paramount when added to the thoughts of the rest of the team.

By this time, icemakers Leif Öhman (Sweden) and Teo Frans (Canada) had "dished" the ice (scraped it so it was slightly lower down the centre than along the sides) so there was a bit more curl to it than during the preliminary games.

Finally, with the combination of the best stones available and ice with more swing to it, spectators were treated to curling, as opposed to the "straight-ing" that had been featured in the early games.

In the semifinal games, Canada downed the United States 11–5, while Finland beat Great Britain 4–3. That meant the Gushue-Howard combination would challenge for gold against U-15 and his fellow Finns. It would be David and Goliath redux, except it was hard to say who was who. Physically, the 39-year-old Markku Uusipaavalniemi was a 6' 6" Goliath, but competitively he was a David, repping a country with fewer total curlers than some Canadian clubs have. And while Howard had the Goliath experience, Gushue was still a young David in the world of international curling.

By this time, Kleibrink's team had won a bronze medal and was on hand to cheer on the youthful rock stars from The Rock. What had been expected to be a tight, taut struggle turned into a rout. After each side scored a deuce in the opening two ends, Canada stole a single in the third end and again in the fourth. What many considered the turning point came in the fifth end, when Finland looked to score a deuce that would tie the game at the halfway mark. But a measure to determine who had second shot went in favour of Canada; Finland counted only a single point, and instead of a tie game, Canada held a 4–3 lead. The sixth end saw a series of small Finnish mistakes, and by the time Gushue came to deliver his final stone of the end, Canada had six stones counting. With a chance for a score of seven, and the gold medal in his grasp, the youthful Canadian, adrenalin pumping, eased his final stone through the rings! Still, that six count made the score 10–3, and had it not been for the regulation that required the teams to play a minimum of eight ends, the Finns would have shaken hands and conceded at that point. As it was they played the next two ends to finish with a 10–4 final verdict that gave Canada its first-ever official Olympic men's gold in curling, a formidable feat that had eluded the best curlers in Canada's past.

Winning a men's gold in 2006 was quite different from winning gold in 1932. That long-ago event in Lake Placid was only the second year of the modern Winter Olympics. The Great Depression was still gripping the world, and more men were jumping off high buildings than were jumping forward to pay their own way to Lake Placid. The curlers could throw practice stones only in the times

When Newfoundland and Labrador school children sent encouraging posters and artwork to Pinerolo, Mark Nichols and the rest of the Canadian team posted them on the walls of their dressing room and found inspiration in them. Photo courtesy of Jim Waite

when Norway's glamorous Sonja Henie wasn't practising her figure skating on the outdoor ice. Canada's 1932 curling gold medal, won by a Winnipeg team skipped by William Burns, is as far removed from the Howard–Gushue gold of 2006 as today's curling is removed from its early days.

There was one other factor at work for the Gushues: superstition. Before the start of the competition, before any fan could even suggest that Canada should emulate the 2002 hockey Olympians in Salt Lake City and bury a loonie in the centre of the house, that idea was firmly vetoed by officials. Nothing was said, however, about putting a newly minted loonie (with the Olympic rings on it) somewhere where it could exert an influence. So, unbeknownst to any of the curlers, an Olympic rings loonie was pressed into the ice at the split between the foam bumpers along the side of sheet B, at the hog line (for the semis), and similarly at the hog line of sheet C for the final. When the dollar coins were pulled out after those games, one was given to Mark Nichols, whose playoff shooting was spectacular (97 percent in the final game). The other coin went to Gushue. Subsequently, on their return to Canada, I made sure that five more loonies were handed out to the rest of the team, plus to coach Toby MacDonald and national Olympic coach Jim Waite.

It is impossible to overestimate the impact of the Pinerolo gold medal victory by the Newfoundland and Labrador squad. Sure, it was Canada's first official men's Olympic gold medal in curling. Yes, it shoved four young shooters (and a grizzled veteran) into a nation-wide and blinding spotlight of success. Of course you choked back a tear when the first thing Gushue did after the final game was to grab a cell phone and call his mother at home, where she was undergoing cancer treatment. But the golden success of the Canadian team was, and is, much more than that.

It's a fact that Newfoundland/Labrador is not exactly Canada's hotbed of curling. In fact, there are only 18 curling clubs in the entire province, fewer than the number of clubs in Winnipeg, or in Toronto. The province has won only one Brier (Jack MacDuff in 1976), so the prospect of an Olympic title was like an impossible dream. Schools across the province sent hundreds of hand-drawn posters of encouragement to Italy, where they were pasted on the walls of the team dressing room. Emails by the thousand rained on the team. The premier, Danny Williams, declared a half-day holiday for every school in the province so that students could watch the final against Finland. Most businesses in St. John's declared their own siesta so they could watch the action. The bars along George Street were packed. And when the team arrived home a couple of days later, at 1:30 in the morning, gold medals looped around their necks, there were over 2,000 fans jammed into every available inch of the St. John's airport, from whence they headed downtown to the St. John's Curling Club, where the party was in full swing.

The golden team gathered in the St. John's council chambers to get their first glimpse of the street signs bearing their names. Photo courtesy of Jim Waite

To be sure, Newfoundlanders have a deep and powerful feeling for their gale-lashed, fisheries-challenged province, and that pride exploded when the golden boys returned home. As former federal finance minister, John Crosby, from St. John's, once said; "You can always tell who the Newfoundlanders are in Heaven. They're the ones who want to go home."

Shortly after the team's return, the mayor and city council agreed to name a new St. John's subdivision road "Gold Medal Drive" and to christen six streets leading into it with the names of the five team members and coach Toby MacDonald.

In so doing, the city was only creating a modern adaptation of a practice from the ancient Olympics, where a new gate in the city walls would be opened to honour their homecoming Olympic heroes.

But wait, there was more. The icing on the Torino cake came a couple of weeks after the close of the Winter Olympics. Canada sent a large contingent of athletes to the Paralympic Winter Games, including a team of curlers skipped by Chris Daw of London, Ontario. Wheelchair curling was relatively new, having begun in 2002, and

Before the arrival of gold, the team gathered for an identifying photo, complete with Olympic rings and Torino identification. From left to right are: National Olympic Coach Jim Waite, Brad Gushue, Mark Nichols, Russ Howard, Jamie Korab, Mike Adam and coach Toby MacDonald. Photo courtesy of Jim Waite

Daw, Canada's top shooter in the event, had always finished behind Scotland in international play. 2006 marked the first time wheelchair curling had entered the Paralympics, and as in previous years, the final game, this time a gold medal game in the Pinerolo Palaghiaccio, was between Canada's Daw and Scotland's Frank Duffy, representing Great Britain. On this occasion, Daw had his regular lead, Karen Blachford of London, and they were joined by three west coast curlers: third Gerry Austgarden of Westbank, British Columbia, second Gary Cormack (Surrey, BC) and alternate Sonja Gaudet of North Vancouver. Coach Joe Rea looked on as the Canadians won the Paralympic gold medal with a 7–4 victory over Duffy's Great Britain foursome.

Torino 2006 provided a glorious curling summary. Three teams to Pinerolo: three medals (two gold, one bronze). Throw in the bronze and silver medals that Canada claimed at the 2006 World Curling Championships—thank you Kelly Scott and teammates in Grande Prairie, Alberta; merci Jean-Michel Ménard et votre équipe in Lowell, Massachusetts— and all of Canada could bask in the glory of its elite curlers from coast to coast.

Chapter Two

AH SCOTLAND.
AND CURLING. AND GOLF.
AND WHISKY.

A FEW YEARS AGO, AT CHRISTMAS, I RECEIVED A BOOK ENTITLED *How the Scots Invented the Modern World* by historian Arthur Herman and subtitled *The True Story of How Western Europe's Poorest Nation Created Our World & Everything in It*. Herman describes in great detail the many Scots who have enriched the world with their discoveries, philosophies, education, literature and political thought. It's a wonderful book, well researched, persuasively written and full of insight into the many gifts Scotland has bestowed upon the world.

But the book may have a failing—for nowhere does it mention curling. Perhaps Mr. Herman was unaware that Scotland is the birthplace of the game? Could it be that Mr. Herman didn't know that the Royal Caledonian Curling Club is universally regarded as "the Mother Club of Curling"? And don't give me that blather about the game having been invented somewhere else, simply because Bruegel painted a couple of scenes ("Hunters in the Snow" and "Winter Landscape") that included something that might be a curling look-alike. That's pretty flimsy evidence. I put the omission down to the fact that Mr. Herman is an American, and curling in the United States has yet to find the same kind of resonance it has in Canada. So maybe I shouldn't be too hard on him just because he doesn't rank curling up there with James Watt's steam engine, or Adam Smith's *Wealth of Nations*. But it was Scots who invented the game, and it was Scotsmen who brought it to this continent over two hundred years ago.

Okay, you say, tell us about some of the famous Scots in Canadian curling. Hmmm. That's a hard one, and I think I know why. Perhaps it's because in Canada we do not specify Scots, or Irish, English, Ukrainian or Cantonese names, when it comes to curling; we call all curlers, simply, Canadian.

It seems that wherever Scots settled in Canada, they introduced curling to their newly adopted country. Today, you could open up the phone book (for any city, town or village) and pick out all the McHaggises or MacDiddlys or other readily identifiable Caledonian names, and you would be reasonably certain there would be a Scottish curler somewhere in the listing. But you could add all the Ukrainian, Asian, Swiss, Scandinavian and many other names and you'd be pretty sure there would be a curler in there too.

I found out long ago that names can be misleading anyway. I recall asking about the background identity of one name from the first Air Canada Silver Broom in 1968. The name was "Joe LeVine." Joe was president of the United States Curling Association that year, and he was also listed as the fifth man on Bud Somerville's USA team. As director of the event I had to make sure each curler was a national of the country involved, and the name LeVine looked somewhat French to me. So I asked Joe about his family background, mentioning that I assumed he was of French descent.

"No," he said, "my family came from Sweden," and then he proceeded to tell how his Scandinavian ancestry had produced a French-looking name.

He told me his family name was originally Pedersen, and his grandfather had come to America with his good friend Andersen. They arrived, of course, in New York, and settled there. But later they decided to move west to Minnesota, where there were lots of other Swedes, most of them with similar names. Before heading West, they decided it might be a good idea to change their names so they wouldn't be lost in the mob of other Andersens or Pedersens. But what names should they pick? They decided to leave the decision to the New York telephone directory. And when they opened up the phone book, it was at the "Ls" and the whole page seemed to feature the name Levine. He told how his forebear liked the name but decided to add a French touch, "so that's how I came to be Joe LeVine!"

There is one curling Scot whom I think deserves special mention: Chuck Hay of Perth, Scotland. When I first became involved in international curling, before the Silver Broom, I was fortunate to meet Chuck. Over the years, I came to appreciate the many influences he had on the game, many of them unheralded, all of them vital, insightful and useful. When it came time to write this book, I leaned on Chuck for his memory and opinions. He never let me down.

Actually, I had met Chuck at the Scotch Cup series of 1962. A couple of years later, in the middle sixties, I had been recruited by some enthusiastic Toronto Rotarians to organize a cashspiel in Maple Leaf Gardens. The prize money was about $10,000, a not inconsiderable sum for a money bonspiel in those bygone days. Among the teams I recruited was a foursome of Scots, skipped by Chuck. I recall talking to some touring Scots at that time, including Bill Robertson-Aikman, then president of the Royal Caledonian Curling Club. When I outlined the details of the Tournament of Champions at the famed Gardens, Bill said it would not be possible for Chuck to compete, since prize money was involved, and, in particular, money of that magnitude was far too much. "In that case," said I, "if Chuck were to qualify for the money, we'd protect his 'amateur' status by giving him a silver cigarette case or something similar." As I recall, Robertson-Aikman was neither persuaded nor amused. The RCCC at that time held to the Victorian belief that curling was a gentleman's game, and prizes of value were frowned upon.

When I called Chuck in Scotland to tell him of the situation, he quickly replied that he—not the RCCC—would make the decision about competing, and if he made it to the prize table, he—not the RCCC—would decide whether he would accept the prize. He did enter the 'spiel, but missed the prize table, so that decision never had to be made.

A couple of years later, in 1968, Chuck was the reigning Scottish and Scotch Cup champion and came to Pointe Claire, Quebec, for the inaugural Air Canada

Two of the giants of international curling, who played each other in the Scotch Cup of 1963, went on to greater things. Chuck Hay (l) became Scotland's first world champion in 1967, while Sweden's Sven Eklund (r) became president of the International Curling Federation in 1979. Photo courtesy of Chuck Hay

Silver Broom, with his team of John Bryden, Alan Glen and David Howie. There he joined such other international stars as Ron Northcott of Canada and Bud Somerville of the United States. At the end of the week's preliminary play, Chuck was in first place, undefeated. In the three-team playoff series, he earned the bye to the final, leaving

Ron and Bud to battle it out in the semifinal. Northcott won that encounter and then, in the final, handed Chuck his first and only loss.

An aside here: in later years, whenever an unbeaten Canadian team happened to lose in the final, and a Canadian fan lamented on the unfairness of it all, I used to say "Where were you when the shoe was on the other foot, when the undefeated Scots lost to Canada in 1968? I didn't hear you bemoaning their fate on that occasion."

In later years, when Chuck ascended to the president's office of the RCCC, he proved to be a tower of strength, not only to the Royal Club, but also to the International Curling Federation.

He always had the best interests of curling at heart. I recall once when I was a member of the Toronto Curling Association executive, we decided to encourage junior curling by holding a youth bonspiel during the Christmas holidays. What kind of prize should we offer? Austin Palmer, who chaired the 'spiel, suggested an all-expense-paid trip to Scotland, and since I had some contacts there, would I set it up?

When I got a damp, unenthusiastic reply to my initial enquiry ("I'm not sure we could arrange it," said the RCCC secretariat), I decided to bypass officialdom and called Chuck. If we sent the team to Scotland and paid their expenses, I asked, could he arrange some games, some sightseeing, some parties for the visitors? "Send 'em over" was the enthusiastic reply, "we'll be glad to look after them." So we did, and Chuck did.

A few years later, I needed his help again. The East York Curling Club in Toronto was attempting to turn their junior bonspiel into an international event. Again Hay assisted, and eventually that competition became the Uniroyal World Junior Championship. That story is told in greater detail in Chapter 33.

Over the years, I've been given the opportunity to travel to Scotland many times, and I must say that each time is as wonderful as the one before. "How was your trip?" was the usual query when I returned, and I soon discovered a reply that has stood the test of time. "How was my trip, you ask?" and then I pause for just a moment before offering my stock answer, "The hospitality was relentless!"

To return to the opening paragraphs of this chapter—I doubt that I would have penned this tale were it not for the efforts of a host of unknown Scots who emigrated to a new land in the 1800s, and who brought with them this "honest, sensible game."

Do I need to continue this paean to Scotland and deliver encomiums to the Scots' gift of golf? Or whisky?

Well, perhaps I could add one note about the whisky.

The year was 1962, and I was sent by CBC Radio to Scotland to send back dispatches on the fourth Scotch Cup series that had grown from a two-country event (Canada and Scotland in 1959) to four countries, by adding the United States and Sweden. I had never travelled abroad before, but I soon discovered the "relentless hospitality," which always seemed to include the nectar of the Highlands. After all, it was the Scotch Whisky Association that sponsored the event, so it is little wonder that there was a fair amount of product available during the series. I was not then (nor am now) a professional quaffer, no matter what you may have heard. An amateur, yes, but back then I had little knowledge of, or inclination to, Scotch whisky. But since that was the approved tipple of the tour, I dutifully became acquainted with it. Everywhere we went—local farms, curling clubs, hotels—we were offered a wee dram. It would have been impolite, I'm sure you would agree, to decline the offer.

At the final banquet I was quietly surveying the scene with a few of my media brethren when a waitress approached our table and asked the usual question—did we wish something to drink before dinner? I remember that there was more than the usual bedlam in the dining hall, and I had to ask her again what she wanted. She repeated the query, "Something to drink before dinner?" in a much louder voice. And I thought I should respond, over the din, with an equally loud reply. Because I had already, over the past week, imbibed a not inconsiderable number of different Scotch whiskies, and because I now had a greater choice open to me, I thought I might revert to my Canadian nature and so loudly proclaimed my request, at which point the entire hall suddenly turned silent. My booming request, "I'd like a rye and ginger please," echoed throughout the room, and I swear the head of every one of the five hundred-or-so Scots present swivelled in my direction. I quickly realized how badly I had erred and tried to hide behind the nearest potted palm!

I still love to visit Scotland, and I think my Scots friends (or most of them) are happy to see me arrive. And yes, I still appreciate a dram, either blended or single malt—although there are some occasions when I ask for a rye.

Chapter Three

THE SCOTCH CUP YEARS

TECHNICALLY, THE WORLD CURLING CHAMPIONSHIPS DIDN'T BEGIN until 1968 (for men) and 1979 (for women). What about the Scotch Cup, you ask? Don't the Scotch Cup years (1959–1967) count for anything?

Of course they do, and the key word above is "technically." The Scotch Cup, which began in 1959 and was sponsored by the Scotch Whisky Association, was never officially sanctioned as a world championship. Come to think of it, there was no way it could have been, for the International Curling Federation didn't even exist when Ernie Richardson and his Regina rink ventured to Scotland to play Willie Young in the series that introduced curling at the world level. Nor was the Canadian Curling Association asked for its endorsement or involvement. But that's nitpicking. The other technicality is that the Scotch Cup was an invitational effort, involving just Canada and Scotland in that first year. But all of this is mere persiflage—let's forget the technicalities and focus on the more interesting aspects of the first bona fide world curling event, in 1959.

A drum roll please, and then add a distant skirl of the pipes as the curlers come into view, for the setting is Scotland and there's no denying that the World Curling Championship began in the very birthplace of the game. At first the event was simply a two-country promotion for a fine product—more spin than substance. But then it began to expand. Today, curling might not yet rank among the world's top sporting endeavours, but wait for it, because it's coming, for a' that. Curling is now an Olympic sport. The World Curling Federation currently lists some 46 member nations (maybe more by the time you are reading this), even if some of them do have trouble mustering a quorum of actual stone slingers.

You want one man's opinion of who the catalyst was for this continuing evolution of curling? The Richardsons, that's who. The family rink out of Regina. The first four-time winner of the Brier, Canada's national men's championship. First four-time winner of the Worlds. Ernie, Arnold, Sam and Wes. And then, at the end of their reign, Mel Perry.

Four of the first five Scotch Cups were built around the Richardsons, so perhaps this is as good a place as any to pay tribute to them. Their mastery of curling got the Scotch Cup off to a smashing start, and their personalities helped rejuvenate the game, first in Canada and then in Scotland. I think it could be argued that without the Richardsons of Regina, the Scotch Cup might well have faltered and failed.

When I first started to cover curling, the Richardsons were starting their magnificent run to four Canadian and world titles. There was tall, patrician Ernie at skip. 'Twas said at the time that any team was two shots down before they even stepped onto the ice against Ernie; he appeared that formidable and intimidating.

His brother Sam (can anyone remember when he was called Garnet, the name on his birth certificate?) was the spark plug of the foursome, the team motivator and a strong sweeper. He is also one of the funniest and most entertaining speakers on the curling-banquet circuit today. On the media bench we got as many quotes from Sam as from anyone.

Cousin Arnold, at third, was the quiet one of that quartet, and may have been the deadliest shooter of the foursome. It would be Arnold who would clean up a sticky situation, rare as they were. The Richardsons were so proficient a curling squad that they seldom got into trouble, but if they did you could count on Arnold to bail the team out. And if he didn't, Ernie could and did.

After the 1963 Scotch Cup, some of the players and spectators visited Paris, where they met the famed Eartha Kitt, backstage. In addition to Ernie Richardson (far right), Kitt welcomed an unknown spectator (l) and Sweden's Rolf Arfwidsson. Photo courtesy of *Canadian Curling News*

Cousin Wes (cousin to Ernie and Sam and also to Arnold) was big and strong and wielded a corn broom as if it was a toy. As the lead he usually got the team off to a strong start. But Wes moved to Hawaii after three Brier crowns and world championships, and in 1962 Mel Perry took over at lead and never missed a beat with the other three. Mel was also a practical joker, the funster who once put an advertisement in Regina's *Leader-Post*, indicating the advertiser had a number of post holes for sale, and then gave Sam's phone number as the one to call!

In 1959, when the Richardsons arrived at the Brier in Quebec City, they were unknown rookies. They left that city as conquering heroes, having turned back the challenges of co-favourites Herb Olson of Alberta and Dick Bird of Manitoba. And then, a few weeks later, with little fanfare, they flew to Scotland to play the Scots champions, skipped by Willie Young, in something called the Scotch Cup. It was the first year of an event that would eventually lead to a fully sanctioned world championship for men, later another for women, and eventually acceptance as a medal sport in the Winter Olympics.

I'm not too certain of the details surrounding the beginning of the Scotch Cup, other than it was a venture of the Scotch Whisky Association. In Scotland, Jock Waugh and Norman Tod were the key organizers and the event had the informal blessing of the Royal Caledonia Curling Club. In Canada, the Whisky Association retained John Hull and his Toronto Communications firm, Public Relations Services Limited (PRSL), to organize the Canadian side of the promotion.

The Scotch Cup was an invitational event, involving the Canadian and Scottish champions. The main stumbling block to its acceptance in Canada was the fact that the CCA was never asked to approve or sanction the event, an oversight some CCA members resented. To overcome that perceptual problem, PRSL recruited two of Canada's best-known curling names: Ken Watson and Colin Campbell. Watson was the first three-time Brier champion, a syndicated curling columnist who had been a key organizer of junior curling in the West. Collie Campbell had been the 1947–48 president of the Dominion Curling Association, was a Brier trustee, and had been a high-ranking Canadian officer in the Second World War. Nor did it hurt that Campbell was an Honorary Life Member of the RCCC. The enormous cachet provided by Watson and Campbell was all that was necessary to make the Scotch Cup an instant international hit.

But there was more. In addition to the impact of the Richardson rink, there were the newspaper stories provided by some of Canada's key curling writers, and the striking photos of Michael Burns, who began his lengthy service to curling by carting his camera to Scotland on behalf of PRSL. And I'm certain that his wife, Helen, the lovely, winsome Helen, whose laughter and good humour have adorned the world event and the Brier for many years, was there too. Michael's photos, sent to every major paper in Canada, helped gain instant recognition of, and acceptance for, the new championship.

The Scotch Cup years (1959–67) saw the competition domiciled in Scotland, with two exceptions. In 1964 Calgary hosted the Scotch Cup, and in 1966 the event moved to Vancouver. While in Scotland, the games moved from one community to another: Ayr, Glasgow, Edinburgh, Falkirk, Kirkcaldy, Perth. And until 1965, the result was always the same: Canada won. Handily.

Then in 1965, the United States Hall of Famer, Bud Somerville, and his rink from Superior, Wisconsin, became the first foursome other than a Canadian one to win. Their victory came just four years after the United States had been invited to participate.

Sweden entered the lists in 1962, which was also my rookie year as a set of tonsils for CBC Radio. (I'm told that if you visit the CBC archives on the Internet, you can hear one of my reports from that year.) Three years later, Switzerland and Norway were added to the roster. France joined in 1966, and Germany was added a year later. When the Scotch Whisky Association elected to retire as sponsor in 1967, there were eight countries participating in the title-shoot.

In that span of nine years, Canada won seven Scotch Cups, the United States one, and Scotland one, with Chuck Hay in 1967, the same year the Whisky Association decided it should bow out of its sponsorship role—a decision, I was once told, that many Scots lamented. Then and now.

The stage was set, not only for a new sponsor but also for a new plateau of activity in world curling. There had been sporadic, inter-country competitions, and one or two bonspiels that included the word "world" in their titles, but it was the Scotch Cup that showed how successful a world championship might become.

Chapter Four

ENTER THE SILVER BROOM

WHEN THE SCOTCH WHISKY ASSOCIATION WITHDREW ITS SPONSORSHIP of the Scotch Cup, many Scots (and Canadians too) thought world curling had come to an abrupt end. "A sad day" was the prevailing opinion. After all, curling at the world level was pretty small potatoes then. There were only a few people who saw an opportunity for a new sponsor. Doug Smith was one of them.

Doug, from Montreal, was one of Canada's legendary radio broadcasters who had built an illustrious career covering all sports, including the Olympics, golf and curling. With Bill Good of Vancouver, he had broadcast the Macdonald Brier on countless occasions. As much an entrepreneur as a sportscaster, at the time of the Scotch Cup he had convinced the aluminum producer, Alcan, to sponsor an international golf series. With his flair for promotion and his media background, he quickly saw the opportunities for sponsorship when the Whisky folks opted to bow out of curling.

Not all the Whisky nabobs were in favour of dumping the Scotch Cup. Lord Bruce, the newly elected president of the Royal Caledonian Curling Club (the Mother Club of curling), was one who wanted to see the event continued. "It was the first element of discussion when I became president," he explained in a letter to me later.

"Jack Anderson, a member of council," he wrote, "knew Doug was at St. Andrews [in June 1967], and we discussed making an approach to him [about finding a sponsor]. When we met with him," he continued, "he made a very trenchant and forceful presentation and said he would need six months

As much an entrepeneur as a sportscaster, Doug Smith (r) provided live radio coverage of the Macdonald Brier with Bill Good (l) from 1948 on. Photo courtesy of *Canadian Curling News*

to put the plan together. We agreed on the end of December as a deadline.

"During this period, however, the Royal Club decided it would be unwise to let the time go by without planning a 'fail-safe' operation. We planned the next event (if no sponsor materialized) for Scotland, and while visiting teams would be required to pay their own travel, once with us they would be looked after.

"It shocked us," he continued, "that nothing appeared to be happening during the six-month span, so it was quite a surprise when an Air Canada representative got in touch with me and proposed to take over the sponsorship. He also made it quite clear that if we were to accept the airline's support, we would have nothing further to do with Smith. We were told it was not proper for them to use an intermediate agent for a sponsorship of this size.

"My father had met Gordon McGregor [president of Air Canada] on one of his earlier visits to Canada, so I immediately got in touch with him by phone to assess the integrity of the offer, and was very pleased to find the offer was firm.

"The contract was ultimately signed at Broomhall [the Bruce ancestral home]. There were several alterations which

I initialed and, of course, expected a clean copy soon after. But this did not happen. The document on which I had worked was copied as it stood and it was this that was sent to the other seven nations. I must say I was not too pleased that the amended contract, with my initials all over it, had gone out. I would have preferred a clean copy."

In early December 1967, Don Carlisle, Air Canada's public relations executive in Toronto, called and invited me to join him for lunch. He knew I had been involved in organizing the Tournament of Champions cashspiel at Maple Leaf Gardens and that I had also organized the inaugural Canadian Mixed Curling Championships in 1964 and '65 and other curling events in and around the city over a number of years. At lunch he introduced me to an airline executive from Montreal who told me that Air Canada had agreed in principle to assume sponsorship of the World Curling Championship— the announcement would be made shortly—and would I be interested in organizing and promoting it?

Would I be interested? Do turtles lay eggs? I was then sworn to secrecy, because, according to the Montrealer, the contract had not yet been finalized, and any premature hint of sponsorship could deep-six the entire deal. What I did not know at the time was Doug Smith's sponsorship search, nor his December deadline.

Smith, I learned later, took the world event to a number of potential sponsors, including Air Canada. Remember, this was before the acceptance of event sponsorship as a valuable tool in a firm's public relations and/or marketing policies. The airline (then a Crown corporation) found the idea attractive, or at least the executive with whom Doug was negotiating did. He recommended the sponsorship to his superiors, but then, suddenly, decided to tarry awhile. You may wonder why, as I did when I heard the story later. The suggestion voiced to me—and I have no proof of this—was that he knew Smith's end-of-December deadline was fast approaching. And if that was the case, perhaps he could out-wait Doug and negotiate directly with the RCCC, consigning Doug to the sidelines. We'll never know, but it seems a reasonable assumption.

As soon as the sponsorship deal was finalized and the formalities executed, the road map to the Air Canada Silver Broom was speedily laid out. After all, if continuity was to be maintained and a 1968 world championship held in March, then fast action was necessary. A Montreal press conference was quickly put together. Air Canada flew in the presidents of the curling associations of the competing countries, including Bill Lumsden of Winnipeg, president of the Canadian Curling Association, and Chuck Hay from Scotland. I was also flown into Montreal for the announcement, along with a number of other members of the Canadian curling media.

Lumsden was one of the better presidents of the CCA, and at a private meeting held the day before the official announcement he asked for key details of the event, but the answers were not forthcoming. He asked Hay if he knew what the new event would be called. Chuck said he had no idea. He asked the same question of the Air Canada representatives and was told, somewhat cryptically, that he'd have to wait for the press conference to find out. He was told that they didn't want any leaks to occur.

Lumsden promptly reminded those assembled at the meeting that, number one, he represented the largest curling body in the world; number two, he knew that the RCCC and some of the Montrealers who were present knew the proposed name; and number three, if the airline wanted the support and co-operation of the CCA, then he should have the information immediately, if not sooner. If it was not forthcoming, he said, he would not be present for the public announcement the following day. No doubt he had in mind the lingering fact that the Scotch Cup had never been endorsed by the CCA, a fact that still rankled some of the CCA membership.

Faced with that ultimatum, he was quickly told it would be known as the Air Canada Silver Broom. He then politely thanked his informant—"that is all I want to know," he said—and having made his point in typical Lumsden fashion, became one of the strongest boosters of the new event.

After the private meeting, Lumsden approached Hay and asked if he had any plans for dinner, since he, Lumsden, had not been invited to go out with any of the Air Canada execs or the local curlers. Hay replied that he had no other plans, so, along with a couple of others, they headed out together. Hay told me years later, "Although I had met Bill before, we discovered we had similar views on how world curling should progress, and it helped cement a lifelong friendship."

In those first months before the start of the Silver Broom, with hardly any time to catch my breath, I was thrust into the whirlpool of world curling. Curling I knew—or thought I did—but the world was something else. Back then, trying to put together a world event was, I realize it now, like trying to learn tightrope walking by correspondence course. I've been trying to keep my balance ever since.

How to put together that first Silver Broom? There were no policy files to follow, no checklists, no "past practice" to fall back on—nothing. I did have a few remembered moments from my media days with the Scotch Cup. And I had a good example of how to do things right from watching Frank O'Brien and Reg Geary, key organizers at the Brier. In addition I had the support and assistance of some key Air Canada marketing and public relations executives. But basically, we had to make it up as we went.

The nightmarish part of it was the lack of preparation time. Publicly, I was happy to be involved with the new event.

Three of the key figures in the inaugural Air Canada Silver Broom of 1968 join me in studying the program. From left to right: Pointe Claire town councillor Larry Marsh, organizing chair Bill MacKay, Jack Bowen of Air Canada and the author. Photo by Michael Burns

Privately, I was daunted by the enormity of the organizational job. It's one thing to organize a local, or even national, event. But a world event, involving (at that time) eight different countries, six different languages, a wide disparity in skills ... the mind boggled.

Today organizing a world event is a two-year operation involving hundreds, perhaps thousands, of volunteers. And organizers today have the benefit of attendance at, and records from, past events to help them prepare. Back then, with no wellspring of experience to draw upon, precise planning was impossible. My approach was to start as early as you can each morning, and work until you're ready to drop late at night. Then continue the next day. Don't spend much time on "what if" or "you can't do that." Cover the most important things first and hope the lesser items will take care of themselves. In short, do what you can. And keep your fingers crossed.

The best thing I had going for me—I now know—was the fact I didn't realize how tough it would be! I just went ahead as if I did that sort of thing every day. My partner at that time (in Douglas D. Maxwell Limited) was A.J. "Pete" Esling, and he dropped as much work as he could for other clients. Together with our office manager, Connie Partridge, we scheduled 18-hour workdays, plugged away on the essentials and hoped the rest would fall into place. I also had the assistance and PR smarts of the Air Canada Public Relations department, without whom I never could have managed.

During that three-month period, I would learn of Doug Smith's efforts the previous year and would hear rumours that a miffed Smith was threatening legal action. To the best of my knowledge—I was told I needn't worry about it—nothing ever came of the threat. Perhaps the matter was settled privately; perhaps it never proceeded at all. And truth to tell, I was so deeply involved in trying to rush a whole new event into operation that I didn't have time to fret over a rumour. To this day, this part of the story has never been told.

Somehow, we managed to get the essentials in place. With Jack Bowen, the first chair of the newly formed Silver Broom Steering Committee, I completed a whirlwind tour of the European curling nations ("if it's Tuesday, this must be Oslo"), to give them full details of the new event, and to get their approval of the Air Canada Silver Broom as curling's official world championship, an approval that was formally sanctioned by the International Curling Federation at the time of the 1968 competition. I also found time to negotiate a television contract (a "no" from Johnny Esaw at CTV, a "yes" from Gordon Craig of the CBC), prepare the various competition details, outline a proposal for media coverage and develop a long-term promotional plan designed to turn the Air Canada Silver Broom into a model international sporting event. And, of course, I met long and often with the arena staff at Pointe Claire, Quebec, site of the first Silver Broom, plus the late Bill MacKay, chair of the Pointe Claire organizing committee, and his hard-working corps of volunteers. Remember, this was in the days before faxes, email and the Internet. We relied on Canada Post, the telephone and the Air Canada telex network.

I also convinced Air Canada they should retain Michael Burns as official photographer for the new competition, and it was one of the best moves I ever made. I knew Mike was a world-class photographer who could not only shoot outstanding photos but also develop them quickly, at the arena, and then, with the help of his wife, Helen, speed them on their way to newspapers across Canada and around the world. Michael's dramatic photos, as much as anything else, helped establish the Silver Broom as a key event in world curling. Not only that, it helped elevate him as the first photographer to be inducted into the Canadian Curling Hall of Fame.

As you can imagine, that first Silver Broom is etched indelibly in my memory and even today, 37-plus years later, those memories sparkle like a diamond with the light glinting off its many facets.

That's due, in large part, to the fine play of three of the giants of world curling: Ron Northcott of Calgary (who had just won his second of three Briers); Perth's Chuck Hay (who had won the Scotch Cup in 1967 and the Scottish national championship in 1968); and Bud Somerville of Superior, Wisconsin (Scotch Cup winner in 1965, and US champion in 1968). The other five national champions present (Kjell Grengmark of Sweden, Franz Marti of

Switzerland, Norway's Thor Andresen, Pierre Boan of France, and Germany's Werner Fischer-Weppler) were fine curlers and gentlemen, to be sure, but it was the trio of Hay, Northcott and Somerville that gave the event instant credibility and set the Silver Broom on its sparkling 18-year journey.

Let me be clear about one thing. I don't want to leave the impression that it's the organizational components that make an event, an event. Those components can help create the ambience in which the players can do their thing, but when you reduce it all to its bare essentials, the players are all that really matter. It's the players, the competitors, the shooters on the ice that make an event, *an event*. Take it from me: have I ever lied to you before?

Chapter Five

LORD, LORD . . .

INEVITABLY THERE WERE GLITCHES IN THE RUN-UP TO THAT FIRST
Silver Broom. But there were also godsends. And occasionally some unexpected guffaws.

I recall learning in the planning stage, from the biographies of the competitors, that the German second, Rolf Klug, had a birthday at the start of the Silver Broom week. So I ordered a huge slab birthday cake, brought it to the opening soiree (note the bilingual touch) and we all sang "Happy Birthday" to Rolf. Nice. The guffaw came shortly after.

There was still a considerable chunk of cake left when the evening ended, so I brought it back to our hotel-room office, where the only spot we could find to set it was atop a small table. The room was packed. Some were media people, including Harry Lewis (reporting to an Ottawa radio station). He couldn't find a place to sit but desperately wanted to perch somewhere. I don't know how he could not be aware of the cake, but somehow he missed its location. Someone yelled "Don't sit there!" as he sat down, but it was too late. Just as quickly as he settled onto the confection, he stood up again, icing all over his pants. And as he twisted around to check his trousers, he left some of the icing on others present. You might say he was the butt of the joke.

In a conversation we had years later, Chuck Hay recalled one of the glitches: what flag and national anthem to use for Scotland? After countless consultations with experts, the protocol people from Air Canada pronounced that the anthem would be "God Save the Queen" (which, I was told, had the exact same tune as the Swiss national hymn in those days!).

And the flag would be the Union Jack. I don't think I need add that the English anthem and flag were not popular choices for the Scot-on-the-street, nor for most of the Scots contingent in Pointe Claire. As Hay recalled, "In spite of protests by our team, Air Canada insisted on 'God Save the Queen.' Fortunately that problem was resolved by the following year."

Hay also recalled that the International Curling Federation (formed only the previous year) was in disarray and had seemed unable to reach agreement on anything during their mid-week Montreal discussions. "It looked ominously as if the fledgling ICF would fall apart before it could get any traction," Chuck wrote me in 2005. But RCCC president Lord Bruce, at that first closing banquet in 1968, called on them to meet again the following morning, at which time he emphasized that the future of world curling depended on agreement being reached before everyone headed home. "This they did," Hay continued, "and 37 years later world curling has progressed by leaps and bounds. Who would have thought back then that Australia, New Zealand, Russia and China (among a considerable number of others) would be a part of the world game today. All thanks to Lord Bruce's impassioned plea."

Hay continued on a personal note: "On reaching our room after the banquet, there was a message from Lord Bruce to call him immediately. It sounded serious, so I called. He asked if we [the team] were alone and I said we were. He then said he wanted to see just the four of us, no one else. 'Well, well,' I thought, 'this is when the president tells the team how useless they were, having won all the games in the round robin and then losing the final—the headmaster coming to deal with the bad boys.'

"As he entered the room I noticed he had a bottle of Scotch in each of his coat pockets. He said, as he poured out five hefty drinks, 'It's like a morgue in here.' I was still speechless as he handed 'round the five glasses. As he sat down on the bed he said, 'I just wanted to thank you for the way you played all week and sorry you lost the final.' He then went on to say how much he had enjoyed the week and asked if we could bring our wives to Broomhall [the Bruce ancestral home] for dinner at a date to be arranged on our return to Scotland. I was still speechless but absolutely delighted at his kindness and attitude. He was so understanding and comforting. We were, of course, delighted he came to the room, especially as we were feeling a bit low after losing the final to Ron [Northcott]. The visit ended when he said, 'Let's go down to the hospitality room and enjoy ourselves,' which we did. How lucky we were to have him as our president.

"On our return [to Scotland] we had a great evening at Broomhall, especially since our wives could be with us. They had missed Pointe Claire, most of them being pregnant at the time."

It's difficult to know where to place that first banquet in my litany of glitches, guffaws and godsends. There had to be a banquet of course. Every curling event I've ever attended has a banquet of some size and stature, and the newly minted Silver Broom would be no different.

The banquet was planned for the end of the championship week at the Queen Elizabeth Hotel in downtown Montreal. Lord Bruce was there not only as president of the RCCC, but also as the principal who had negotiated and signed the contract establishing the Silver Broom as the official men's world curling championship. As the number one member of the Mother Club of curling, it was automatic that he be named as guest speaker. Beyond that the detailed planning of the banquet had to wait until the games began. In fact much of the preparation was done, even as the games were being played, by marketing guru Jack Bowen, with help from Hal Cameron and Mike Hildred, two of Air Canada's public relations experts. Inevitably, in the rush, a couple of things fell through the cracks.

Lord Bruce recalls one such oversight. "At the lineup going into the dinner," he wrote me, "the Air Canada organizer (when getting the head table in proper order) read out the name of the Reverend so-and-so, and there was no response. So it was read out again, a little louder. *The Reverend so-and-so.* Still no response. Jack Bowen was summoned, and it was discovered the Reverend so-and-so had never been invited, so as we moved into the banquet hall, Jack turned to me and said, 'I would be grateful, m'lord, if you would give the Grace before we sit down.' I remember anxiously passing towards my seat when there came a flash of remembrance of Dr. Penecuik's transcription from the seventeenth century: '*To curle upon the ice does greatly please, Being a Manly Scottish exercise. It clears the brains, stirrs up the Native Heat and gives a gallant appetite for meat,*' and having got through that without fault, I thought it would be appropriate to add 'Amen.'"

My own most vivid recollection of that banquet also involved Lord Bruce, whom I had just met but who would (as so often happens in curling) become a lifelong friend. (The following year, on the death of his father, he assumed the hereditary title of the Earl of Elgin.)

About midweek he came to me with the query that went something like this: "Do you suppose the hotel would have a piano available?" I reassured him that a world-class hotel like the QE definitely would. Then I ventured a somewhat timid and hesitant, "Why, what do you have in mind?"

"Well, my sister lives in Montreal and plays the piano," he said, "and I thought it would be nice if she played at the banquet and I sang a song or two."

An interesting presentation was made at the 1968 closing banquet, when Lord Bruce (r) gave Air Canada president Gordon MacGregor (l) an original Krieghoff painting. Photo by Michael Burns

My heart sank. Here we were at the start of what I perceived to be a precedent-setting event, an event I hoped would set some kind of glorious standard, and suddenly I was faced with an awkward request—from nobility, no less. It mattered little that he was the direct descendant of Scotland's legendary King Robert the Bruce; I reckoned the occasion would be more like "Amateur Night at the Rialto."

And there was nothing I could do about it.

I needn't have worried. I discovered that his sense of occasion, to say nothing of his lilting tenor and love of curling, would come through. Sensationally. And his sister

Alison (the Lady Alison Stewart-Patterson, who would soon after be ordained a Presbyterian minister) provided a superb accompaniment.

That recollection gave Lord Bruce a chuckle of memory. "My sister and her husband, Cleve," he wrote, "had been seated among the members of the press, and when it came my turn to speak, one of them (looking at his program) said, 'What's next?' to which another answered, 'It's that Lord from Scotland.' On that note my sister escaped to the piano and on her return the same character said, 'How the hell did you know he was going to sing?' and she turned to him and said, 'He's my brother.'"

If you gather from all this that the evening was a huge success, you're absolutely right. There was a presentation to Gordon MacGregor, president of Air Canada, of an original Krieghoff painting—given by the artist to an earlier Lord Elgin and brought from Broomhall. There was the usual conviviality of such an occasion. But it was the Laird's songs that turned out to be the hit of the night and put a magical cap on the evening. There was a sense of history being made that night.

There was also a freezing rainstorm that night, so getting back to the Airport Hilton, the headquarter's hotel, was an adventure in itself. Somehow, in spite of icy roads, everybody made it back without mishap, even though it seemed to take hours.

One of the first to return was Don Fleming, better known as "Buckets," the highly respected and somewhat Runyonesque curling writer from the *Edmonton Journal*. After filing his story, and to put in time while waiting for the rest of us to arrive, Buckets repaired to the hospitality room, where he stayed busy fuelling for the remainder of the evening.

Eventually everyone returned and headed to the hospitality room. When Lord Bruce and the Scots team arrived,

Buckets sauntered over. He threw his free right arm (the left held a much-replenished glass) around the Bruce's shoulders and loudly proclaimed, "Lord, Lord, you saved the f--king show."

There was a horrified and stunned silence, for in 1968 the f-word was, well, just not used. Never. Ever. That may not be true today, but it certainly was then.

Everybody waited for the response. After all, this was not another member of the rag-tag curling media being addressed, but the president of the RCCC, and Scottish nobility at that. We quickly learned the meaning of "savoir faire" and "noblesse oblige." We also learned about the ready Bruce wit.

"Well, Buckets," said Lord Bruce after a suitable pause, "after all (pause) it is the Lord's job (pause) to save."

Need I add that "the Bruce" and "Buckets" became instant best friends? And remain so to this day.

THE CURLER'S GRACE

In addition to Lord Bruce's grace at the banquet, there are two others he could have chosen:

GRACE 1

O Power abune whose bounty free
    Our needs and wants suffices.
We render thanks for barley bree
    And meat that appetises.

Be thou our skip throughout life's
    game
    An' syne we're sure to win,
Tho' slow the shot and wide the aim
    We'll soop each ither in.

GRACE 2

O Lord, whose luv surrounds us a'
    And brings us a' together,
Wha writes your laws upon oor hearts
    And bids us help each other.

We thank thee for thy bounties great
    For meat and hame and gear,
And thank thee too for snaw 'n ice
    Although we ask for mair.

Gi'e us a hert to dae wha's richt
    As curlers true and keen,
To be guid friens along life's road
    And soop our slide aye keen.

Chapter Six

SILVER BROOM SEMANTICS

I HAVE A CERTAIN AMOUNT OF RESPECT FOR OLD HUMPTY, FOR I TOO
ran into semantic difficulties with the newly minted "Silver Broom."

In January 1968, only two months before the first Silver Broom, it was
decided we needed a poster to trumpet the fact that (1) yes, there would be a
world curling championship that year, (2) Air Canada was the new sponsor,
(3) it would be known as the "Air Canada Silver Broom"; and (4) it would be
held in Pointe Claire, Quebec.

It wasn't hard to design a poster with those basic elements in it. What
turned out to be difficult—and in one case disastrous—was the translation into the four main languages of the world event: Norwegian, Swedish, Swiss–German and French. The latter was the trickiest. Would it be the
French of France, or of Quebec?

True, we had little difficulty in translating "Silver Broom" into "*Balai
d'Argent*," and "World Curling Championship" into "*Championnat du
Monde de Curling*" (although there were some who held out for "Championnat Mondiale"). In my unilingual naïveté, I assumed that whatever
translation was okay in Canada would also be okay in France. Hah! It is to
laugh—c'est risible. Or should that be *c'est ridicule*?

Members of the French Curling Association, when I met with them in Megève for the 1971 World Championship organization meetings, hadn't wanted it translated at all. Their argument was: "you Anglais call it the "Grand Prix," and not "the Big Prize," so why not stick with "Silver Broom"? They felt that "Silvair Bruhm" (with that marvellous Maurice Chevalier accent) was much preferable to "*Balai d'Argent*"! The latter was, well, more Canadian than international.

To be sure that each poster would be correct in the language of the target country, the translation agencies were called in. Their work was impeccable, except in the case of Germany. There they ran into a problem. The problem was the word "curling." In each of the other countries, "curling" was easily translated as—"curling"! But when the translators checked their German dictionaries, they found "curling" equated to "*Eisstockschiessen*." So "World Curling Championship" became "*Eisstockschiessen Weltmeisterschaft.*" Now, contrary to many preconceptions, I am not fluent in any language other than English (and there are some who would say that is open to question), so if the experts said curling was *Eisstockschiessen*, who was I to argue?

As soon as the posters reached Germany, I received a phone call from the German Curling Federation. Was it resignation in the caller's voice, or a chuckle? *Eisstockschiessen*, I was told, was a game very similar to curling, sometimes called "*Eisschiessen*," but it was not—definitely not—curling. There was, they said, little similarity between an *Eisstock* and a curling stone. In addition, the game did not use brooms or brushes. "Then what is the correct translation for curling?" I asked, and was told that "curling" (as in every other country) would do just fine, thank you. The posters, of course, had to be scrapped, and if I'd been smart back then, thinking I might be writing this book a bunch of years later, I would have kept one of those offending posters as a collector's item. But I wasn't, and I didn't. Some years later, when the Silver Broom journeyed to Garmisch-Partenkirchen, Germany, I tried my hand at *Eisstockschiessen*, outside at night, under the lights and the stars, and found it to be a kissin' cousin to curling, particularly in Bavaria. But it wasn't curling.

There have been countless other occasions when linguistic ability (or inability) has proven, well, exhilarating. Take the 1978 Silver Broom in Winnipeg as a for-instance. Two of the visiting spectators to that seminal event were Jack Petrenko and his wife, Bente Hoel, of Norway. Bente's English is perfect. Jack? He spoke at least seven languages and could be deadpan funny in all of them. Jack died a number of years ago (or I would have checked this yarn with him directly), so I'll let Bente continue the story.

"In 1978," wrote Bente, "Jack and I came to Canada for the first time. Before arriving in Winnipeg, though, we were invited to stay, for a few days ahead of the event, with our friends Harriett and Laurie Artiss in Regina. They wanted us to meet their friends Shirley and Jack Klein, and we all went out to dinner one night to a lovely restaurant. It was a very festive evening. Everybody had a great time, and of course stories were told. After a while, Jack K., wanting to shock his new Norwegian friend, Jack P., with some colourful language, told the story of how he had been golfing in some exotic place: '... and there, suddenly, on the green, I saw this f--king snake.' And then he stopped and looked at us to see how we would react. Jack P. never blinked. There was no hesitation; his reply was immediate: 'I don't understand this word ... snake??'

I should add that the winsome Bente was a fine curler who played for Norway at a couple of women's world championships. The year before the Winnipeg event (and the snake story), I was in Oslo for the European curling championships, where Bente was one of the key organizers. Pierre Jerome, chair of the Silver Broom Steering Committee, was with me, and our main reason for being there was a PR one. We wanted to support the event with our attendance, but we also wanted to do some promotion for the upcoming Silver Broom in Karlstad, Sweden. But, once again, let Bente pick up the story, because her recollection of that occasion matches mine.

"Yes, in Oslo, I was part of the organizing committee, and at the closing banquet I was lucky enough to be placed at the head table. Next to me sat Doug Maxwell—he and Pierre Jerome had travelled all the way to Oslo from Canada—something that was greatly appreciated by our committee. Anyway, Doug wanted me to teach him some Norwegian, and of course we had to start with the most important words in any language, namely 'I love you.' In Norwegian this is *Jeg elsker deg* and sounds (in English) something like '*Yi elska dye.*'

The magnificent (and second) Air Canada Silver Broom trophy replaced the hurriedly prepared initial trophy. Photo courtesy of Air Canada

It was, as you might gather, a memorable evening—the kind of party that only curlers can produce, but then I'm biased. I should also add that, as I was practising my newfound phrase, looking deeply into Bente's eyes (I thought I might ask her to dance, if I got the nuance of the phrase right), when Jack approached from the wings and advised me that while I was getting close to the correct pronunciation, I still had a long way to go to make it stick!

I should add that, ever since that day, *Jeg elsker deg* has been our greeting to each other. All this was (and is) with my wife's blessing, of course. Anne thinks Bente is pretty special too.

Inevitably I would return home from such a European trip wishing I was at least semi-bilingual ("after all, isn't your country bilingual?" I was asked, mock-innocently, on more than one occasion). Trust me, it's somewhat embarrassing to attend a meeting in which the chair and other members of the organizing committee are fluent in three, four or five other languages, and then to have to sit there with a frozen smile as the chair opens the proceedings with the words "We'll conduct today's meeting in English, since our good friend Doug is with us today."

Most of the time language difficulties can be problematic, but on occasion can be beneficial. Let me illustrate. Early in the preparations for the Silver Broom of 1971, I decided I should brush up on my high school French. And I was coming along not too badly, so I thought, until I hit one particularly icy patch at a committee meeting in Megève. The chair of the committee, Gilbert Le Bescond (he was also mayor of the town), asked a question, in French of course, to which I quickly responded, "*Oui, d'accord*" (yes, okay). He looked at me in a funny way, and then kindly said, "*Je répète la question*" (I'll repeat the question). This time I waited for the translation, and when I realized he was asking for something that was clearly impossible and which I had not understood, I quickly blurted out "Hell no." Gilbert was a delight and was very gracious in his offer to repeat the question. After that I always waited for the translation, conveniently forgetting my Grade 10 French, except when in the local cafés and restaurants.

You can understand why, after a while, I could identify with Humpty D.

Chapter Seven

THE GLASS HOUSE

THE SECOND SILVER BROOM WAS HELD IN PERTH, SCOTLAND, ARGUABLY the site of more world curling tourneys than any other location on the globe. The year was 1969, the late Tom Stewart was chair of the organizing committee, and I was still riding my learning curve.

Two experiences stand out in my memory. The first is one that only now can be told; the second became famous at the time, but perhaps I can add a couple of little-known sidelights to the story.

A NEW CANADIAN FLAG "WAIVED" IN SCOTLAND

I don't think I need go into chapter and verse of Canada's flag flap—you probably know it better than I do—but it's an integral part of our country's history. Prime Minister Lester B. Pearson began to promote a distinctively Canadian flag in 1965 and was battled at every turn by Opposition leader John G. Diefenbaker. The new flag was finally unveiled in February 1967, and most Canadians rejoiced. I recall looking at that stylized 11-point maple leaf and committing it to memory. And a couple of years later I was glad I had done so, for it figured in my event management apprenticeship.

It was in Perth where I learned the lesson *don't assume anything; don't take somebody's word, check it out yourself.* The incident happened just before the opening ceremonies of that long-ago Broom. In earlier meetings with the Perth committee, I had asked about the signs that would identify the teams during their entrance in the opening ceremonies.

In a reversal of roles, a Perth '69 Silver Broom publicity photo saw Scotland's Chuck Hay (l) don a Canadian coat and Stetson, while Bill Lumsden of Winnipeg put on the kilt to hold the broom. Photo by Michael Burns

I was told they would be using the same ones from the earlier Scotch Cups, and in addition the signs would be surmounted by a small painted flag of the country. I thought that was a great idea and told the committee so.

But I didn't bother to check out the signs.

About a half hour before the opening ceremonies were scheduled to begin, I saw the signs. They looked great—all but one. To my horror (which was immediate) and amusement (which came later) I discovered that the sign for Canada's Ron Northcott team was surmounted by the new Canadian flag, complete with red bars on either side, and the red maple leaf on the white central background. But wait—what kind of maple leaf was that in the middle? Red, yes. White background, yes. But why was there an almost-complete circle surrounding the maple leaf?

It was, of course, the Air Canada partial circle or rondel, the airline's logo of the day, added by a Scots committee member who, understandably, was not as familiar with the new Canadian flag as Canadians were.

What to do? By now the opening ceremonies were less than 25 minutes away, and there was no time to paint the proper maple leaf into place.

By sheer good luck I happened to have a red felt marking pen in my briefcase, so I grabbed a piece of paper, quickly sketched in the outline of the stylized maple leaf and left a committee member with instructions to shade in the rest, paste the paper over the Air Canada logo, and tell no one about the quick edit job. The proper leaf could then be added later, in time for the closing ceremonies.

No one caught my artistic effort, and the ceremonies went off without a hitch. But not before I had digested the lesson: *check everything yourself.*

THE EMPTY GLASS HOUSE AND THE ENRAGED WIVES

You can't see it now, because the old Perth Ice Rink (built when hockey first took hold in Britain in the mid-thirties) was torn down in 1989 to make way for a supermarket mall. But in the old rink, upstairs at one end, there was a dining area, glass-fronted, where the CBC had set its television cameras and commentator positions for the '69 Silver Broom. At the other end of the rink, also behind floor-to-ceiling glass, were several rows of seats that were without doubt the best in the house for watching curling. Locally this prize location was known as "The Glass House." But for some reason or other, as the Silver Broom got underway, no one was sitting there. I never thought to wonder why, but would soon be enlightened. One of the committee members came to me and told me that the Canadian team wives had left the arena and were congregated in the bar, more than a little mad. "Steam coming out their ears," I believe was his phrase.

It should be added here that, apart from the wife of one of the Scots curlers, the four Canadian women were the only wives present for the second Silver Broom. The presence of great numbers of Silver Broom supporters, team wives and media was yet to come.

So there I was, still a rookie organizer, contemplating a new and potentially disastrous situation. I ventured into the bar and soon found them sitting off to one side, wearing glum faces, and, yes, I believe I did see some steam coming out their ears! As I approached it was evident all their frustrations were about to be spilled over onto me.

So I took the coward's way out. "Whoa," I said. "Before we talk I get to buy each of you a drink." It wasn't long, once the tall glasses had been set in front of them, before I found out what had upset them.

Being ardent curling fans and being accustomed to watching their husbands play from "behind the glass" in Canada, they had noted the empty seats in The Glass House and had made their way to the area, only to be turned away by a local committee member.

"Sorry, no one allowed in here," said the embarrassed Scot. "Air Canada instructions," he added.

"But our husbands are playing, the seats are empty, and we want to watch the game," they chorused. The local was polite but firm. He had instructions that no one was to be allowed in. The instructions had come from the sponsor, and he would see that they were carried out. The wives left, probably vowing at that moment never to return.

I agreed that the restriction was dumb and they should be permitted to sit in the empty seats. I told them I would check it out and be back shortly.

They were right; the Scots guard was polite but adamant. No one came in without the say-so of Jack Bowen, the senior Air Canada representative present.

I couldn't find Bowen, so I approached Gordon Craig, the producer of the CBC telecasts, later to become the founding president of The Sports Network (TSN). Don Chevrier and I would be providing commentary for the telecast from a tiny "booth" area off to one side of the main restaurant section.

We were located directly behind "home" end, in some ways an even better location than The Glass House. When I told Gordon the situation and suggested that, since we weren't televising anything at that time, we invite the wives to view the game from our vantage point, he readily agreed.

On my way back, I sought out the lone Scottish wife present and asked her to join the Canadian wives in our somewhat crowded commentator position. That way all the wives would have the same privilege. Needless to say, the close quarters created instant friendships. I then had a bit of breathing time to address The Glass House situation so that the wives could watch subsequent games from that vantage point.

The essentials of that story quickly became known to many of the interested general public, so that part of the yarn is no surprise. But it's the postscript that has never been told, till now.

At the reception prior to the closing banquet, Bev Gerlach, wife of Northcott's third man, Dave Gerlach, approached me. A former flight attendant (though not for Air Canada), Bev was beguiling, attractive, sophisticated.

"Who is that man over there?" she asked me, pointing to Bowen. I told her, and she went on, "Isn't he the one who made the ruling about The Glass House?" I allowed as how that was the case. She thanked me and drifted away. I noted, however, that she began to work her way through the gathering toward her target. I was standing nearby when she "accidentally" bumped into Jack and introduced herself.

"And I'm Jack Bowen of Air Canada," he beamed in reply.

"Oh," she said, all sweet and coy, as if the light had just dawned. "You're the man who kept us out of The Glass House!"

Well, Jack began to splutter about the reasons for the move, muttering something about keeping the seats reserved for a variety of VIPs and other bigwigs expected later in the week. Bev remained quiet until he finished.

"Horseshit," she said sweetly, complete with radiant smile. And, pirouetting smartly on her high heels, she moved on. Was it my imagination, or was there just the hint of a satisfied smile on her face?

Chapter Eight

DREAM JOB

SOME YEARS AGO, WHEN I WAS MASQUERADING AS PUBLISHER AND editor of the *Canadian Curling News*, and the *Scott Tournament of Hearts* was coming up to its twentieth anniversary (in 2001), I asked Robin Wilson, who was coordinator of the Scott, to send me some memories or small vignettes from her time as Numero Uno of the Hearts. Or should that be Numera Una?

You should know that Robin has "been there, done that" in practically every aspect of curling you care to mention. Back in 1976 and again in 1979, she played second on Lindsay Sparkes' team that won the Macdonald Lassie (Canadian women's championship) crown. The other members of that squad were Robin's sister Dawn Knowles (third) and lead Lorraine Bowles. In 2006 all four were inducted into the Canadian Curling Hall of Fame and Museum, recognition that was long overdue. The year 1979 was the last year of the Macdonald Tobacco company's sponsorship, but it was also the first year of the world women's championship in Perth, Scotland. And so Lindsay and squad flew off to Scotland, where, as you might expect, they were favoured to win that inaugural women's world title. Somehow the Canadians finished behind the Swiss team skipped by Gaby Casanova, much to the Canadian team's chagrin. I never had the heart to ask Robin her reaction to that disappointment. Until recently.

"It was totally disheartening," she wrote to me. "With international curling in its infancy and Canada seen universally as a powerhouse, we went to Scotland to win and that's what our many fans back home expected. When we lost to Gaby, it really hurt. I can sympathize today with subsequent Canadian champions who lose big events.

"We just never figured out the ice. The hacks were several inches above the ice and we had to move them for Lindsay and me to throw left-handed, and we forgot to move them a couple of times. The crowd was standing within two feet of us. There were no boards, no dividers, and the ice had recently been used for hockey. We wanted to match rocks but none of the other teams even knew what that meant so we were not allowed to do so. However, when it came right down to it we didn't curl well enough to win. It was definitely embarrassing.

"Looking back on it today, though, it was an unbelievable experience and we made friends that have lasted a lifetime."

As mentioned, 1979 was the year Macdonald Tobacco ended its support of both the Brier and the Lassie. Two years later, Scott Paper came onto the scene with the Scott Tournament of Hearts, and today, Scott Paper holds the impressive distinction of being the longest-running corporate sponsor of amateur sport in Canada.

When Robin sent me her 2001 Scott vignettes, I was struck by something she said then, for it mirrored what I had always wanted to say about my own good fortune, but had never been able to find the right words. She wrote, "I don't know who it was who said, 'Find something you love to do, and then figure out how to get paid for doing it.'"

That's exactly how I felt about the Silver Broom, except I didn't find the Air Canada Silver Broom; it found me. But let's allow Robin to continue with her reminiscences. Although those thoughts were from the 20th anniversary and we're now past year 25, her recollections haven't changed much between then and now, and I know that for a certainty, for I asked her if she still felt the same way today, and she told me "even more so."

The remainder of this chapter belongs to Robin, who continues with memories from her 25-year reservoir of anecdotes. Take it away, Robin Wilson.

I HAD WORKED FOR SCOTT PAPER FROM 1972–79 BEFORE leaving when I became pregnant with my first child. One summer day in 1980, John Leonard (head of Scott's advertising agency) asked me to lunch, where we discussed the fact that Scott was looking into sports sponsorship and women's curling was currently without a sponsor. He suggested Walker Leonard Advertising and I join forces and see if we could put Scott Paper and curling together. So we did.

The vice-president of marketing at Scott Paper at the time was Bob Stewart. He was to become the patron of women's curling in Canada for quite some time, including his stint as president of the company. Others who would figure prominently in the early partnership between Scott and the Canadian Ladies Curling Association were David Stowe, Dave Doherty and Don Pettit, and although the company has been sold three times over the years, it is still the people at Scott who make the difference. Today it is Don Cayouette, John McClelland, John McPherson and Stephen Blythe in head office, as well as Len Bosgoed, John Thornton, Dave Ronald and Hilton Moore, to mention just a few of those in sales. Let's see what else I can remember as I travel back down memory lane.

The first Scott Tournament of Hearts was in Regina in 1982, with three terrific women in charge: Evelyn Krahn, Eva Kerr and Marj Mitchell. Ev was Chair, Eva was CLCA president and Marj was head of transportation for that very first Scott event. In those days, everything was new and there wasn't a lot of help. You had to do a lot of things on your own, like putting together a hundred media books (who were we kidding, thinking that many media people would

Robin Wilson. Photo by Andrew Klaver

show up?) on the floor of my hotel room. Marj was there to help and around 3:00 a.m., we moved downstairs to the hotel lobby to set up the Scott display; you should have seen us trying to master this folding monster with only the help of an instruction booklet printed in French!

"The next year—Prince George, BC—saw another trio of women arrive: Noreen Delisle, CLCA president (with a smile that never fades), Deb Kennedy (product manager at Scott Paper and the classiest woman I have ever known) and Helen Knowles, supermom. In those days a church service was held on Sunday morning. The minister at the non-denominational service had been carefully chosen by Noreen to meet the needs of all curlers, no matter what their religious background. How was she to know he would give a sermon on circumcision!

For the victory banquet we had invited an international sports star (who shall remain nameless) to be the guest speaker. We had also invited the mayor and the minister to sit at the head table. The mayor, unfortunately, fell asleep. Deb told me I had to go and wake him up, which I did by crawling on my hands and knees (hidden by the table skirting) and tugging on his pant leg under the table. And then the guest speaker used the awful "f-word" throughout his speech, which caused the minister and his wife to wince each and every time.

It was especially nice to be in Winnipeg in 1985 because all my 1976 teammates were there—Lindsay Sparkes as a coach, Lorraine Bowles as a player and my sister, Dawn, to help out. Gloria was also there. Gloria? An incredible lady who was our driver when we won the Canadians. Back then, she had indulged all our superstitions (which included a rather large and mangy stuffed animal) and here she was again, ready to help wherever needed.

The Scott has always had its share of personalities, and one of the best was (and is) Marilyn Bodogh, of St. Catharines, Ontario. To my mind, she was the catalyst that rocketed women's curling onto the national scene with her win in 1986. Her enthusiasm, her green bloomers and short skirt took the curling world by storm. It would take her 10 years to win her second Canadian title, but in the interim she established herself as a leading motivational speaker.

I remember Lethbridge in 1987 when a chinook played havoc with the ice. But Shorty Jenkins and cohorts made major adjustments to ensure the ice was restored. Dancing with Shorty: now that's something you do once and never forget!

Bob Stewart always had an active hand in the menu selection for the victory banquet. For years he had suggested beets as a vegetable, but I had always managed to ignore his request, as I hate beets. In 1988 (by then he was president of Scott Paper) he insisted. However, we had a major challenge moving our 500 guests from the reception area up a narrow staircase to the ballroom. As a result we ran late, and all of the vegetables (including the beets) were burned and had to be replaced. I'll never forget Bob's remarks that night when he said, "I have been trying for years to get Robin to put beets on the menu. I have accomplished that. I still have to find a way to get her to put them on your plates." Ten years later, when Bob had his gall bladder removed, I sent a bouquet of beets to his hospital room.

There are another three special ladies in Canadian curling (they all seem to come in threes...) who are so entwined that it is impossible to talk about one without the others: Vera Pezer, Joyce McKee and Sylvia Fedoruk—all from

Saskatoon. All of them were Canadian curling champions: Sylvia once, Vera four times and Joyce five times.

Vera was our on-site contact in Saskatoon, 1991. An amazing curler, she is still one of the key people in the history of women's curling in Canada, and her 2003 book *The Stone Age: A Social History of Curling on the Prairies* is a must for curlers everywhere.

I still remember the first time my skip, Lindsay Sparkes, met Joyce McKee. She was speechless, embarrassingly so. She couldn't say a word. It amused Joyce, who always had a twinkle in her eye. Sadly, we lost Joyce—and that twinkle—shortly after.

Sylvia Fedoruk is a remarkable individual. A brilliant woman who once graced the cover of Time magazine, she was also a CLCA president, a championship curler (with Joyce) and later a lieutenant-governor of Saskatchewan. When she hosted a government reception for curlers, she gave each of her guests a jar of "Syl's Dills" (yup, dill pickles).

Along with the great moments, there are always disasters waiting to happen. One of mine happened at the victory banquet in 1994, in Kitchener-Waterloo. When we were assembling the seating list for the teams, media, special guests and head table, the copier broke down. Once repaired, we didn't have a collator, so we set up a manual sorting system in the hallway of the hotel. Four of us were running up and down the hallway, madly sorting, staplers in hand. After a maniacal 10-minute drive (with Joe Mior, my partner at Whitewater Communications, at the wheel), we arrived quite late. Bob Stewart was furious. He asked me who was in charge and I said, "You. You're the president!" That will stand as my boldest statement ever to a CEO of a major corporation!

I'm sure you remember, as I do, 1998 and the return of the Hearts to Regina, where it had all started for Scott. In

1982 the attendance was less than 10,000. In 1998 it topped 150,000. That was also when Sandra Schmirler and her team arrived home from their Gold Medal Olympic performance—with barely enough time to get ready, as Team Canada, for the championship. I will never forget Sandra and her teammates walking into the Regina Agridome as a full house stood on their feet, cheering wildly ... and for so long. We were so proud of them and their accomplishments. It was probably too much to expect them to repeat their win from 1997 after all they had gone through. But what they did do was sign every autograph, shake every hand and kiss every cheek that was proffered to them.

I remember vividly when we lost Sandra to cancer. She phoned me on the media bench on the last day of the championship and asked me to read a message to the curlers at the victory banquet that night. I couldn't manage it, but Vic Rauter did. We celebrated Sandra that evening and we continue to do so today. The Sandra Schmirler Foundation was created to ensure that Sandra's legacy—her love of family and children—will live on through donations to neonatal facilities across Canada. The Foundation continues to grow with the help of an incredible group of dedicated volunteers. A truly remarkable person, Sandra was wife, mother, daughter, competitor and friend to so many of us. I will always cherish her memory.

When I look back, I realize how incredibly fortunate I have been to have had an opportunity to indulge my passion and to enjoy the thrill of helping to build women's curling in this country. However, one relationship is set apart from all the others: the one between me and my mother. Mom came along as a babysitter for several years, then later as accountant to manage expense accounts. In 1986 Bob Stewart asked me who paid for Mom to come to the Scott Tournament of Hearts. I said "I do." He said he wanted to

STAY HEALTHY

I know what Robin means when she talks of a dream job. Mine was with Air Canada and the Silver Broom, and it took me all across Canada and the United States, to Scotland and every curling outpost in Europe and Scandinavia.

Inevitably, whenever I let drop the news that I would be off shortly for (fill in name of your favourite curling destination), someone would ask if they could come along and carry my bags. Or sometimes it was "how can I get a job like that?" to which my answer was always the same: "stay healthy." I recall one occasion when, as usual, we were scheduled to fly into our target community on a Friday, meet throughout the weekend with the various local subcommittees and then fly home. One of our contingent mentioned on the flight to Europe that he was feeling a bit queasy. By the time we arrived at our destination he was running a temperature so he retired to his hotel room bed where he stayed until it was time to board the plane and head home.

"Fat lot of good you were," was the unsympathetic comment from one of our number as we settled into our seats for the long flight home.

Yep, if you want that kind of a job, priority number one is to stay healthy.

change that and gave me a cheque for her expenses, retroactive to 1982. At Scott Paper's 10th anniversary in 1991, Scott presented her with a diamond pendant in the shape of the four hearts. Mom continues to come to the Scott Tournament of Hearts (she hasn't missed one yet). I continue to cherish those two weeks I have with my mother every year. It's another reason I am thankful to Scott Paper.

In 2006 we celebrated the 25th anniversary of the Scott Tournament of Hearts in London, Ontario. Much has happened in the last five years. We survived a major brouhaha as curling fans expressed their displeasure with the CCA over their switch in television coverage. The prospect of full TSN coverage in 2008 now has everybody happy.

That 2006 celebration was not just about longevity. The Tournament of Hearts was all about celebrating champions: champions on the ice and off. It was about saluting our fans, our host committees and their volunteers, and the curling associations, both provincial and national. It was about our customers, and the media who have provided incredible support through their coverage over the years.

Scott Paper may be the longest-serving corporate sponsor of amateur sport in Canada, but we're not finished yet. Scott Paper has signed a new agreement to sponsor women's curling through Canada's Olympic year of 2010. I'm proud to have been associated with them since the beginning.

Okay fans, as author of this here tome, let's hear it for Robin Wilson (applause and a standing ovation).

Chapter Nine
CURLING AND TELEVISION

IN ANY SPORT THERE ARE SEMINAL EVENTS THAT HELP TO DEFINE IT OR to change it indelibly.

In baseball it was Curt Flood and the reserve clause. In hockey it was in the summer of 2005, following a year's lockout of players by owners, when the National Hockey League and the NHL Players' Association agreed to a new collective bargaining agreement.

And in curling, if you want my opinion, the game was altered forever with the arrival of television in the 1950s.

Before the advent of the TV camera, there were two common similes associated with curling: "Watching curling is like watching paint dry" and "Curling is like sex: better for participants than spectators" (although someone else opined that curling and sex were alike in that you didn't need to be expert in either to enjoy them).

The arrival of television moved curling from the periphery of sport to the forefront. Any sport is television-friendly, because it involves an unknown result. Even so, many of the major TV sports are not as boob tube-friendly as curling.

Think about it for a minute. Most major sports involve relatively small objects (hockey puck, baseball, golf ball) travelling at a very fast speed within a large playing area. The sight of a golf ball soaring against the backdrop of a blue sky is not particularly exciting. That, of course, changes when that same ball returns to earth, particularly if it veers into the woods at Augusta, or the waters off Pebble Beach, or a pothole bunker on the Old Course at

St. Andrews. But, let's face it—a golf ball against an azure sky is not high drama.

In hockey, before the advent of slo-mo replays, a slapshot was nothing but a blur. "Did you see it hit the goalpost?" "No, but I think I heard it." The FOX network's experiment of putting a meteor-like trailer on a slapshot was quickly dumped.

Baseball has no trouble with a close-up of a collision at home plate, but often the viewer at home has no idea where all the other players have moved to back up that play. A close play at first base is still a mystery to the television viewer until a slo-mo replay shows what the umpire sees and hears (the slap of the ball in the first baseman's mitt just before or after the runner's foot touches the base).

So where does curling fit into all this? First, let's acknowledge some obvious but not oft-mentioned facts. A curling stone is not small. It is definitely not moving at warp speed. And the game's action is confined to a relatively small area. As soon as you paint a bullseye onto the ice (and show it in an overhead shot), even the most obtuse fan can figure out that the object of the exercise is to get your stone closer to the centre than your opponent's. A curler's delivery (long, elegant slide, handle oozing out of the fingers) and even the frenetic, noisy sweeping of two corn brooms (later changed to the quiet scrubbing of brushes) have an artistic and graceful quality.

"Why do the players put the stone where it doesn't seem to do any good? Why do they want to hit that stone over there instead of this one over here? Wouldn't it be smarter to try this instead of that?" And so on, as the viewers at home, whether curlers or not, ask what seem to be very sensible questions. And, of course, the commentators (mostly former champions) are there to answer those queries or outline the strategy of the moment. Think Vic Rauter, Linda

1969 CANADIAN
CURLING CHAMPIONSHIP

The year after the start of the Silver Broom, Don Chevrier (l) and the author provided commentary for one of the many CBC special curling series. CBC photo by Robert Ragsdale

Moore, Ray Turnbull on TSN; or more recently Don Wittman, Joan McCusker, Mike Harris on CBC. Or, to be a mite immodest, out of the past, Don Chevrier, Don Duguid et moi.

There's another major appeal to televised curling. The fact that the curlers on view could be your neighbour or your buddy from work helps add a touch of familiarity to the coverage that may be missing in other professional events, in which the competitors are apt to be millionaires imported from elsewhere. Add the fact that the players are fitted with microphones so the viewer can eavesdrop on the action, and the curling telecast has a dimension that is missing from most other sports telecasts—an appealing air of immediacy and unpredictability.

Don't take my word for it. Bob Weeks gives a good example of this aspect of the televised game in his marvellous book, *The Brier*, when describing the Sudbury Brier of 1983. That was the Brier where the CBC fitted the curlers with microphones for the first time, warning all players, of course, to be aware of their language, because it would be caught by the live mics. In an Ontario–Alberta game, 'twixt Ed Werenich and Ed Lukowich, the entire nation listened in as Werenich discussed a key shot with his third, Paul Savage. It would be tricky, almost impossible. The rock had to barely clear a front guard, but if it did, it could be lacking in strength to reach the rings. Take it away, Bob: "So the Wrench said he would release his rock on the narrow side of the broom, 'and let the boys sweep the piss out of it.' In the mobile studio outside the arena, the CBC technicians fell out of their chairs, some stunned, others howling."

There is no record of the reaction of millions of fans across the land, but it can be assumed they learned, first-hand, how delicate a Brier shot can be. And how necessary it is to have heavy sweeping at exactly the right moment.

For these and other reasons, television producers and program executives soon discovered that watching curling was not as much like watching snail races as some had thought. Early on, when the viewing numbers began to come in, it was fascinating to discover there were more people tuned in to the Brier than there were registered curlers across the land. Indeed, the mailbag often contained letters from folks who said they didn't curl, had never curled, but loved to watch the game on TV.

I was lucky enough to be there at the start of curling on the tube. It should be noted that television's production pioneers in the various curling precincts of the land—Winnipeg, Edmonton, Calgary, Toronto—all discovered the allure of the game locally. And I imagine the same held true in Halifax and other curling locales in Atlantic Canada. Trying to decide which city was first to provide local coverage is a waste of energy, but I do know when the first live coast-to-coast telecast of a Brier game took place, and where—'cause I did it. It was in Kitchener's Memorial Auditorium on Saturday, March 10, 1962.

Here's the story. When the regular round robin that year finished on Friday afternoon, March 9, there was a three-way tie for the top (7 wins, 2 losses) between Alberta's Hector Gervais, Manitoba's Norm Houck and Saskatchewan's Ernie Richardson. It was only the third time in Brier

The answer, Alex, is ... (l–r) the author, Hector Gervais and Johnny Wayne. The question, in true *Jeopardy* fashion, is: Who are those other three talking to famed *Jeopardy* host Alex Trebek, when he worked at the CBC? CBC photo by Robert Ragsdale

history that three teams had tied for first place. In 1928 Gordon Hudson of Manitoba had emerged as winner in the playoff. In 1946 it was Alberta's Billy Rose. Would it be Saskatchewan's turn in 1962? Certainly, in those days, the three Prairie provinces were ranked as prime Brier favourites.

Two things happened after the 10th round of play. The first was a draw from the hat to decide which foursome would get the bye to the Saturday final. Saskatchewan won the draw, leaving Alberta and Manitoba to fight it out in the Friday night semifinal. The second was a phone call I received from the CBC's Gordon Craig. Gordon and I had been involved in some of the local curling telecasts in earlier years and subsequently in the CBC's "Cross Canada Curling" series (later called "Championship Curling"). Gord's message was succinct. "I've made arrangements," he said, "to do tomorrow's final playoff game, live, so I'll be rolling a truck down [Highway] 401 in the morning. We'll set up as soon as we arrive, and I want you to find a place where you could do the play-by-play." I found a location in the stands (there was no dedicated booth as in future years), and I can't recall if we even had a monitor to show the camera shots. But it was historic because, for the first time, curling fans across the entire country could follow live, via television, the same action, the same excitement, the same drama, that the fans jammed into the Kitchener-Waterloo Auditorium were watching. It still gives me goosebumps just thinking about it.

The results? Big Hector, the defending Brier champ from Alberta, beat Houck of Manitoba Friday night, 8–6, but was outgunned in the final as the Richardsons of Regina won their third Brier crown, 14–7. I seem to recall Norm playing the first playoff game in a white dress shirt, complete with cufflinks. I don't think his attire had anything to do with the playoff result.

Since then, of course, television technology has soared—with overhead cameras, split-screen coverage, freeze-frames, slow-motion replays, the telestrator (the device that allows commentators to diagram strategy options on the screen) and the many other items of technical wizardry that

THE OVERHEAD CAMERA

Back in the early days of the CBC "Championship Curling" series, one of the things the television viewers never heard was the plaintive request from the overhead camera operator in Winnipeg. Today, of course, the overhead camera is a remote-controlled robot whose operator would be a whiz in any video arcade. Back then, though, the overhead camera was a regular camera, set on a platform above the rings and controlled by an operator who, before the game, climbed up to his perch via a ladder that was then roped up away from the ice.

On this occasion, Don Chevrier and I, listening on our earphones, and awaiting the imminent start of play, heard the overhead gentleman ask to have the ladder lowered.

"What for?" asked the producer in the truck.

"I gotta go!" came the anguished reply.

"Tough luck," said the producer, "you're up there till the end of the game!"

If there was a moan from on high we didn't hear it, and as the game began we ceased to worry about the overhead camera operator. Until the end of the game.

We waited to see how quickly he would climb down from his crow's nest location. It turned out to be a leisurely descent, and as his feet moved slowly down the ladder, we could see why.

Clutched in one hand was one of his zipper galoshes, held at some distance from his body. Seems necessity really is the mother of invention.

have combined to produce coverage that is now considered essential to any major curling event.

And other countries around the world have discovered what Canada has known for over 50 years: curling is the most couch-potato friendly sport of them all!

Chapter Ten
CULTURE CLASH

YOU'VE ALL HEARD OF CULTURE SHOCK. WHAT I WANT TO TELL ABOUT now is culture clash. Not the same thing. Culture clash is a flash of recognition that the way you do things in your culture and the way other cultures do the same things is different. Not necessarily better or worse—just different. And after working with committees in all parts of the curling world, I say *vive la difference*. Learning about other cultures was one of the greatest benefits of working all those years organizing curling events, including the world championships.

You want a couple of for-instances? Okay, I've got a pair: one from France, t'other from Sweden.

Let me preface the France story with this query: When you were a child, did your parents teach you the same thing mine tried to? One of my father's dictums was "Clean up your plate; think of the starving Armenians." For the longest time, I never knew who the Armenians were and why they were always starving. Maybe in your family it was some other nation. Anyway, my parents were pretty successful in their clean-up-the-plate teaching, and I always did my best to eat everything put in front of me, whether I liked it or not. Still do, to this day.

Fade to France, 1971, as preparations are being made in Megève during the week prior to the first Silver Broom in Europe. Along with my wife, Anne, and a few Air Canada planners, I have arrived in that beautiful Alpine setting. One evening, a couple of the committee members suggest dinner at a tiny restaurant way up the side of one of the mountains.

We traverse a local goat path to arrive at the chosen *estaminet* and enter through the kitchen—the better to inspect the chef's handiwork. As dinner progresses we are all enjoying ourselves immensely. Our hosts are the epitome of kindness, the chef is inspired and, although there is a bit of language difficulty now and then, the abundance of wine helps us find the needed words. In short we are having a marvellous time.

The only trouble is that as fast as we honour the teachings of *mes parents* ("clean up your plate") and finish the ambrosial offerings in front of us, our hosts are just as quick to replenish our plates—and wine glasses—until finally I can heed my father's strictures no longer. We are pleasantly buzzed with *le vin du maison*, and stuffed to the plimsolls with the chef's best.

As we groan our way back to our hotel we learn that all the time our parents had been drumming that particular eating lesson into our tiny little heads, our hosts' parents had been drumming into their heads that it is impolite to have a guest with an empty plate in front of him or her.

As dutifully as we followed our parents' instructions, they followed theirs—and loaded more victuals onto the plate and more wine into the glass. We, in turn, would clean off the plate and drain the wine, whereupon they would replenish. You get the picture, I'm sure.

After that experience, we knew enough to leave a little wine in the glass and a little food on the plate to signal that we were satisfied. Being France, the food was always imaginatively prepared, enticingly presented and superbly delicious. And the wine, ah, the wine....

My Swedish cultural experience was neither clash nor shock, but was certainly new and delightful—and one that the Maxwells have, on many occasions since, incorporated into our Canadian life.

The "winsome foursome" from Sweden: (l–r) Elisabeth Branäs, Britt-Marie Lundin, Eva Rosenhed and Anne-Marie Ericsson. Photo courtesy of *Canadian Curling News*

We're all familiar with the custom of toasting someone or something, on a special occasion. "Here's a toast to Charlie, on his 21st birthday." Or "Let's drink a toast to Janet, the hero of that last game." In Sweden, the custom is much more formalized, as I discovered in Örebro one time—1976, I think it was. I do know it was June 21st, Midsummer Night's Eve, for the sun in that northern part of the world dipped below the horizon only for an hour or so that night.

A group of us led by Pete Jerome from Air Canada were heading to Karlstad (via Örebro) for meetings regarding the 1977 Silver Broom. We had been invited to play golf with Elisabeth Branäs's 1976 European championship team. Elisabeth's winsome foursome (Eva Rosenhed, Britt-Marie Lundin and Anne-Marie Ericsson) had come to Canada the previous winter to play in the CBC's televised curling series.

They were the first non-Canadian team invited to do so and had proved to be outstanding ambassadors for Sweden.

When we arrived in Örebro, the day was bright and balmy, perfect for golf. But it proved to be an embarrassing day for me. It will come as no surprise to my friends that I am not ranked among the top golfers at the club. But on that day I skulled more balls, shanked more drives, found the woods more often and plunked more balls than I thought possible into the narrow stream that meandered back and forth across the fairways and, of course, was more than somewhat embarrassed by it all. Even more so since our Swedish hosts, as fine golfers as they were curlers, shot superb rounds.

After we changed, it was time to attend the dinner that the Branäs team had arranged for us. By that time, their husbands and other guests had arrived, and when it came time to go to the table, we were given easy, but explicit, instructions. "Pierre, would you accompany Eva; Sven, would you escort Anne-Marie; Doug, you will sit to the left of Elisabeth," and so on. We were then formally welcomed to the table with a toast from the host, and throughout the meal, there were individual toasts proposed. I say "individual" for strangely (to me), the toasts were usually raised just between two of those present.

What a delightful custom it is. And at times, what a sexy one.

When Anne-Marie says, "Doug, I'd like to drink a toast with you," it's just the two of us who raise glasses. Then, while sipping the nectar, it is imperative that the two of us look deeply into each other's eyes. When finished sipping, still maintaining eye contact, the glasses are lowered to the same level as the outset of the toast. God bless the Swedes for this lovely custom.

At that Örebro dinner, the first time I ran into this situation, I blundered badly. I toasted as we would in Canada;

that is, as the toastee, I would raise my glass, take a sip and then lower the glass, hardly bothering to look at the toaster at all.

Fortunately for me, Sven Eklund (later to serve as president of the International Curling Federation, but then the secretary-general of the Swedish Curling Federation) set me straight on the details of the Swedish custom and how it had originated in the military.

"A senior officer would toast a junior officer and, on conclusion of the sip of wine, the glass would be lowered to the level of the second button down from the collar," said Sven. "If the junior did not return the toast within a minute or so," continued Sven, "then his career was on rocky ground."

The toast can also work in a crowded room. One evening at a banquet in Sweden, where there were 500 or more present, an old friend across the room caught my eye. Raising his glass, he indicated a long-distance toast. Having learned of the custom earlier, I was able to respond as if I had been doing so all my life.

From the military the custom came into general use and is still used today at any Swedish dinner party of eight or more. "Except," said Sven, "you don't toast the hostess."

"Why not?"

"Because if every gentleman present, in obvious good taste, saluted the hostess," he explained, "either she'd be so busy quaffing wine she wouldn't get around to serving the meal, or..." and I'm sure you can work out that reason.

However, when it comes time for the post-dinner coffee, then the gentleman to the left of the hostess (it's the honoured position) rises and, on behalf of all present, offers a special toast to the lady, thanking her for the lovely meal. But even here, Sven told me, you have to be careful. If you praise the dinner too fulsomely, it might be interpreted as a suggestion that normally our lovely hostess's meals are somewhat ordinary, but tonight she has really outdone herself. I don't think I was ever able to get it quite right, to find *les mots justes*, the perfect words. Oh well, I tried—and that should count for something, shouldn't it?

And if you ever wind up in that honoured position, don't try to foist off the job on someone else, someone more polished than you, as I did the first time I ran into the situation. You're in the position of honour; get used to it. Think of it as a chance for you, as skip, to throw the last rock of the final end of the title game; you'd better deliver.

I found this out the hard way, at that post-golf dinner in Örebro, being seated to the left of our hostess. When I finally accepted that I was in the honouree's role, I casually asked one of my Swedish male friends for some Scandinavian words that approximated our Canadian "May I have your attention please." I then used the word he provided, which I cannot possibly reprint here, since it was, so I learned later, a rather rude and indelicate term. It did, however, have the desired effect, for everyone immediately ceased talking and, yes, I did have their complete attention, or perhaps I should say their shocked attention. Somehow, unaware of my verbal gaffe, I stumbled through the occasion with only minimal damage to Canada's reputation, although I'm sure the Swedes present wondered where I had picked up that particular word.

Earlier in the Örebro meal, I discovered how sexy the Swedish toast can be when the lovely lady across the table said, in her sultry voice, "Doug, I'd like to drink with you," and raised her glass. Looking deeply into her eyes, as the vintage wine trickled over the tongue, it was hard to tell whether it was the drink, or the moment, that created the flutter of excitement somewhere within the rib cage. There were just the two of us, all alone, amid the others. At least I think there were others.

My good friend Håkan Sundström, who first came to the Silver Broom as a journalist, but who later went legit and became secretary-general of the Swedish Curling Federation (and World Curling Federation media man), reminded me of another occasion when I rose to offer the after-dinner toast. I had written him to check my facts on the Swedish custom, and he replied that I was pretty close with my memory.

"Do you remember," he asked, "the advance media tour in September of 1976?" The tour was what the airline people call "a Fam," or familiarization, tour: A small group of travel agents and media are shown the championship site in advance, so they can relay suitable details to their readers or clients.

"We had a dinner on the cruise boat on Lake Malaren," Håkan recalled, "an 'upside-down' dinner, where we started with coffee and cognac; and you stood up immediately and thanked the committee for a lovely meal."

Now that you mention it, Håkan, it did turn out to be a lovely meal ... the *skål* (toast) was followed by dessert, then the main course, hors d'oeuvres and ended with the pre-prandial punch.

Is that when I learned to say *skål*, you ask? No, I had learned that one earlier, as you will discover in Chapter 22, which tells how I learned to say *şerefé*.

Chapter Eleven

MEMORABLE, MAGICAL MOMENTS IN MEGÈVE

WHENEVER A FEW OF US ANCIENT SILVER BROOMERS GET TOGETHER and pour out a flagon of nostalgia, it's not long before we recall our memories of Megève, that picturesque Alpine town in the French Haute Savoie. Megève, as mentioned earlier, hosted the 1971 world championship—the first time the event was held in Europe, and it was also, quite simply, magical. A brace of stories come to mind.

You may already know that Megève was, and is, one of the top-class winter destinations in Europe. "Quaint" best describes the village, with its narrow, cobblestone streets, small shops and intimate restaurants. The surrounding mountains are stunning. While it does have a sheet of curling ice within the arena and off to one side, Megève is best known as a ski resort, and host to many international ski competitions, which leads into my first story.

WHEN THE WAR CAME TO MEGÈVE

The accompanying photo shows a group of curlers posing in front of Megève's finest and most famous hotel, the Mont d'Arbois, our home away from home that Silver Broom week. The photo was taken sometime between the World Wars, and there is a fascinating story about the hotel and its long-time manager, Monsieur François Parodi, who stands second from the right.

The famed Rothschild family, who usually vacationed in St. Moritz, Switzerland, for their winter fun, was apparently concerned about anti-Semitic

The early days of curling in Megève brought together a world-famous group of automotive and aviation pioneers. From left to right are Monsieur Santos Dumont, the
Wright brothers (Orville and Wilbur), Monsieur Voisin (automotive), Mr. Farman (aviation),
two unidentified men, Monsieur François Parodi (with beret, director of the Mont d'Arbois
hotel) and another unidentified player. Photo courtesy of Tourism Megève

German army clientele making their winter vacation difficult in St. Moritz during the Great War of 1914–18. So
they elected to move their custom to Megève, then a small,
quiet Alpine village. Winter sports were just beginning to
attract visitors and, as the town grew, thanks in large part to
the Rothschild pocketbook and patronage, Megève became
a fabulous, high-society winter resort. And later, as it had
been in St. Moritz, curling was added to the sporting roster.

Shortly after the Winter Olympics of 1936, the Rothschilds recruited Parodi, a Swiss ski champion and Olympic competitor (one story had him as an Olympic medallist),
to be the manager of the Mont d'Arbois. Turning Megève
into an outstanding winter sports community was quite to
Parodi's liking.

World War II saw the Nazis overrun France, including Megève. The story goes that when the German commanding officer arrived in Megève, he went directly to the Hotel Mont d'Arbois, high up the mountainside, intent on commandeering the facility as his personal headquarters. While standing in the lobby, he spotted a photograph on the wall and began inspecting it. It was of a ski jumper, in soaring flight, against a mountain backdrop.

The commandant demanded to know who it was.

Proud Monsieur Parodi, suspecting he might be the soon-to-be deposed hotel manager, nevertheless stood up and announced that it was him and explained that the photo was taken during the 1936 Winter Olympics in Garmisch-Partenkirchen, where he had been a Swiss Olympic competitor. The commander reportedly looked again, then turned to Parodi, narrowing his eyes and said that he too had been an Olympic skier, for Germany. Legend doesn't say if the two became true "Olympic friends" or merely exchanged stories over a bottle of wine, or even if they spoke further. What is known, though, is that the commanding officer decided to find another location for his HQ. The Olympic bond between the two saved the hotel, and M. Parodi's job. In addition, I was told (though I can't vouch for the accuracy of the information) that the brilliant copper roof of the hotel, which gleamed brightly in the moonlight, was often used as a navigational checkpoint or beacon for Allied bombers on the way to their targets.

When I was researching this small story, Chuck Hay helped to confirm my information. "Not only did he [Parodi] ski well," wrote Chuck, "but for several years he was captain of the French Golf team. After World War II, I understand the Rothschilds gave him the hotel as a gift for looking after them so well." Hay also reported having been invited to visit the private room where Parodi kept his medals, trophies and souvenirs.

When the Silver Broom began in 1968, three of the Parodi sons—Guido (Guy), Martino and François Jr.—provided the support for French skip Pierre Boan.

THE HAPPENING AT LE VIEUX MEGÈVE

You've heard of a "happening," I'm sure. You know, that occasion when suddenly, unexpectedly, the stars are all aligned and something unique happens. It's impossible to plan one; you just have to experience it. It's a fragile thing, and fleeting, but if you're part of a "happening" you never forget it. Let me tell you about the happening in Megève.

It started out as a normal mid-week day of games during that 1971 Silver Broom. Mike Taylor was, as usual, directing the film being made of the event and said to a number of us before we left the hotel for the evening games, "Be sure you get back right after the games. Leo and Bob [Thompson and Mason, number one camera and soundman] will be shooting the party scene in the pub area, and I want you guys to be in it."

How often do you get that kind of a summons from a Hollywood director? Well, maybe not a Hollywood director, but perhaps a National Film Board honcho? Okay, then a gifted filmmaker working in Air Canada's PR department? Not very often. We told him we'd wrap up the activity at the arena as quickly as possible and then race back so we could be at the pub, complete with combed hair and captivating smiles.

What we hadn't counted on that night was the weather. Midway through the games, it began to snow. Big, wet, white, fluffy, dinner-plate-sized flakes that blanketed the roads, in particular the winding road up the mountainside leading to the hotel and the pub. Many of the spectators left the arena early, and the teams hurried into their vans as soon as the last rocks were thrown. Those of us who were left behind were either finishing up the administrative side of the

Two of the heroes of Megève: "Cactus" Jack Wells (l), catalyst for "The Happening," and Don Duguid, 1970 and '71 Silver Broom World Championship skip. Photo by Michael Burns

draw or sending back media reports to Canada or Scotland. By the time we hurried out of the arena, the snow was deep, the driving treacherous. We were told the road to the hotel was closed unless you had a four-wheel-drive vehicle equipped with chains on all four wheels. Better, we were told, to wait downtown till the snow let up and chain-equipped cars could collect us.

So about 10 of us, maybe more, found ourselves in a small café called Le Vieux Megève, where we ordered some finger food and wine. Among our group was "Cactus Jack" Wells of Winnipeg, one of curling's most famous of blithe spirits. The restaurant was filled with locals, some Scottish spectators who were staying in downtown hotels and a few members of Les Binous, the Breton bagpipes (first cousin to Scots bagpipes) who had led the players onto the ice earlier in the evening. We put together a couple of tables for our group and, till then, it was a scene typical of any boîte in the land.

And then Cactus asked if any of us had some extra curling pins, the lapel pins that are a staple at every curling event from a local bonspiel to a world championship. Pretty soon he had collected enough for Les Binous. Then he sashayed over to their table, and in his best Winnipeg sign language, mimed that he would like to bestow the pins on them. Somewhat sheepishly they allowed him to decorate their uniform jackets, and then he finished off the presentation with that Gallic kiss-on-both-cheeks salute. And not willing to leave it there, he mimed that perhaps they might play something on their pipes. Which they did. Followed by applause from all in the café.

Well, it didn't take much more for someone to order a few bottles of wine to be sent over to Les Binous's table, and for some of us to unlimber our Grade 10 French, while the locals gamely tried to reply in their tourist anglais. And the Scots did what Scots always do so well—display a hearty appreciation of the occasion.

Then, with the snow still "shawling out of the ground" (isn't that how Dylan Thomas put it?), the proprietor got into the act. Locking the doors of the restaurant—in his opinion, it was past closing time—he uncorked more of the house wine, on the house, and pushed back the tables. Music suddenly commenced, and then we were all arm in arm, singing and downing the wine and, just like that, we were in the midst of a "happening," as locals danced with Canadians, and Les Binous, with maybe a Scot or two, doing their version of the Highland Fling, and time stood still. I tell you, it was magic, sheer magic. A happening.

And all because Cactus had bestowed his own brand of goodwill on the young Breton pipers, who probably didn't know one end of a curling stone from the other.

Eventually a car equipped with chains to get us up the mountain road appeared, and somehow we got back to our hotel, unable to wipe the smiles from our faces.

"Too bad you missed the party scene," said Mike and Leo and Bob.

"Too bad you missed the happening," we countered. "Your party scene was probably contrived; ours was the real thing. That was what you should have caught on film."

Except, of course, it was the kind of experience you can never wholly capture on film. You can only play it back from the happy parts of your memory.

DIVERS/DRIVERS

There was one instance when quick thinking and a hastily contrived translation proved a boon. It happened like this. In his Megève hotel room one evening, a visitor spent an enjoyable interlude with the "social hostess" of the hotel, and discovered he could charge the expense to his hotel bill. When he returned home and submitted his expense account, including the hotel bill, the company accountant challenged the 300-franc expense, shown as *divers* (pronounced *dee-vairs* and meaning "miscellaneous").

"What's this "divers" expense?" he queried, giving the name the English long-"i" pronunciation that suggests an aquatic connotation. Our fast-thinking hero looked at the account and then, as if the light was just dawning on him, calmly replied, "That? Oh that was a misprint, a mistake. You see, they took up a collection for the drivers who ferried us back and forth to the arena, and I charged it to my hotel account. That should read "drivers"... they left out the "r.""

Chapter Twelve
CURLING BEATS FUN

Larry Wood

Calgary's Larry Wood arrived at the Brier about the same year I did, 1960, and has logged as many air miles as I have—nay, probably more—covering curling for the Calgary Herald. When we sat down to lunch a year or two ago, the reminiscences started flowing faster than the wine, and so, when this book started to take shape, I asked him to contribute some of his memories. I'm glad to say he did, and his contributing words include this chapter. Carry on, Woody.

ONCE UPON A TIME, BACK THERE IN THE SIXTIES, AN ENTERPRISING Western Canadian pitchman named Ted Thonger penned the three-word slogan "Curling Beats Fun" and transferred it to an array of buttons, banners and bumper stickers. It was a grabber in its time and, some say, it wasn't stretching the truth a great deal.

Curling is a "people" sport, accessible to anyone who can walk, squat and think. It is considered by some to be in a league with darts, shuffleboard and bowling—several media cynics have referred to it as Eskimo bowling—but this ancient Scottish import is actually more diverse, more technically, physically and mentally taxing than people think. It combines some of the physical and technical demands of bowling and golf with the mental demands of chess and, yes, even baseball and football.

Most curlers answer their critics by reasoning that, like anything else, you have to learn something about it to appreciate it. But they may be underselling their product. CCA officials estimate there are 1.25 million curlers in Canada, yet CBC television ratings for each year's world championships, as well as the Brier and Hearts, regularly indicate viewer totals up to five times that number. In fact, couch curlers have outnumbered participants since the 1970s.

The time is Tuesday afternoon, late March, 1970. The place is the brand new Memorial Auditorium in beautiful downtown Utica, New York. The occasion is round three of Silver Broom III, otherwise known as the World Men's Curling Championship sponsored by Air Canada. Save the curlers, a smattering of officials bedecked in tams and badges, a dozen or so glassy-eyed reporters and a noisy group of school children absorbing for the first time (in the name of physical education) this strange spectacle of "guys throwing cobblestones," the building is empty. On Sheet D, the cream of Canadian men's curling is in debate with the flower of the game as it is played in Germany. It is the seventh end, and the scoreboard reads Canada 322 023—12, Germany 000 100—1.

A Canadian player kneels at mid-ice to inspect a glint that has caught his attention. He reaches down for the thin wire object that appears to be embedded in the freeze. He grasps it with thumb and forefinger and holds it up for the inspection of a teammate. It is a paper clip. Further inspection reveals another such object on the ice. And another.

"Migawd," says Jim Pettapiece, the aforementioned Canadian, to himself, readjusting his gaze to the adjacent swarm of kids, laughing and restless, "those kids are throwing paper clips at us." Such was the impact of international curling and the underwhelming respect its stars received . . . in the beginning.

"The silver broom telecasts from Regina [in 1983] drew a 46 percent share of the total TV audience," the late Jim Thompson, then the producer of "CBC Sports Weekend," was quoted as saying in a 1986 article on TV sports coverage.

"Back in 1977, the Broom telecasts from Karlstad, Sweden, drew 48 percent, or 1.9 million viewers, which was a record high figure for any kind of weekend sports coverage," Thompson continued.

Almost from the advent of televised curling, CBC curling shows have drawn 50 percent more viewers than other sports events. Coverage of the Brier, Scott Tournament of Hearts and World Championships, along with World Juniors, National Juniors, Mixed and Seniors Competition, have enjoyed an appeal range of 30–46 percent over the last 30 years. The CBC's normal share of the Saturday afternoon audience usually tops out at half that level, 15–20 percent.

Its live gates haven't been too shabby, either. At the 1983 Broom in Regina, the organizing committee showed a record profit of $201,485. It was the second World Championship to log an advance-ticket sellout. A total of 248,243 watched the 1991 World Renewal (men's and women's championships) at the Winnipeg Arena. Of more recent vintage, the 2005 World Men's Championship in Victoria drew a total of 116,167 through the turnstiles of the brand new Save-On-Foods Memorial Centre.

When curling was finally embraced by the International Olympic Committee in 1993, rules stipulated that a sport must be played in at least 25 world nations on 3 continents in order to receive Games recognition. What epitomizes the sport today is its rapid growth at the global level. Today, the World Curling Federation boasts 46 member nations on 4 continents. Truly, it has as much to do with people and fun as with competition. More than one Canadian champion curler participating at the world level has been heard to ponder his or her subsequent return to the event as a spectator "just to find out what I missed."

The time is late evening, a Tuesday, late March, 1978. The place is the Holiday Inn, Winnipeg, and the suite of the Royal Caledonian Curling Club of Scotland. The occasion is the Scotch party, a perennial "must" for invitees at the World Curling Championship.

A youthful Scottish piper is divesting himself of his pipes and reaching for a long-awaited wee dram of the finest, over ice.

"Is it true what they say a Scotsman wears under his kilt?" inquires a young female guest, sidling over to the piper.

"Aye!" roars the piper as he unfastens his sporran, reaches therein, produces a pair of jockey shorts and presents them to the lady.

"With my respects, ma'am," he adds, "but you'll be aware o' the tradition which deman's that the recipient of a gift reciprocates in kin'."

"But of course," replies the lady who, with nary a blush, turns away, bends over, lifts her skirt, and in an impressive manoeuvre resembling an elaborate curtsy, produces a pair of nylon pantyhose.

Since the champion teams of Scotland and Canada waged a five-match duel for the first world curling title under the sponsorship of the Scotch Whisky Association in 1959, the World Men's Championship grew in magnitude to that of a European-style festival.

It boasted its own tour package, its own family of organizers, media representatives and an ever-burgeoning number of followers who considered the annual trek to the event as much a requisite holiday as the summer month at the cottage or the winter week at the ski lodge. Today arenas are decorated in a kaleidoscope of flags and banners, the pomp and pageantry of the opening and closing ceremonies borders on the spectacular, there's always an opening-night soiree complete with feast, footwork and frolic, and a closing clambake that usually goes the opener one better.

Sandwiched between the feasts is a crowded program of 17 draws of round robin competition plus tiebreakers and playoffs. In addition, the festival also includes sundry ancillary functions, industrial and geographic tours and cultural events, most of them unique to the nation or region of a particular venue. And loaded tables fit for King Arthur. Always that.

Take Silver Broom VIII at Perth, Scotland, in 1975, as a for-instance. The activities that supplemented the championship play at the old ice rink included tours of a knitting mill, two distilleries, the Royal and Ancient Golf Club at St. Andrews, Scone Palace, plus shopping in Edinburgh and a middle-of-the-night curlers' initiation ceremony with Celtic food and strange rites conducted in an abandoned castle dating back centuries.

"Attired in the obligatory ranchland duds" in 1972 were Regina committee members (l–r): Kay Hoffman, Gerry Schneider, Harriett Artiss, Win Pike and Harold Painter. Photo by Michael Burns

The time is mid-morning, a Wednesday, late March, 1972. The place is an ornate banquet hall in the centre of gorgeous Garmisch, across the river from pristine Partenkirchen, in Germany's Bavarian Alps. The occasion is the first promotional party ever tossed by the organizing committee of a subsequent world championship, in this case Silver Broom VI, slated for Regina.

An assembly of 30-odd Canadians from Saskatchewan, attired in the obligatory ranchland duds, has encountered one small problem in the arrangements for its western-style breakfast. There are no suitable carafes for the maple syrup!

"But," a gentleman wearing a Tyrolean hat, and who presides over the kitchen, has suggested, "vee haff plenty of deese." The "deese" to which he has referred are shot glasses. Now, the breakfast is underway, and a local Fräulein is selecting her seat, placing her plate of flapjacks, bacon and sausage on the table and observing with curious interest all the shot glasses filled with brown liquid.

"Aha!" she exclaims at length. "Regina schnapps!" and then immediately, "Bottoms up."

Although the World Curling Federation strives to elevate today's world championships to the highest class, it's no secret their heyday was the period from 1968 through 1985 when Air Canada sponsored the Silver Broom.

Back in those days, a committee composed of world federation and sponsor's officials toured aspiring sites at least 26 months in advance and announced its decision on the eve of that year's event.

In 1984 at Duluth, Minnesota, Toronto was awarded the hosting rights for the 1986 event over bids from Seattle-Tacoma, Vancouver, Ottawa and Chicoutimi. It's fair to say the event, which was melded with the world women's in 1989 and remained a two-pronged attraction through 2004, has undergone a rebuilding process since Air Canada's sponsorship ceased after 1985. The men's and women's events were separated again in 2005, but the longevity of the current Ford of Canada sponsorship will determine how long the separation will remain.

"Pinch me, I've never been pinched by an Italian!" Renato Ghezze of Italy (with his 1973 teammates Paolo Da Ros, Lino Mayer and Andrea Pavani) wasn't sure how to react to the Canadian matron's request. Photo from Italian Curling Association

The time is mid-evening, a Sunday, late March, 1973. The place is the Regina Inn, a swanky hostelry serving as the headquarters for Silver Broom VI. A giant of a man, a campground operator from Cortina d'Ampezzo, Italy, strides across the hotel lobby with a purpose and follows a middle-aged lady into the crowded elevator. He is Renato Ghezze, the first Italian skip ever to compete in a world curling championship.

"Are you Canadian?" asks the middle-aged lady as the doors slide closed and the elevator commences its ascent.

"Italiano," booms the big man, smiling politely.

"Oh my," chirps the middle-aged lady. Whereupon she

whirls, bends forward and, without benefit of a drum roll, thrusts a hip at her newest acquaintance. "Will you pinch me, please?" she asks, grinning. "I've never been pinched by an Italian before."

The big man from the Dolomites, his face the colour of grappa, bows politely, retreats to the back wall of the elevator and then hurriedly exits at the next floor.

"Canada—mamma mia!" he is heard to mutter in his hasty retreat.

The danger of physical injury so prevalent in most sports has been relatively non-existent in curling, but one observer remembers "probably the worst on record for the world championship." It occurred at the inaugural Silver Broom in Pointe Claire, Quebec, in the days before the Europeans began to emphasize conditioning, and it happened to a European. Franz Marti, skip of the 1968 Swiss champions from Thun, heeded a resounding call of nature in mid-game and dashed off the ice for a spot of relief. But, in even greater haste on the return trip, he slipped on a stairway, fell and fractured two bones in his left hand.

"Fortunately," recalls the observer, "he was still able to direct traffic and deliver his stones, but of course, he couldn't achieve much with his brush."

In case you missed my point: Curling Beats Fun!

Chapter Thirteen

HANSI, YOU TALK TOO MUCH

AFTER THE FIRST COUPLE OF YEARS OF THE SILVER BROOM, AIR CANADA began to receive indications from a number of curling centres around the world that perhaps we should consider bringing the Broom to their city. So suddenly we found ourselves in the site-selection business. I was asked by the airline to develop a set of criteria for choosing a host city and a procedure to follow. Other criteria grew naturally until we had a pretty sophisticated process.

We originally established a committee of three, which later grew to include two or three others who had special expertise we wished to draw upon, but for the most part, the latter acted as consultants to the original trio. And with an airline as sponsor, the travel part of the process was easily handled.

So what three were included as the key partners in the committee? First there was representation from the sponsor. Then there was a representative from the Royal Caledonian Curling Club, with whom the original contract had been established. And as the permanent person on the committee, and the one who had to work with the chosen city, there was me. Later, when the International Curling Federation ceased being a committee of the RCCC and became an independent body, we added the ICF president, an ice technician and a representative from the travel agency that would prepare the tour to the host site.

After a few experiences choosing sites, we soon developed a set of principles that we found important: (1) do not go into the visits with preconceived ideas—just let each bid city put its best foot forward and go from there; (2) do nothing to indicate to anyone—especially to the other committee members—any opinions you might have, until the end of the tour when we meet to make our decision; and (3) our decision must be unanimous—there will be no vote taken. Ever. That meant we would hold an often lengthy discussion at the end of the site tour, out of which would come a unanimous decision. We would not begin the discussion with each person indicating a choice of best site, because to do that would turn the meeting into a debate in which each would try to defend his or her view rather than arrive at a reasoned decision.

It was easy to adhere to item 3, for we all knew that if we were ever to take a vote, it would be impossible for the member who lost the vote to keep quiet about it. Oh, nothing would be said in the beginning, but the first time something went wrong at the chosen site, that member would simply be unable to keep from blurting out some variation of "I knew it...I could see it coming...I tried to tell them all along that something like this would happen, but they wouldn't listen."

It was for this reason that when we met to make the decision on the host city, we kept talking and talking (like Quakers), discussing the merits and drawbacks of each element of each site until one of the group, usually the newest member, would blurt out some variation of "Why do we keep discussing this? I think it's obvious we're all in agreement as to which would be the best site." It was usually true; we did seem to reach a common conclusion each of us could support. The beauty of this method was that, while it took a rather long time to reach a conclusion, it was one that each of us could support unanimously and wholeheartedly.

The first time Garmisch-Partenkirchen sought to host the Silver Broom was 1970 (for 1972). We had just begun to use the new site-selection process, and the system was still in its infancy. If it hadn't been in its early stages, we never would have encountered one of the famous names of Canadian history.

Here's what happened.

We were headed toward Garmisch-Partenkirchen to hear the submission of the famed Bavarian winter sports centre and had added Tony Schoen to our small group. Tony was Air Canada's PR rep in Frankfurt at the time, and we certainly needed his translating abilities. On the way to the Bavarian resort city, we received word that Munich also wanted to bid for the Broom, and they asked if we would meet with them following our visit to Garmisch-Partenkirchen. The Garmisch-Partenkirchen bid, incidentally, was superb and well-prepared. We were entranced by the famous Bavarian tourist centre and by their people.

That should have been the end of it. We should have told Munich that the deadline for bid entries had passed and, sorry, some other time perhaps. But since it was early in the site-selection process, we hadn't made that kind of policy decision yet. So we agreed to meet with the Müncheners.

On our arrival in Munich we were ushered into the city's historic council chambers, where a delegation had been hastily assembled to meet us. It soon became evident that the Munich bid was as capricious as it was ill-prepared. In fact, even though much of the conversation was in German, it was obvious to us that some of the council members present were asking some variation of "Just who are these people anyway? And why are we here to meet them?" I guess there were about 10 or 12 of us around the council table, all of us male, except for Frau Wagner, whose husband was one of the curlers spearheading their bid.

At some point in this awkward meeting, Don McLeod, chair of the Air Canada Silver Broom Steering Committee (and an airline vice-president) sensed that the Munich pitch was more a personal effort of Herr Wagner than anything else and stood absolutely no chance of success. Besides, most of the others present were more concerned about preparations for hosting the 1972 Summer Olympics. So Don suggested, diplomatically, that perhaps they might like to throw their support behind the Garmisch-Partenkirchen bid (there were two other bids outside Germany that year). The resulting agreement was like a sigh of relief. It got everybody off the hook, and then it was suggested we all retire for lunch.

But before we left the city chambers, Frau Wagner, in support of her husband, and speaking in German, tore a verbal strip off the deputy mayor, the main political figure present. I, of course, had no idea what she said to him, but her tone and gestures left little to the imagination. Seldom have I seen a more forceful hectoring job done on a politician.

At lunch I was seated next to her and, switching to perfect English, she conversed about Canada in general, and Montreal in particular.

"Do the Royals still play at Delorimier Stadium? Are the Canadiens still as powerful as ever?" she asked, and I told her the Delorimier days were long gone (I had spent many a pleasant summer baseball day there, when with the CBC in Montreal). And the Habs, I told her, were as powerful and popular as ever. And so it went.

From time to time her husband muttered, "Hansi, you talk too much. Hansi, you talk too much." His mutterings might just as well have been aimed at the ceiling.

So I asked her where the name Hansi came from and added, "I thought Hans was a man's name."

"Oh," she replied, "Hansi is just a nickname. My real name's Gerda."

Later, on the train, as our selection committee travelled to our next destination, I mused about Hansi/Gerda with Don and Tony. "She seemed to know so much about Canada and Montreal. Her English was perfect. She was such a dynamic person ... do you suppose Gerda Wagner is really Gerda Munsinger?"

"Oh migawd!" exploded Don, "and I suggested that the next time she comes to Montreal she should stay at our house! Tony," he commanded, "find out."

Later we discovered that "Hansi Wagner" was indeed the same Gerda Munsinger whose sex scandal involved at least two cabinet ministers and almost toppled the Diefenbaker government in Canada's version of the Profumo Affair. And Don needn't have worried about hosting her, since she was *persona non grata* in Canada, and would never have been allowed into the country.

That should have been the end of it, but two years later, "Hansi" showed up at the Garmisch-Partenkirchen Broom and proceeded to captivate many of the males present. It should be added she didn't seem to have the same effect on the females.

Even then, she caused Don a problem.

Part of the week's events was a reception promoting the next year's Silver Broom, slated for Regina. You might recall Larry Wood's description of the Regina breakfast in the previous chapter. Gerda was in attendance at the various Regina promotional events, including an evening reception where she asked Michael Burns if he would take her picture with the two Mounties present, who were resplendent in full uniform. Michael obliged, of course, and I'd use that picture here if only Michael had a print, or the negative. But Don, consummate PR pro that he was, insisted the negative be destroyed. "If that picture ever got out in Canada," he thundered, "it could cost those Mounties their job."

Flanked by two Mounties in Garmisch-Partenkirchen, 1972, are Gerda Munsinger, Laurie Artiss and Harriett Artiss. Photo courtesy of Laura Argue

So where did we get the photo of Gerda, the two Mounties and Laurie and Harriett Artiss? Not from Michael Burns's files, that's clear. No, we got it from a Regina committee member who took her own shot that day in March 1972. Don didn't know about that negative, and neither did I until some years later.

There's a PS to this story, not from 1972, but from 2002. I was in Grande Prairie, Alberta, where the annual McCain TSN Skins Game was being held. After the weekend series was over—with Randy Ferbey's incredible Edmonton foursome as winners—our TSN crew was at the airport awaiting our departure.

"Excuse me, but aren't you Doug Maxwell?" asked a uniformed security chap. I allowed as how that was so.

"Well, you may not remember me," he continued, "but before I retired from the RCMP, I had the pleasure of going with the Regina Silver Broom Committee to Garmisch-Partenkirchen in 1972."

"And you were one of the Mounties who was photographed with Gerda Munsinger," I replied.

"That's right," said Hank Jantzen. "My partner and I were on hand because we spoke German, and we were an integral part of the Regina '73 promotion."

We chatted until we heard the boarding call, recalling long ago memories of Garmisch-Partenkirchen. And the days from then till now. And Gerda. Or perhaps I should say, Hansi.

Chapter Fourteen

WHEN THE ICE GOES WONKY

LET ME SAY, RIGHT AT THE START, THAT I KNOW VERY LITTLE ABOUT THE intricacies of arena ice. So all you icemakers can relax; I'm not about to pass along some esoteric lore that is essential to your craft.

I know that water freezes at 32° F, or 0°C. And if that is the case—and I assume we're all agreed on that—then why was it, in 1972, when the Silver Broom rolled into Garmisch-Partenkirchen, Bavaria (West Germany as it was then called), there was a stretch of water that refused to freeze?

The teams were due to arrive within the next few days. The fans would arrive soon after that. The first floods were being put onto the arena floor. All was going well, and the water was freezing nicely. Icemaker Don Lewis would soon be putting in the hacks and painting the circles, except there was this stubborn streak of ice—well, it should have been ice—that refused to freeze. Across the rest of the arena floor there was ice—beautiful, pristine. But behold, running from one end of the arena to the other, about 24 inches (61 cm) wide, right through the 8-foot circle of Sheet B, there was this strip of water, a veritable canal, where no canal was intended.

It was, of course, late at night when this paradox came to my attention, because late at night is always when these kinds of things happen. It's a curling variation of Murphy's Law. Late at night is also when icemakers shine. There's nobody around to bother them with dumb comments or silly suggestions. But when the water doesn't do what it is supposed to do—namely

Cartoon by John Dunnett, courtesy of *Canadian Curling News*

freeze—then guess who gets called.

As I mentioned, I know very little about ice, so the ensuing conversation was not about what was happening, but about what should, could, might happen, if the situation persisted. The conversation went something like this:

DON: Can we (heh, heh) call the whole thing off?
ME: Don't be silly.
DON: Is there any way we could hide it?
ME: You mean, rearrange the sheets so that the watery bit could be disguised as carpet between sheets A and B? I don't think so.
DON: What do you suggest then?
ME: I suggest we all go to bed and we'll ask for some local help in the morning. Maybe one of the good guys of Garmisch, or a perceptive pal in Partenkirchen might know something we don't, and can help us.

So we did, and they did. Sure enough, someone (I still don't know if he came from Garmisch or Partenkirchen) came to our rescue. He was an old-timer, and told us, through our resident interpreter and Jill-of-all-trades, Erika Kornmüller, that a number of years earlier there had been a leak in the pipes, and the repairs that were made included putting the new pipes on a separate circuit with its own thermostat. When Don was shown the replacement technology, it was a simple matter of matching the temperature in the repaired piping to that of the rest of the freezing equipment. And lo, the shimmering stretch of water through the eight-foot circles on Ice B, from one end to the other, quickly froze in time for the arrival of teams, none of whom knew (till now) how perilously close we came to sending sailboats down Sheet B instead of stones.

The fact is that making ice in an arena, any arena, especially at the end of the curling season, is one of the trickier propositions in the curling world. Although ice-making has improved about 1000 percent over the past 35 years, it is still an inexact science, as any top icemaker will tell you. And in an arena the problems are magnified many times over. There are a multitude of factors involved: the outside temperature and humidity; the air exhaust fans and dehumidifiers (if any, and, if so, where they're located); the human fans and where they're located; the hardness or softness of the water in the local community; the experience and knowledge of the icemakers; and on it goes.

Let me tell about some of the other challenges I can recall.

There was the Brandon Brier in 1963, where they had buckets on the ice to catch the drips from the leaks in the roof, and where, on one memorable occasion, one of the Richardsons (Sam, I think it was) swept a Richardson rock *out the front of the house* (after hitting an enemy counter in the eight-foot) in order to blank the end!

I recall arriving in Utica in upstate New York for the 1970 Silver Broom to discover there was no ice and, it appeared, little chance of having ice. That's not the sort of thing designed to appeal to a rookie organizer, still riding his learning curve. Why was there no ice, you ask? Utica had a beautiful new civic arena, but it seems the freezing plant in that beautiful new civic arena was not working because a certain valve was kaputski. Even worse, I was told, the municipality's credit was so precarious that the valve supplier was insisting on payment up front—cash please—before delivery. It required a state senator and the urgent blandishments of the organizing committee's outstanding chair, Art Cobb, to work out a deal with a touring ice show, due to play the arena the week after the curling. The figure skating impresarios were persuaded to "twin" their portable ice plant with the arena plant and, hooray, it worked.

Three years later, we were faced with suddenly mushy ice for the close of the final game of the Silver Broom in Regina. Although the experienced Don Lewis was icemaker there (it was his hometown), none of what happened that year can be laid at his doorstep. In fact, I suspect—nay, I know—he was more sinned against than sinner.

The problems of the ice in Regina started long before the event. The ice plant in the old arena was a 95-ton effort, judged to be too small for an event like the worlds. So the organizing committee, under Laurie Artiss, sought and bought another ice plant, with a $75,000 tab, which they knew they could sell after the event. In fact they had it sold about the same time they suggested to the local arena board that they would handle the $75,000 cost if the board would handle the $15–$20,000 tab for additional exhaust fans.

As Laurie told me recently, "They thought we were being pretty generous taking the bigger cost and leaving the smaller one to them. Later, when they found out we had a buyer, they weren't quite as impressed. In fact, they said they would split the ice plant cost, and we were still negotiating when the Silver Broom began."

About the same time, some SaskPower engineers on one of the Regina committees hauled out their slide rules, calculators and various reference books—for all I know they might also have used a Ouija board—and then predicted that a full house of spectators would provide enough body heat to raise the building temperature a full 14 degrees over the course of the opening game and probably more if you took into account the extended opening ceremonies. There wasn't, they said, enough exhaust capacity to handle that many spectators, and it was obvious (to them, anyway) that the ice would suffer. You can imagine the reaction they received from the finance committee, for one: "Are you certain of your facts? How do you know that will happen? The cost of the additional fans would be how much? Can we afford the expense?" and so on. The executive, worried about finances, declined to follow the engineer's advice.

When the opening draw got underway, all was well. Midway through the opening games, the temperature had risen significantly. By the end of the game, the temperature was exactly as predicted, 14 degrees higher. The ice was barely playable. However, halfway through the draw, Artiss and his key executive members met in an emergency session, and the decision was quickly made to install the additional fans.

As soon as the last rock came to rest, the committee shifted into high gear. The Regina Fire Department was standing by, and when the last spectator left the arena, a number of the department's huge smoke exhaust fans were put to work, pumping out the warm arena air into the cooler night air outside. High above, a repair crew was chopping a hole in the roof to install the new exhaust fans. The whole thing was completed by the time the fans (of the human variety) returned for the evening draw. And the fans (of the mechanical variety) worked perfectly throughout the rest of the series.

But Regina's ice-making woes weren't over. When it came time for the championship final, the committee had one extra item on their worry list. The arena would be needed the following day for the start of a winter agricultural fair, so there would have to be a fast disposal of the ice and a quick turnaround of the facility.

In the media room, we were well aware of the upcoming event, for truckloads of cattle were being brought into a building adjacent to the media workroom from mid-week on, and the media were working awfully close to the cattle boudoir. I know, I know—"we in the media" should be able to recognize that stuff easily since we've shovelled a lot of it over the years. But still...

Anyway, faced with this extra bit of urgency, someone (to this day, I don't know who) was delegated to ensure that when the final stones came to rest, the ice temperature would be higher, it would be easier to melt the ice, and the transformation from curling to agricultural exhibition would be relatively easy. At least that was the theory.

The trouble was that the alteration in temperature didn't work out quite as planned, and by the seventh end of play in the Sweden–Canada final, Kjell Oscarius, on reasonably good ice, held a 5–2 advantage over Harvey Mazinke. The ice was becoming increasingly "heavier" with each succeeding end, and Mazinke adjusted quickly to the challenge. After 10 ends, Canada had tied the score 5–5, sending the game into an extra end, when the ice was, to be charitable about it, "kinda mushy."

Sweden had last stone in the extra end, and when Oscarius's first shot ground to a halt in the back 12-foot ring of an empty house, Mazinke was faced with trying to draw and use the Swedish stone as backing, and force Oscarius to win with his final shot of the game. But the increasingly heavy ice defeated Mazinke. His final stone, even with heavy sweeping, shuddered to a halt before it reached the rings; Oscarius didn't need to throw his final granite. Kjell Oscarius, who had finished dead last at the Silver Broom of 1972, rebounded in '73 and became the first European to win the worlds.

It should be pointed out that ice-making at that time was somewhat haphazard by today's standards. If I remember right, Regina, in what was, I believe, a first for a major event, installed temperature sensors in the ice. In fact, Marcel DeWitte, who was to make the ice for the Brier the following year in London, spent consider-able time digesting the huge manual that Don Lewis and his ice-tech cohorts prepared following the 1973 Broom.

The ice in the final end of the playoff was critical to the outcome of the 1973 title game between (l) Harvey Mazinke (Canada) and (r) Kjell Oscarius (Sweden). Tom Schaeffer of Sweden is the partially hidden Swedish player. Photo by Michael Burns

The Bern ice problem, in 1974 and subsequent years, is really an overall Swiss problem, for many arenas in that country (including the one in Geneva, which hosted the 1993 worlds) have a concrete floor that is not level, but tipped, so the ice is higher at one end than the other. The Swiss arenas, I was told, are built that way so that melted ice can be removed quickly, if necessary. The tipped ice surface is not necessar-ily a problem with hockey or figure skating, but it is with curling, which demands level ice. In Bern, if memory serves me right, the ice at one end of the arena was about 10 cen-timetres thick, but only 2–3 centimetres at the other end. Since ice is an insulator, the surface ice at the thick end was softer than the surface ice at the thin end. The net effect was an uphill–downhill feeling to the play, and the curlers were rightfully concerned about it.

A similar thing happened at the 2005 Women's World Championship at the Lagoon Leisure Centre in Paisley, Scot-land. There the combination of mild and humid Scottish weather, a lack of dehumidification equipment and a concrete base that had heaved over the previous year created problems for all the curlers. Interestingly enough, curlers from countries who always curl under near-perfect conditions—Canada and Scotland—had trouble adjusting, while the other competitors, with sometimes less-than-ideal conditions at home, were able to change their game to take into account the difficult surface. And, as ever, when the losers complained (it's always the losers who complain), the winners just grinned.

One of the worst-ever ice scenarios for curling came in the 1992 Winter Olympics, when curling was still a demonstration sport. The World Curling Federation was lobbying hard to get curling accepted by the International Olympic Committee as a medal sport. But when the Olympic pooh-bahs arrived in Pralognan la Vanoise (the Alpine village where the Albertville curling was being contested) the ice was close to, if not, impossible. But for that story, you'll have to wait for Chapter 30: Curling Goes for Gold.

You can always be certain of one thing: at any major curling event in an arena, the icemakers never can win. If the ice has the slightest imperfection, the curlers will blame the icemakers. If the ice is perfect, the curlers will agree that it's just the way it should be.

Chapter Fifteen

THE BEAUTIFUL INGE

ONE OF THE FEATURES OF THE SILVER BROOM WAS THE YEARLY FILM of the event produced by Briston Films of Montreal. The films were used in a variety of ways, sometimes on TV, but mostly in curling clubs around the world, not only to show what happened the previous year, but also to help promote the next year's event and host site. Two of my particular favourites were the film of the Megève Broom in 1971 and the first Garmisch-Partenkirchen event in 1972.

With Mike Taylor of Air Canada's Montreal office as producer/director and with such outstanding cinematographers as Briston Film's Leo Thompson, Bob Mason, Ernst Michel, Peter Bennison and Jim Grattan, the films were bound to be good. Not only did these filmmakers understand curling—they'd been filming the Brier for years—but they were also highly professional, and the results of their annual efforts played a major role in the growth and development of the Broom.

In the autumn of 1972 a few of us returned to Garmisch-Partenkirchen to premiere the film of the happy times from the previous March. Hans Thaut, chair, and his organizing committee were due to be joined by local media and assorted civic VIPs for the gala showing. It wasn't quite Hollywood red carpet, but pretty close. The timeline was tight. The German version of the finished film was due to be flown from Montreal to Zurich, where Air Canada's local PR honcho, Tony Schoen, would get it and drive it to Garmisch-Partenkirchen. Don McLeod, Air Canada's vice-president of public affairs, was our leader and we were joined for the occasion by Willie Wilson, president of the Royal Caledonian Curling Club.

Two parts of that visit are still vividly fresh in my memory.

First of all, Tony was nowhere to be found when Don and I drove into Garmisch-Partenkirchen. We checked into the Post Partenkirchen Hotel, but no Tony. I seem to recall that, feeling the effects of jet lag, we crashed for a few hours. When we awoke, and met for an aperitif, we found Willie, who had just arrived from Scotland. But no Tony.

As the minutes crept by, Don became more and more concerned. Here we were, only hours away from premiering the film and Tony had the only copy. Where was he? Don't ask me why neither Don nor I had the film. For some reason it was with Tony, and we didn't know where Tony was.

I knew that, while Tony may have been a free spirit, he was very reliable. Some of his PR moves might have been, shall we say, slightly unorthodox, but the results were always outstanding. But as the time approached for the film to be shown, even I became worried. For his part, Don was almost apoplectic. He had rehearsed his "Tony, you're fired" speech several times.

I won't go into our Plan B scenario or any of the other options we considered. Suffice it to say that Tony finally arrived, film in hand, but with only minutes to spare. He had encountered a sudden snowstorm (it was the Alps, after all) that slowed him down, but, hey, he got through. I think we may have delayed the start of the film by a half-hour, but in the end, it all worked out.

Incidentally, one of the highlights of that film was the original music written and scored by Frank Mills. If you have that CD with the "Theme from the Silver Broom" on it, then you'll know the haunting and lovely background music that enhanced the Bavarian scenery.

After the premiere, after the guests had left, after we rewound the film, the four of us—Don, Tony, Willie and I—returned to our hotel. Don said he was tired from the overseas flight, but I think he had drained himself by worrying about Tony, what with firing him eight times and then re-hiring him nine. He said he'd see us in the morning.

Tony and I were ready to unwind back at the hotel, in the Bar Barbarossa, where the beautiful Inge held court nightly. Willie joined us.

The beautiful Inge was not only a visual delight behind the bar, but was also a talented and sparkling entertainer. She spoke six or seven different languages, was a master storyteller, sang beguilingly with her own guitar accompaniment, and kept her customers enthralled as they watched her draw a large glass, inch by inch, of the foaming beer on tap.

She looked as if she had just stepped out of a Bavarian travel poster, poured as she was into her low-cut Bavarian blouse and dirndl. Tony and I were among her wor-

The beautiful Inge Elb. Photo courtesy of Bob Picken

shipful throng, and over the year of our committee meetings in Garmisch-Partenkirchen, we had willingly joined her legion of fans.

As we entered the Barbarossa that evening, we indicated that Willie was a Scots VIP, here for the premiere, and suggested she might dust off a few of her best stories for him. She did, and he too quickly joined Inge's army of admirers.

We were about ready to leave for the night when Willie asked Inge if she had been at this bar during the Silver Broom a few months earlier. Of course she had, every night, right here, she told him.

The conversation then went something like this:

"Did you know any of the Scots ... Andrew Williamson, for example?"

"Tall, handsome man from Edinburgh?" she answered, "Yes, I know who you mean."

"How about David Duncan?" Willie asked.

"From Glasgow, his wife's name is Janette?" replied Inge.

"Tha's right," said Willie. "What about Andrew Wilson? Did you ever run into him?"

"Andrew Wilson," she replied, her voice rising, "Andrew Wilson...just a minute..." and she delved into her purse, finally extracting a photo. She handed it to Willie.

"Is that who you mean?" she asked.

There in the photo was a smiling Andrew, happily posed with Inge. It was one of those tourist photos that were regularly taken in the Barbarossa, of a patron cosied up to the beautiful Inge.

"Aye, tha's him," said Willie. "Tha's mi brither! He said he'd had the most marvellous time here last March, but he never did gi' me any details!"

Chapter Sixteen

LABONTE'S BOOT

Bob Picken

It's not hard to select "The Curse of LaBonte" as the biggest curling story of the past 50 years. Not just for me (I was in the middle of it as head official) but also for most curling fans. I wrote all about it in my previous book, Canada Curls, and I suspect most of you know the details already. The famous "kicked rock caper" of the 1972 Silver Broom involved Canada's Orest Meleschuk and Bob LaBonte of the United States. Good friend Bob Picken was there on the media bench and saw it all. Since he is from Winnipeg, Orest's home town, and is close to Grafton, North Dakota, LaBonte's home, he keeps in touch with both principals. Some years after the incident, he filed this follow-up story.

BOB LABONTE DOESN'T SMOKE ANY MORE. DITTO FOR OREST MELESCHUK. In 1972, both of them could have been enlisted to do cigarette advertising. Lucky Strike? Export?

You can't smoke on the ice in any major curling event now, but rarely did the American and Canadian skips have a cigarette out of their mouths during the '72 World Curling Championship in Garmisch-Partenkirchen, that glorious beauty spot in the Bavarian Alps.

The photos taken by renowned sports photographer Mike Burns at the time of the infamous kicked-rock incident in the championship final that year, show LaBonte falling on his derrière, a cigarette sticking firmly to his lips.

For some time I actually wondered if LaBonte took too deep a drag on his smoke. Maybe it made him dizzy, leading to the pratfall on the 10th end before a decision was made on whether or not his team had won the world title.

"No...nothing like that," laughed LaBonte, when I queried him on the subject many years later. "When I saw my third, Frank Aasand, put his arms up in the air, I got too damn excited, started to jump, my feet skidded and down I went. I didn't feel it, but they say I kicked the rock as I hit the ice," he reflected.

Another photo taken on the extra end that followed would be somewhat astonishing for a curling audience today. Meleschuk delivered his last stone on the 11th end of the game with a cigarette stuck in the corner of his mouth. The shot was perfect, a superb draw to the four-foot-circle behind cover that LaBonte couldn't emulate with the hammer, and Meleschuk's Canadian team had pulled out a 10–9 victory in curling's all-time bizarre championship conclusion.

Over the years, the story on what transpired that evening in Germany has been told and retold, often embellished and often inaccurate. I was there, in the Olympia Ice Stadium, and nobody had a better front row media seat than I did on Saturday, March 25, 1972.

Meleschuk had won eight straight games going into the final, adding to Don Duguid's unbeaten records in 1970 and '71, to give Canada 28 victories in a row in the world event. LaBonte, the 21-year-old American champion, had a 5–3 record, emerging from a four-way tie for second place to meet Canada in the showdown.

For six ends it looked like a major upset was in the making.

LaBonte's youthful foursome, with Frank Aasand, 22, at third, his brother John Aasand at second and Ray Morgan at lead, both 21, was curling like international veterans, pouncing on Canadian miscues to establish a 7–3 lead.

With key shotmaking by his front end of John Hanesiak and Pat Hailley, Meleschuk rallied, scoring back-to-back deuces to tie the score 7–7 after eight ends, only to see LaBonte nail two points on the ninth for a two-up edge going home.

On the fateful 10th end, Canadian third Dave Romano made two fine draws, and after LaBonte ticked a guard, Meleschuk drew to lie three. The American skip countered with an excellent double takeout, rolling to the button slightly behind cover. With last stone, Meleschuk had to hit and stick inside the eight-foot ring to cut out another American stone and score two points to tie.

The 31-year-old Winnipeg skip made the takeout, but his shooter rolled away, and after Frank Aasand's vigorous sweeping it settled along the eight-foot ring. Was it second shot? Aasand took a quick look at both stones, raised his arms, and hopped in glee, clear of the stones.

That was not the case for LaBonte seconds later. He came into the house from the rear, started to jump, then slipped and contacted the Canadian stone, moving it a foot or so along the eight-foot ring. Remarkably, the kick barely altered its position in relation to the centre of the rings.

I recall hearing a gasp go through the Olympia and somebody shouting, "He kicked it!!" Everybody seemed to be somewhat stunned, including Canada's Romano, who was checking the position of the American stone, but hadn't moved to compare it with the Canadian rock. In any event, there was no indication of a concession on his part.

In the confusion that followed, neither Frank Aasand nor LaBonte admitted to the head official that the stone had been kicked, and there was some uncertainty on how to resolve the issue. Clearly, Romano saw the contact with LaBonte's foot, but without an American confirmation (of the rock being burned), it was decided the only course was to measure the two stones.

Fortunately, the measurement went in Canada's favour, forcing the extra end. In view of what happened, I believe that was the correct procedure. The American skip was at fault, and there was no agreement on who had second shot before he toppled to the ice.

I remember interviewing Frank Aasand after the game and stating that he was the only person in the building who could make a judgment on the two stones, and asking what he thought. "It was close and might have required a measure anyway," he replied. "But I thought we had it."

The verdict created a storm of controversy. A subsequent appeal to the International Curling Federation by the US Curling Association was rejected, and there was a bitter reaction in LaBonte's home state.

I touched base with LaBonte at various times over the next few years. He said that, at the time, he got over his disappointment fairly quickly. "I was just 21, and I thought I'd be back a bunch of times to win the worlds," he said. "But as the years went by it really began to hurt, because I realized I'd never get another chance."

The two skips crossed paths a number of times after '72, and when the Ford World Championships were held in Bismarck, North Dakota, in 2002, LaBonte was the honourary chair and invited Meleschuk to join him for the opening ceremonies.

Meleschuk has accepted the fact that some people applied an asterisk to his name in the world record book, but he continued to curl at the top competitive level in Manitoba. He won another purple heart in 1989, a provincial senior title in 1996, and the Manitoba Masters crown in 2002.

"Curling can be a game of inches, and sometimes you're on the right side of the inch," he remarked. "I think we *were* in Garmisch, and in my heart I think we deserved that extra end, and we made the most of it."

Chapter Seventeen

LIES, DAMNED LIES AND STATISTICS

IT WAS BENJAMIN DISRAELI, THE FAMED BRITISH PRIME MINISTER OF the mid-1800s, who wrote "there are three kinds of lies: lies, damned lies and statistics." He was also a novelist, but as far as I know, never a curler, or even a curling writer. If he had been so inclined, he might have pointed his stats remark at the curling world.

If I have one regret during my time at the Brier and the Silver Broom, it's the matter of developing player statistics as a part of the game's media coverage. Today, of course, such statistics are a given and, no matter my opinion, are an integral part of today's game. But not, I suggest, as the be-all and end-all of curling media coverage.

I first learned about shooting percentages in my rookie years at the Brier. Buckets Fleming—Donald Schubert Fleming to quote the name on his birth certificate—was the learned and fun-loving curling writer for the *Edmonton Journal* when I first met him, and I was fascinated to watch him score a game. He had a pad of newsprint and a stub of a pencil, and before each game he'd rule off a scoring grid so he could do his math work. I don't know how he managed to see everything that was going on in the arena, carry on a conversation with whoever was seated next to him, and still manage to score every shot of every Alberta player. He didn't worry about the other games. After all, he was writing about his beloved Albertans and, of course, his stats efforts would aid in his subsequent analysis and coverage of the game.

Later, I tried to emulate Buckets and score a game myself, and discovered it definitely wasn't easy. It did have one unassailable advantage, though; it forced you to watch every shot of the game.

Buckets used the four-point system that is in vogue today. But others (Curtis Church was one) favoured a five-point system since it was much easier to translate two shots per end (five points for a perfect shot) over 10 ends, into percentages. On the

Edmonton's Don (Buckets) Fleming was my mentor when it came to percentage scoring. Here he meets with the famous Richardson rink. From left to right: Wes and Sam Richardson, Fleming, Arnold and Ernie Richardson. Photo by Michael Burns

other hand, it was harder to decide whether to give a not-quite-perfect shot two points or three. With the four-point system, it makes the whole matter cut and dried. A hit and roll out, when the skip wanted a hit and stick, is a half-shot: two points. And so on.

The first time we used personal stats at the Silver Broom was 1973, in Regina. Chair Laurie Artiss recruited Al Heron and a crew of experts to look after the details, and they did a masterful job. So much so, that we continued to chart personal stats and soon developed a system that could put a percentage opposite a curler's name as a measure of how well he had played in a given game. At the start, of course, it was all done using a sharpened pencil (and more importantly, the eraser at the other end), plus hand-held calculators.

Later, around the time Ray Turnbull was head official, we were able (thanks to Ray's encyclopedic knowledge of the game and its people) to recruit Winnipeg's Gary Danielson as our computer whiz, and Lorne Knowles (chartered accountant, curling instructor and theorist of the game) to organize our stats group. Our figure filberts (and outstanding curlers) included Terry Braunstein, Bob Christie, John Allardyce, Warren Brooke and Bob Dolishny. Later on, we added international experts like Kristian Sørum of Norway.

But in every Garden of Eden there is always a serpent. I still remember how shocked I was when one European told me that the stats were interesting, but "of course, they're biased towards you Canadians, because it's Canadians who are doing the scoring."

"Not so," said I, "the chaps we have doing the stats are all competitive curlers. They're well trained and pretty rigidly controlled. If they appear biased, we fire 'em...they'd never get back to a Broom again." And since Air Canada was looking after their transportation to the Broom (particularly when it was in Europe), we held the hammer.

Then I had second thoughts, especially when Keith Wendorf related a story from the Ford World Championships in Brandon, 1995.

I'm sure you know Keith Wendorf. A 1972 grad of the University of New Brunswick and son of a Master Warrant Officer in the Canadian army, Keith was, and is, an outstanding curler. Shortly after his graduation, Keith headed to Europe, intending to stay only a year or so, but as sometimes happens, is still there.

While managing the curling club at the Canadian Forces Base in Lahr, he put together a team that won the German title and that brought him (and his squad) to the Winnipeg Silver Broom in 1978, where I first met him.

He was so good that he returned seven times to the world championship, and in Regina, 1983, gained his best record ever, winning a silver medal, losing the final to "the Wrench," Ed Werenich. It wasn't too many years later that he became

 Keith Wendorf. Photo by Michael Burns

national coach for Germany, and today works full time for the World Curling Federation as its curling development officer. His name is honoured in New Zealand, where they compete for the Wendorf Rock (national championship trophy). He and his wife, Susan, have curled all over the world and have taught in most of the new and emerging curling nations. Equally important, he is also a two-time winner of the Collie Campbell Memorial Award, given to the player at the worlds who best combines "playing ability and gentlemanly conduct," as the citation states. I could go on, but you get the picture: Keith is honoured—and rightly so—wherever curlers gather.

Anyway, back to 1995. By now, the Free Guard Zone rule had been in effect for three or four years, and most teams knew how to handle the FGZ strategy in different situations. For example, in the late stages of a game, when your team has a slight lead and the trailing team's lead throws up a centre guard (which, according to the FGZ rule, can't be removed from play) many teams play "the tick shot." That's a shot that is intended to merely tick the centre guard and ease it gently to the side of the ice but still keep it in play. If it goes out of play, the stone, of course, is replaced to its original position. The main thing is to get it off the centre line. It's a delicate shot, and if you make it, it can be a game-saver. If you miss, you're no worse off than if you'd tripped on your scarf and thrown your rock through the rings. It is also a statistician's dream shot. Make the shot and you give the shooter four points (or five if you're into bonus marks). Miss it, and you score it the same as a throw-through, i.e., no score at all. I'm not sure all scorers would agree, but go ahead, sue me.

In Brandon, Wendorf was plotting every shot of his German team as they played Australia, and as he told me later, Holger Hohne (the German lead) made four successful tick shots in the latter stages of the game. And each time he executed the tricky shot, the team would celebrate with high fives, etc. Indeed, after the game, in congratulating Hohne for his prowess throughout the contest, Keith said that Hohne might just become the first-ever player to score better than 100 percent, what with all those bonus points! But when Keith collected the official stats sheet, he was dismayed to find that Hohne had only scored in the 70 percent range.

Keith immediately headed to the stats room, where he found a couple of the statisticians relaxing after the game. He asked if he could see the shot-by-shot evaluations, and was immediately shown the scoring for the Germany-Australia game. He was flabbergasted to see that instead of perfect 4's, or bonus 5's, Hohne had been scored with zeros, zippos, zilches.

Somewhat innocently, he asked who it was who had scored that game. "I did," said one of the relaxers.

"Why did you give him a zero for those tick shots, instead of a 4 or 5?" enquired Wendorf.

"Because I didn't agree with the call," answered the local chap. "It was the wrong shot."

Now I don't want to get into a debate here about what kind of dumb answer that is, but statistical scoring is, essentially, a means of measuring how well a player executes the shot he is asked to play. Nothing more, nothing less. The shot may well be, as the figure fanatic put it, "the wrong shot." Doesn't matter. If the skip asks for the tick shot and the shooter executes it perfectly, he or she is entitled to the full points of whatever system is in use. You might even want to give him a bonus mark if it steers the team to victory.

You can see why I'm hesitant about the benefits of personal statistics in the game. Sure, they're helpful, especially to a reporter trying to file a rush story after an extra-end game, with a looming deadline in mind. But sometimes— and it's only my opinion—there is too much emphasis put on those stats when it comes to the coverage of the game. There's more to the reporting of a game than the easy, and ever-present, percentages.

We still haven't worked out a system that takes into account a skip giving the wrong ice, or the brushers making a sweeping error, or any other of a number of variables. Statisticians (it says here) should only score a curler on the shot that is asked for, and the shooter's response to that request. End of discussion.

It should also be noted that sometimes those personal statistics can sound more meaningful than they really are. For example, at a recent world championship I recall a TV commentator falling into the stats trap by mentioning that "Team A is outscoring Team B, after eight ends, 82 percent to 80 percent." It sounded impressive. But was it?

The total (team) points available in 8 ends of play are 256 (maximum 4 points per shot × 2 shots per player × 4 players, or 32 points per end). So, 82 percent is equal to 210 points (rounded): 80 percent works out to 205 points (rounded). By the eighth end, the team difference was only five points, or a little over one point per player! And that can easily be explained away by a very small difference of opinion by the official scorer. In effect, both teams are not only playing very well indeed, but also are shooting equally well, at least according to the statistician.

Linda Moore, the Olympic gold medallist at the 1988 Winter Games in Calgary and TSN's outstanding commentator, used to say that a difference of five percentage points between players was not especially significant; a difference of more than five points was.

More recently, Canadian curling buffs Dallas Bittle, George Karrys and Gerry Geurts published the *Black Book of Curling*, an in-depth look at a variety of statistics used to measure the efficiency of the top curling teams in the world. Using the power of the computer, the *Black Book* boys looked at game results over many years, and then came up with measurable stats that were based on mathematical facts, not the subjective opinions of scorers.

Some of their new statistics include measures based on game scores (points scored per end, or given up per end, steals or blank ends). They developed new measures of "hammer efficiency," "steal efficiency" and "force efficiency." For example, force efficiency indicates, as a percentage, how often a team without the hammer is able to force the opposition to take a single point, when ('tis assumed) they would prefer to blank the end and hold onto the hammer. By now, you have probably figured out the impact of hammer efficiency (percentage of time a team scores two or more points with the hammer) and steal efficiency (percentage of time stealing an end).

But they have gone further in the field of personal stats. By using a five-point system, adding in a degree-of-difficulty factor, a sweeping component, and a "skip save" element, they can produce a statistical percentage for each player that is, they claim, a more balanced measurement of that player's prowess. But, they readily agree, it still comes back to the ability of the chap with the laptop computer and mouse.

In addition, they have stored game results going back for decades, and so can produce, instantaneously, those little background nuggets that television seems to serve up effortlessly. You know the kind. The announcer casually produces, in an off-handed way, the comment that "this is only the second time in the past 18 years where a left-handed shooter has slipped while coming out of the hack and still been able to ease his inturn delivery through a narrow port, wick off a counter in the 12-foot ring and freeze to the shot stone on the button." Or did you think that the commentator had all that info bubbling away on the back burner of his brain pan?

Yes, all this is possible today, thanks to the speed and power of the computer. Buckets Fleming, or any other member of the pencil brigade (I was a late recruit to that rag-tag army) might have been able to serve up the same detail as the computer of the Black Book boys, but it would probably have taken us a week or more to do so, and frankly, we had other more important fun and games to attend to.

The beauty of these new statistics is that they are mathematical in nature and not dependent on an individual scorer's subjective assessment. And, as such, mark a welcome new era to the statistical side of curling.

I'm sure Disraeli would agree.

Chapter Eighteen
SLAVKA HOGAROCK

IT'S NOT EXACTLY STOP-THE-PRESSES NEWS THAT CURLERS ARE GREAT people. But after kicking around a number of sports in my career, I like to think that you can make more friends in curling than in most other sports. Maybe it's the traditions of the game. Perhaps it's the socializing after the game. Or it just may be that the game attracts the kind of people who genuinely like other people, people like you and me! I don't know. But I do know I made a lot of friends over the years through the Brier, the Silver Broom, the Scott and many other events.

Slavka Hogarock was one of them.

Now before I tell you about good old Slavka, let me say that "political correctness" obliges me to acknowledge that where some would take issue with "ethnic humour," others enjoy a gentle spoof of the various nationalities that made up the annual Silver Broom. We could tickle the Scots funnybone with the tired old wheeze about their parsimony, knowing that the Scots are some of the most generous folks around. We could rib the Swiss about their time-clock precision, or, as was the case in Garmisch-Partenkirchen, 1982, we could interview Slavka Hogarock about the growth of curling in the Ukraine. If I were to be politically correct, you would never realize the extent to which curlers like to poke fun at themselves. Nor would you ever meet Sir Slavka.

I first ran into him when CBC Radio sent me to Welland to cover the Ontario High School Curling Championship. That was way back in the fifties, when it was "school curling," not "junior curling." Slavka was one of the competitors that year and, in later times, he would get mock-mad at me when I would tell him I had absolutely no recollection of him at all at that event. He later became a golf pro and a curling fanatic, first in Kitchener, later in Mississauga. I should also add that he was a highly skilled curler who could do a number of curling tricks, from his between-the-legs delivery to his double-slider delivery. For the latter he would throw the rock and then glide down the ice on both sliders, rotating at about the same speed as the rock.

He had been recruited by Ray Turnbull as an instructor in some of the many curling schools and clinics Ray used to hold all over the

Slavka Hogarock, a.k.a. Bob Dolishny. Photo courtesy of Warren Brooke

world. Then one day he arrived at the world championship as a statistician and a good one too. And when he showed up at the 1982 Silver Broom, I told him, once again, that I couldn't remember his past exploits. Or even his name.

"Slavka Hogarock" he said, but he knew that I knew he was having me on. As a matter of fact, he had many names he would use, and Slavka Hogarock ("first coach of the Ukrainian Curling Association") was just one of them. At the 1986 Brier in Kitchener-Waterloo, he was a Mennonite curler, complete with wide-brimmed black hat and black clothing.

Behind these characters and send-ups of both the game and "the brass" was Bob Dolishny. That was his real name, the one his parents had agreed on, the one on his passport.

He became a popular media interview, usually late at night when the stories and the giggle-juice were flowing. Then Slavka Hogarock would appear and the tape recorders would come out for some impromptu badinage.

"Tell me, Mr. Hogarock, how is curling in the Ukraine different from Canadian curling?"

"Vy, in mine country, vee don't go forth and back like you do, in Canuckistan. Vee haf lots of ice, so vee play one end, den vee keep right on going for de next end, and so on."

"What do you do if you have to play an extra end?"

"Vee take der bus back to der first end and start again."

Slavka also became a curling "translator" in Garmisch-Partenkirchen at the 1982 Silver Broom. In this incarnation, he prepared a glossary of German curling terms that we used in "The Eye-Opener" (the mimeo sheet available each morning that was a sort of bulletin of the day's events and of the previous day's results). Several of the media picked up the glossary and used it that week. I suspect you can still find it somewhere in the curling world, with someone claiming it as their own, but it was really Bob Dolishny's sense of humour that produced it. It goes like this.

Curling	*Das ist rock-chucken*
I'm a curler	*Ich bin ein rock-chucker*
Rocks	*Schtones*
White rocks	*Der schtones like der schnow*
Red rocks	*Das udder vuns*
Hacks	*Der rubber pushers*
House	*Howzen*
Ice	*Eizen (mit der howzens unt der rubber pushers)*

Pebble	*Der little bumpens on der eizen*
Hog line	*Das line of der schveinhund*
Broom	*Schtik*
Corn broom	*Der schtraw schtik*
Brush	*Der pusha-pusha schtik*
Hit the broom	*Pitchen on der schtik*
Skip	*Herr boss*
Vice	*Herr schkapegoat*
Second	*Der fraulein fetcher*
Lead	*Der dumbpkopf*
Substitute	*Der guy who vasn't dere before*
Slide	*Der schlippen on der eisen*
Draw	*Plunken der schtone in ze howzen*
Take-out	*Der quickie pitchie*
Front rock	*Der shorten plunken*
In-turn	*Der in-schpin* (like der tick-tock machine)
Out-turn	*Der out-schpin* (like der tick-tock machine lookink frum der back)
Button	*Potten*
Port	*Dis iddy-biddy hole*
Freeze	*Das schnuggle-up-to plunken*
Come around game	*Das peek-a-boo pitchen*
Last rock	*Der clobberball*
Steal	*Machen der score mitout der clobberball*
Corner guard	*Vee don't underschtand zese tings*
End	*Vat heppens ven der schtones is kaput*
Umpire	*Das schtrike unt ball unt safe or out caller*

Measurement	38-24-36 *(der bossen umpiren ist machen dis vun)*
Sweep	*Achtung! Machen der schtiken moven*
Don't sweep	*Getten losten dumbpkopf*
Good shot	*Gutten pitchen*
Bad shot	*Dumbpkopf pitchen*
Medium shot	1 ½ ounces of schnapps, *bitte*

Then one day, sometime between the Vancouver ('87) world championship and the Lausanne ('88) event, we learned that Bob had been diagnosed with leukemia. He put up a brave battle but succumbed shortly before the Lausanne competition. He was in his early forties when he died, and a very wide circle of curlers lost a wonderful friend.

But Bob Dolishny lives on at the Brier, the Broom, and its successors whenever someone recalls his accents, his laughter, his pranks, his enthusiasm for the game. And his integrity.

One final note. "The Eye-Opener," that daily mimeo sheet, doubled as a bulletin board for spectators in a variety of hotels. It worked so well when it was first produced (in 1971) that we copied the idea (and renamed it as the perfectly bilingual "Journal Canada") for the Munich Olympics in '72, and of course the concept is a given at all the big events today. Except now, with the speed of the computer and gifted journalists (ah there, Larry Wood and Al Cameron) contributing to the mix, the "Heart Stopper," or "Tankard Times," or whatever other worthy name is used (in Germany it was "*Der Wecker*"—the alarm clock), the daily bulletin is more speedily produced but still remains an eagerly awaited summary of the news of the day.

Chapter Nineteen

THE BEST OF BRIERS, BROOMS AND HEARTS

WHENEVER I'M INTERVIEWED ABOUT CURLING (IT HAPPENS EVERY OTHER day, of course) I am invariably asked to list my choice of the best or the worst or the strangest of Briers, or Silver Brooms or Tournament of Hearts—you name it.

I always resist. For three reasons: first, because while I may be dumb, I'm not stupid! Secondly, I would find it incredibly difficult to come up with a quick answer (I've got a built-in lazy streak). And thirdly, because my reasons for "best" or "worst" would be completely different from anyone else's and undoubtedly would be based on completely different reasons. One man's meat is another man's poison, or has somebody else said that already?

What I am prepared to do is to give you my list of best and worst elements in a long litany of World Championships, Briers and Scotts, and as long as you're interested in one man's opinion, and realize it may have little or nothing to do with reality or other people's perceptions, then read on. Bear in mind Jack Matheson's famous and 100 percent accurate observation: "There's never been a bad Brier." He could have expanded that just as easily to include the Broom or the Hearts.

In my mind, there is a definite winner in the category of the most imaginative pitch to host an event: Regina's successful bid for the 1973 Air Canada Silver Broom. The site-selection process that had begun in Garmisch-Partenkirchen continued to develop in the ensuing years, and we added new criteria each succeeding year. For example we discovered, when picking a site for 1973, that it was vitally important that each bidding location tell its own story, in its own way, unimpeded by any preconceptions on our part. It was important not to anticipate anything.

Here's why.

Three Canadian locations suggested we consider their charms for the 1973 Silver Broom: Calgary, Regina and Saskatoon. So now, put yourself in our shoes, "our" being Don McLeod (Air Canada), Willie Wilson (RCCC) and me. It was our opinion, as we began our journey, that Calgary had the edge. After all, it was the stampede city. Banff was nearby. The lure of Calgary to visitors would be huge. The only trouble, as we quickly discovered, was that their bid was a perfunctory, almost a personal, pitch from one or two Calgary curlers, without any club or city-wide support. They even suggested we change the date of the championship because they couldn't get decent hotel facilities for that week! Thus, it was with a rather bleak frame of mind that we boarded our flight to Regina. We wondered if the remaining bids would be as disappointing as Calgary's. That was the setting as we found ourselves preparing to land in Regina.

As the plane started its descent, the head flight attendant came by, handed each of us a large, sealed, brown envelope, and asked if we wouldn't mind waiting till all the other passengers had deplaned. As the other passengers filed down the aisle, we opened the envelopes to discover a copy of the Regina *Leader-Post*, with a huge banner headline across page one that read SILVER BROOM SMASH SUCCESS. The story that filled the entire front page included a mention of all three of us in inspirational and glowing terms, and as we wondered what was up, we noticed that the date on the paper was that of the day *after* the 1973 event, still a couple of years in the future! We were still smiling when we got off the plane to discover an honour guard of Regina police (white gloves, no less) along with Laurie Artiss and some of his key committee members ready to whisk us away somewhere in stretch limousines. That was the start of a mighty impressive visit and in my memory is still one of the slickest opening stunts to impress a site selection committee.

It wasn't long before we were at the Regina Exhibition Stadium, or it may have been called the Queen City Arena. Whatever its name, that building, mercifully, is no longer with us. And no one mourns its passing. If you remember it at all, you'll recall it was a tatty, rundown, decrepit old shed, and probably one of the worst arenas ever to host an international championship. It was also dark and locked when we arrived, save for one door. I know I was wondering what had happened to the vaunted Artiss smarts, and I suspect Don and Willie were equally surprised.

Well, perhaps more than "equally surprised." We were aghast. Laurie, seemingly put out and somewhat embarrassed by this glitch in the committee's carefully laid plans, found the open door and guided us through the gloom to an entrance at ice level. He then yelled and wistfully pleaded, with the echo rolling around the empty seats, for someone to please turn on the lights, any lights.

Suddenly the arena was bathed in brightness, and as we tried to get our eyes accustomed to the glare, the massed Pipes and Drums of the 10th Field Regiment, Royal Canadian Artillery, entered from one end of the arena. We were marched to the centre ice area as they blew into their pipes and thumped their drums with gusto. I can't remember, but I suspect it was "Scotland the Brave" they were playing. Willie loved it. Then we were told we should inspect their uniforms or something equally embarrassing. Of course we were dazzled by this bit of creative showmanship on the part of Artiss and Company and almost forgot about checking the arena in complete detail.

You guessed it—this bit of Hollywood flim-flammery disguised most of the old barn's deficiencies. Following the arena visit, the committee proposed a bunch of imaginative and captivating new ideas for the Silver Broom, but the thing I remember most was the arena bit. In truth, we discovered through that visit just how important it was to let a bid committee make its pitch, unencumbered by any preconceptions on our part. That old arena was a liability in the committee's overall presentation, a liability they managed to disguise. To this day I realize that if we had checked the arena completely, we might not have chosen Regina, which would have been a mistake of epic proportions. It wasn't that Saskatoon, which we scouted a day or so later, didn't present a strong pitch. They did. But they were beaten by a better one.

Nor did Regina's efforts stop there. When we returned a year later, the arena was, of course, completely sold out and, for the first time, the Silver Broom was decorated with wall-to-wall people. It was also decorated with wall-to-wall murals that had been prepared by Regina school children, and that too was a first. But in the cold light of day, and 30-plus years later, there's no doubt in my mind that the worst arena we ever played in was that Regina Stadium of 1973.

A few years later, it was replaced by a brand-spanking-new arena, which has been home to several national and international events and is superb in every respect. In fact, it became the home of the inaugural Scott Tournament of Hearts in 1981, the 1983 Broom, the Briers of 1992 and 2006, the 1997 Olympic Trials, another Scott Tournament of Hearts the following year, plus the inaugural Continental Cup, so you get an idea of how good the new arena is and more importantly how good Regina volunteers are when it comes to staging a big event. Regina never disappoints. Regina's pitch to host the 1976 Brier included chair Laurie Artiss riding a horse, somewhat tentatively, for while I'm sure you could easily dress Artiss in western garb, I'm not sure you could ever convince anyone he could handle the horse if it began to canter. All in all, the Regina committee of 1973 was one of the best I ever encountered, and their opening gambit on that site selection visit was the best I can ever recall.

My nomination of the old Regina arena as the worst is not unanimous. I know that Michael Burns, for example, would probably ordain the old Central Scotland Ice Rink in Perth, particularly in its 1969 clothes, as his personal worst arena. It too has felt the impact of the wrecker's ball and is now a fast-receding memory to Scots. But not to Mike.

We had just got the Air Canada Silver Broom comfortably underway in 1968 when it was time to start preparing for the '69 Broom in Perth. When Mike, Canada's superlative curling photographer, arrived there before the start of the competition, he learned that the only spot he could put his darkroom was an unused, former coal storage area. And no matter how hard you scrub such a room, you can always find a vestige of its former life. It didn't matter that the 1969 world championship in Perth was an outstanding success; for Mike, the '69 Silver Broom will forever be a coal bin.

Eventually it was torn down and the land sold to make way for a new supermarket. And to replace it, the curlers, led by Chuck Hay, put up the beautiful new Dewars Centre. It was built for curling, carpet bowls, banquets and the like and is a marvellous addition to civic life in Perth, the gateway to the Scottish Highlands, and to the curling life of all Scotland.

Well, if we can agree that the Regina arena of 1973 was the worst, what was the best arena? Bern's Allmend Arena? Duluth's Entertainment and Convention Centre? Utica? Moncton? Winnipeg? Victoria? London? Any one of them could qualify as numero uno. Bern's arena is a marvel no matter how you look at it. Moncton's new Agrena (where do they get these names?) is just about perfect for curling, with its sightlines, additional facilities, parking and other amenities. You could also add the Harbour Station in Saint John, scene of the 1999 Ford Worlds, to the "best" list. Utica's arena (in 1970) was pretty good, until we ran into problems with the freezing plant. The Bern arena, built to withstand atomic attack, can house a battalion of soldiers, possesses full hospital facilities (including an operating room) and set a single game record attendance of 13,123 back in 1974. But of them all, I think Duluth's arena was the best we ever used for the Silver Broom. Not only did it have outstanding facilities, excellent parking, and easy access from the downtown hotels (via a covered walkway), it was also attached to their convention centre, had comfortable spectator amenities and outstanding sightlines. It also had a wonderfully congenial facilities committee and a superbly co-operative staff, under Joe Sturkler, with which to work.

Some other "bests" and "worsts"? It isn't hard for me to nominate the Winnipeg Silver Broom of 1978 as one of the most exciting and vibrant Brooms of them all. First of all, there were the spectators, jammed into 9,374 sold-out seats each draw, for a week-long total of 102,193, at that time a world record. They provided a stunning atmosphere that felt electric. The committee, under Vic Palmer, was a dream to work alongside, and 10 years later, when they held a reunion for the organizing committee they kindly invited me to attend, and the nostalgia that flowed that night was like chilled and vintage champagne: bubbly and intoxicating. Indeed, every time I flew into Winnipeg for any kind of curling event, it was great. Every time "Winterpeg" staged a world event, or a Brier, or any number of CBC curling championships, it was, as Yogi Berra phrased it, "deja vu all over again." Not for nothing does Winnipeg call itself the curling capital of the world.

If you think I'm nominating 1978 in Winnipeg as one of the most significant Silver Brooms, you're right. The Palmer-led committee established a new plateau of excitement for the world event. But wait—great as it was, you'd better also spare a moment for the 1973 event in Regina that set the original plateau of excitement and excellence.

Don't forget it was in Regina that the world event expanded from eight to ten countries, as Denmark and Italy joined in the world fun. There was the enthusiasm of an entire city when Regina's citizens turned on their Christmas lights and kept them ablaze throughout that week. Topping it off was the storybook victory of Kjell Oscarius, who gave Sweden (and Europe) its first-ever world curling title, the same Kjell Oscarius who had gone winless the year before in Garmisch-Partenkirchen. Talk about moving from outhouse to penthouse!

Another best from my memory bank is International Day, Regina, 1973. I don't know who first thought of it, but I liked the concept when Laurie Artiss and his International Day committee chair, Don Turner of Weyburn, first presented it. The idea was that each of 10 communities around Regina would adopt a team from the 10 competing nations, and their supporters, and host an event on the Saturday before the start of the competition. Each community would put on its best bib and tucker and organize the day as a people-to-people event.

Some of the towns held curling matches, followed by community dinners, complete with local entertainment. Others organized farm visits. Every community adopted "their" team, not just for that day but for the entire week, and provided a cheering section of Canadian enthusiasm for the visitors. It was an idea that leapt off the drawing board into the hearts of the visitors and teams alike. And many friendships were formed then that endure to this day.

After being feted during International Day in Strasbourg 1973, German skip Mickey Kanz was fated to finish in a seventh-place tie. Photo by Michael Burns

On International Day, Laurie and Harriett Artiss insisted that Anne and I should accompany them to Strasbourg, the town that was entertaining Germany. Laurie and I were unable to go for the full day—there were too many last minute things still to be done—but we figured we could manage the evening dinner. So off we went, along with Terry Denny of Air Canada's Montreal office and Erika Kornmüller, who had been such a help to us the previous year in Garmisch-Partenkirchen and who was helping us again in Regina.

It was a vintage Saskatchewan farm-community social. There was plenty of good food, a happy crowd, and the German team (skipped by Mickey Kanz) basked in the spotlight. They lapped up the enthusiasm, and then it was time for the speeches. You can guess how many there were and who gave them.

Somewhere along the line, Terry Denny was informed that since he was the senior Air Canada person present, he would be expected to say something on behalf of the sponsor. As I recall, he had only a few minutes to collect his thoughts before he heard his name called.

Terry was captivated not only by the moment, but also by Regina and its committee, and he wanted to get that fact across. Even though he was a gifted and natural speaker, he did make one innocent mistake, one minor boo-boo. And it cost him. Boy, did it cost him! On such an occasion, enthusiasm and hyperbole can overwhelm a person and create that "slip of the lip" that is remembered long after the rest of the speech is forgotten. As he neared the end of his soliloquy, he ventured into the realm of personal impression. As I recall, the finale of his speech went something like this: "When I arrived a couple of days ago," he intoned, "it was late in the afternoon, and I went up to my room in the Regina Inn. I looked out from the height of the hotel's top floor, at the setting sun. What a view! It was really something for a guy from Montreal to stand there and look out across the prairie, across miles and miles of nothing, and see that sunset."

He sat down to polite applause, and then it was Laurie's turn to speak.

"I want you to know," said Laurie softly, but then with voice rising, like a pipe organ in crescendo, opening up all the stops. "I want you to know, Terry, that when you looked out of your hotel room window (and now he lowered his voice so that all strained to hear him), that wasn't miles and miles of nothing you saw, that was (voice rising again) miles and miles...of SOMETHING!!"

The Strasbourg burghers erupted into a standing ovation. The applause was deafening, and at that moment, Laurie could have run for premier and garnered every vote in town. Terry was looking for a place to hide. An innocent-sounding phrase had undone all the rest of his oration. To this day I can't remember what else he said, though I know he said it very well, but I do remember—and I'm sure Terry does too— his "miles and miles of nothing."

That same year, 1973, I encountered one of the strangest of reactions of all my time at the Silver Broom. It happened when the Italian team, newcomers to the world championship that year, arrived in Regina.

"Our brushes have not arrived," I was advised when I greeted them, and I think I detected a small note of desperation in their voices. Well, missing luggage is a fact with any airline, but this was only missing equipment, which we could easily replace.

"Don't worry," I said soothingly, "we'll get you some replacement brushes." But I could tell my answer was not what they wanted to hear. What they wanted to hear was that we would move heaven and earth to find those particular brushes. Of course, the missing brushes arrived on the next flight, or the next day, I can't remember.

What I do remember was the look of relief when the brushes were delivered to them. Included in their carry bag were their regular brushes, plus a couple of thick, hollow-handled scrubbers into which had been stuffed wads of money—lira—which, I believe, their local currency regulations said they could not take out of the country. No wonder they seemed a little desperate on arrival.

Chapter Twenty

MORE BEST AND WORST

LET'S CONTINUE FROM THE PREVIOUS CHAPTER WITH A FEW MORE observations of "best" and "worst." Purely personal, I hasten to add.

BEST NEW ADDITION TO THE WORLD PROGRAM

That's an easy one: the Grand Transatlantic Match (GTM) in Karlstad, Sweden, in 1977, and still going strong today, under a revised name—The Grand Transoceanic Match—but still the GTM. Take a bow, Lennart Hemmingson; it was your idea and a superb one at that. Chapter 35, "The Swedish Solution" describes the event in detail.

Mind you, Regina came close with its innovative International Day in 1973 (described in the previous chapter) and again in 1983, when they pulled off another dandy in "The World's Biggest Dinner Party." That was when Reginans opened their doors so that every guest from outside the city could enjoy a specially cooked dinner in a Regina home! With thousands of visitors, it was a logistical nightmare for the organizers, but a never-to-be-forgotten evening for the visitors. World curling fans are still talking about that one.

Among Brier events, I'd tip my sombrero to Don Pottinger's idea of The Brier Patch, first unveiled in 1982 in Brandon, and a staple of every Brier since. The Brier Patch? What started out as a smallish "watering hole" for fans, visitors and locals alike, is now an immense "party central" where there is ongoing entertainment and thirst-reducing potions available.

The 1985 Glasgow Organizing Committee worked a minor miracle in transforming the Kelvin Hall from a heritage building into an ice palace for the final Air Canada Silver Broom. Glasgow Organizing Committee photo by Stephen Gibson

MOST INNOVATIVE ELEMENT OF A WORLD CHAMPIONSHIP

I'd nominate Glasgow's Wizardry in 1985, turning the heritage Kelvin Hall into a curling arena by installing a temporary ice plant. Imagine an empty heritage building, rather dusty, and with sparrows and pigeons fluttering under the roof. Now close your eyes, and when you open them, bingo, there is an ice pad with instant spectator seating for 5,000 and an adjacent refreshment area. The original idea sprung from the mind of Richard Harding, and it worked superbly.

What happened to the birds, you ask? Well, it was obvious they had to be relocated. Why? Let me cue the front page story Doug Gillon wrote in the *Glasgow Herald*. Headlined "Pigeons to be shot to clear curling ice," Gillon penned, in part, the following:

"Marksmen will move into Glasgow's Kelvin Hall tonight to shoot pigeons threatening the success of the world curling championship. The birds are constant inhabitants of the hall, but their presence, with the Air Canada Silver Broom imminent, is most unwelcome. Not only do they foul the ice, but their springtime antics in the rafters have been sending down dust and dirt which can have a disastrous effect on the playing surface... (so) the pigeons must go."

Gillon's story went on to detail how the pigeons would be shot (with gas-powered air rifles), but the story so aroused Glaswegian bird lovers that they vowed to disrupt the championship by throwing rock salt onto the ice, if even one pigeon was potted. Eventually the birds were captured using medicated meal offerings, released outdoors, and the Silver Broom proceeded. You might say they were winging it.

BEST/WORST CHAIR OF AN ORGANIZING COMMITTEE
Did you really think I'd commit professional suicide in such a public way?

BEST HEADQUARTERS HOTEL
No contest: a tie between Megève's Mont D'Arbois in 1971 and the five-star Beau Rivage in Lausanne, 1988. No Canadian hostelry even comes close—sorry about that.

WORST HEADQUARTERS HOTEL
Again, no contest: the hotel/motel Utica. I think the building was condemned shortly after the 1970 Silver Broom—maybe even before. When our growing contingent of world curling

followers assembled there in 1970, it was definitely not one of your five-star inns. Interestingly though, the fact it was such a lousy facility didn't seem to bother anyone. Perhaps it was because, to quote Jack Wells, "we were all in the same rotten dump together." He was absolutely right. On the plus side, it did have a great short-order cook (more about him in a bit), the Black Bear Lounge and trumpeter Rio Pardo who could get anybody involved in a fun time.

There's another hotel that could give Utica a run for its money in this category, namely the hostelry in which the media were imprisoned at the 1969 Oshawa Brier. The Hotel Genosha had paper-thin walls, was dingy and dirty, but, hey, that was 35-plus years ago. Both hotels, as you might guess, have long since been demolished.

BEST VOCAL EFFORT AT AN OPENING

I nominate Bill Lumsden, chair of Winnipeg's 1970 Brier and a past president of the CCA. When the recorded anthem failed to materialize on cue, Bill calmly invited the packed house of spectators to join him in singing "O Canada," and his rich voice and engaging suggestion provided an a capella anthem that produced goosebumps. Right beside the Lumsden nomination would be the choir from Regina's Campbell Collegiate, under the direction of Stewart Wilkinson, at the 1998 Scott Tournament of Hearts, who provided a fresh and vibrant version of our anthem— the best I've ever heard. Again, goosebumps.

BEST WEATHER

Easy. Garmisch-Partenkirchen in 1972. The balmy, sun-filled days, sparkling mountain air and frosty nights combined to produce a fantastic week. Ask any of the 2,000 or so people who were there, and they'll remember it to this day. (Mind you, the number who will claim they were there has now probably climbed to more than 10,000!) And, if you don't mind, I'll take full credit for arranging the weather. Next item.

WORST ICE

That's a tough one. In the running is the ice for the 1973 final in Regina, the pre-competition ice in Garmisch-Partenkirchen in 1972, and also the ice in Bern, 1974. (You probably already read about them in Chapter 14, "When the Ice Goes Wonky.") But far and above any other, was the indescribably bad ice at the 1992 Winter Olympics in Pralognan la Vanoise, France. I got the scoop on that horror story some 13 years later. You can find those details in Chapter 30, "Curling Goes for Gold."

BEST SHORT-ORDER COOK

The unknown chap at the small breakfast counter in the Hotel Utica in 1970 wins this one. This guy could whip up a breakfast in mere seconds, serve a lot of people quickly, and he also had a never-ending flow of quips. I was mesmerized watching him prepare scrambled eggs and bacon, handle the toast, flip the flapjacks, pour the coffee, seemingly all at the same time. It was a culinary tour de force, and I was in awe of his dexterity. I've never run across his like since.

WORST CEREMONIAL MOMENT

1969. Perth, Scotland. We were still in the process of working out ceremonial concepts, but we knew that one of the key elements would be the raising of the winning country's flag and the playing of their anthem at the closing. But how could the flag-raising be accomplished in Perth, where there was a false ceiling? We decided we could drill a hole in the ceiling, run a line from one end of the arena to a pulley at the hole, and lower the line so that the flag could be attached to it. John

Foster, arena manager, would be on the line and, to make sure it moved smoothly, he fitted it onto one of his fishing reels, so he could "reel up" the flag. In rehearsal everything went perfectly. The flag was set into the back of the winner's dais and, on cue, it would be raised to a point just over the heads of the winning team, so that television could frame the flag and the champions together. Perfect plan, wot?

When the actual moment came, the flag started to rise as planned but suddenly shuddered and stopped, immediately behind Ron Northcott's winning foursome. But move any further it did not. I can still hear Gordon Craig, producer of the TV show, saying calmly to his switcher, "Fade to black." As mishaps go it wasn't big, and in the great scheme of things, it didn't matter too much, I suppose. But at the time, we thought it somewhat of a calamity. What happened, you ask? The line jumped off the pulley and jammed; the flag, slightly askew, never did reach its proper height.

BEST ENTERTAINMENT FEATURE

The "instant" slide show at the 1973 Silver Broom in Regina, since emulated in other precincts. Mike Taylor of Air Canada worked with Bob Warren, a genius with a camera, to prepare a wide-screen and multi-screen version of "This Was The Week That Was," for the closing banquet. Bob's camera wizardry and Mike's selection of music and overall organization and direction created a dazzling show that garnered acclaim from all of us gathered in the Saskatchewan Centre of the Arts. Mike even included some of Bob's colour shots from the closing ceremonies held just a few hours before, as well as another shot of people arriving at the Centre of the Arts banquet! The whole thing was mind-blowing.

I'd also have to rate the 1975 Bern "farewell" show in the Kursaal, put on by the famous Hazy Osterwald band, as a "best" in its field. That night was pure big-band nostalgia.

Included in the spectacular evening was the appearance of the Winnipeg Pipes and Drums, who rose to view on the huge dance floor, as it was hydraulically lifted, from the basement 16 feet below. The music came first, then the black-bear busby of the drum major, and then the full band of pipes and drums was revealed. Again, sheer magic.

Speaking of sheer magic, you might recall, if you were there, the "Magic on Ice" efforts of the Saskatoon Brier of 2000. Superb.

MOST EMBARRASSING MOMENT

My nomination is for a singular occasion at the 1965 Brier in Saskatoon. I still remember it vividly, and I'm sure Ron Franklin does too. Franklin, skipping Nova Scotia, was up against Harold Worth of Saskatchewan in the 10th draw. Worth was challenging Manitoba's Terry Braunstein for top spot; the Bluenosers were well down in the standings. Franklin won the game, effectively knocking Saskatchewan out of contention. (An aside here: Franklin would later move to Calgary, where he was one of the organizing honchos for the 1997 Brier.) I'm not thinking of Ron's 7–6 win, but rather of a moment in that tense game. There was a stone just biting the 12-foot ring close to the divider. The call was for a takeout of the stationary stone, and as the shooter whistled down the ice, Franklin was right there to catch it if by chance it hit the sideboards first. At the very last moment, Ron reached down, grabbed the *stationary stone*, and lifted it high. As the shooter scooted underneath, Ron realized, as did the packed house, that he had grabbed the wrong rock! After a second of silence, a giggle of laughter began to build in the stands, until a crescendo of guffaws filled the arena, and Franklin stood there, with nowhere to hide, holding the wrong granite in his hand.

BEST CHOICE OF WORDS

Some time ago—can't (or don't want to) remember when—Laurie Artiss was at the top of his game. Not only could he throw a left-handed stone to the button, he also sponsored a local seniors' bonspiel in Regina, where he could display his southpaw talents. And to provide backup, he invited three friends. There was famed Brier lead Fred Storey, along with Ray Kingsmith (before he became CCA president) and an Eastern scribe (in case alibis were needed). Each of us wondered, of course, where he would fit into the Artiss lineup. But in the hotel-room "strategy session" the night before, nothing was said about position.

We were, of course, ready to agree that Artiss should skip. After all, it was his event, and we were mere cannon fodder, a sort of parsley on the fish dish. But who would lead? Who would hand out wise counsel at third? Who would be in charge of excuses? We were left in suspense, none of us wanting to suggest a role for the other, or for self. Nothing was said until just before our first game.

"Okay, you guys," spake Artiss finally, "what position do you want to skip from?"

Chapter Twenty-one

THE KEY TO THE FRONT DOOR

THE PHONE RANG IN THE SILVER BROOM OFFICE IN PERTH AND I PICKED it up. The voice at the other end was melodiously Scottish, quite businesslike, and—was I imagining it?—slightly tinged with worry.

"The key to the front door," said the voice, "is...missing." She couldn't bring herself to say that she thought one of my media friends had pocketed the key during the party the previous night, but I could read between the pauses.

"I'm sorry to hear that," I said in my most diplomatic manner. "Please have a duplicate made, and send me the bill."

"But you don't understand," she continued, voice rising, "there is only the one key. It's ancient and historic. It's 12 to 14 inches long, and there is no spare, no copy. It's the only one in existence."

Oh migawd, I thought, what now?

The year was 1975. The voice belonged to a curator. The front door in question was huge, historic and heretofore locked with the said ancient—and now missing—key.

It was the front door to Scone Palace, hereditary home of the Earl and Countess of Mansfield.

You may not know Scone Palace itself, but you probably know about the famous Stone of Scone, also known as the Stone of Destiny, or, in Gaelic, *Lia Fail*. The stone is some 336 pounds (151 kilograms) of sandstone and has been revered for centuries as the symbol of ancient Scottish monarchy. It had been spirited away in 1296 ("stolen" said the Scots), and put under the throne in Westminster Abbey, where it had been featured in the coronation of English monarchs since 1306.

Scots rightly sing the praises of the island of Ailsa Craig (between Scotland and Ireland) as the origin of the finest curling stones in the world, so they figure they know stones. When the famed Stone of Scone disappeared from Westminster Abbey in 1951, it was front page, big-bold-headline news, paricularly in Scotland. On Christmas Eve, three Scottish student nationalists had crept into the Abbey, wrestled the stone out from under the monarch's throne and into a waiting van, then had it driven north to Scotland. Four months later, after countless newspaper stories, the Stone of Scone was found in Arbroath Abbey, site of the 1320 Scottish Declaration of Independence.

So Scone—the stone, not the palace—was right up there in the ranks of Scottish history, while Scone—the palace—has a claim on curling history, for it was in the great polished oak hallway of Scone Palace that curling was first demonstrated to Queen Victoria and her consort, Prince Albert. That visit led the monarch, in 1843, to bestow the title "Royal" on the Grand Caledonian Curling Club, and the Royal Caledonian Curling Club has been the Mother Club of curling ever since.

So when Scone Palace was offered to the 1975 Silver Broom organizing committee as the site of the annual media party, the offer was accepted with great appreciation and delight. In planning the party details, I had the chance to meet with the curator. To be honest, I was somewhat apprehensive about it all, for I knew just how historic a site it was, but I also knew how blithe some of the media spirits could be. After all, as one of those spirits, I had enjoyed similar parties in the past, though seldom in such surroundings. I'm sure you can understand why I was concerned about the possibility of cigarette burns on the furniture, glass marks on the sideboards, etc. After all, this was not some function room of a local hotel; this was a historic site of considerable importance to Scottish history—and to the history of curling.

I needn't have worried. My media buddies were all gentility and polish. No one stepped out of line. Why, the committee had even assembled a small string ensemble to provide gentle chamber music while we chatted, munched and sipped. I'd love to say it was a typical media party, but that would be a stretch.

There was one small moment, however, when the members of the chamber orchestra were ready to take a break, and Cactus Jack Wells asked one of their group, an elderly, white-haired violinist, if she would mind staying behind for a moment or two. He thought it would be nice if she could accompany the Leslie Wells Singers (curling's famed media chorale) in their rendition of a ditty used annually to serenade the host city's mayor or top official.

Allow me to detour here. If you haven't heard the choir at a Brier or Broom, you may have read about the singers in an earlier book of mine, *The First Fifty* (now out of print). Wells was the founder, conductor, historian and bon vivant of the group. The lyrics changed with the venue of each championship but only slightly—just the name of the host city in the opening line. Actually, it is the only song the choir knows. Here is the shortened libretto of our signature song, sung to the tune of "Mary Had a Little Lamb":

Perth is a horseshit town, horseshit town, horseshit town.
Perth is a horseshit town, we haven't been laid today.
We haven't been laid today, (softly) we haven't been
  laid today,

(with gusto) "Perth is a horseshit town, horseshit
  town, horseshit town (hold that note).
Perth is a horseshit town, we haven't (pause) been laid
  (pause) today.

Now, where was I? Oh yes, Scone Palace and the party.
Our conscripted violinist did a creditable job of accompanying the choir, although we were told later that the look on
her face as she heard the lyrics wash over her was worth the
price of admission.

Well, the evening went surprisingly well, and when we
boarded the bus for the ride back to the hotel, I breathed a
sigh of relief. There were no cigarette burns, no glass marks,
nothing broken. It was the next morning that the phone rang,
advising me that the key to the front door was missing.

What to do? I put the word out to the assembled media
that the key to the front door—the historic key, the ancient
key, the one and only key—had to be returned as quickly as
possible and even if it showed up in a plain brown envelope,
there would be no questions asked, no recriminations, and
the identity of the culprit(s) would be forever protected.

A short time later, I received another phone call. Could I
guarantee there would be no questions asked, no recriminations, no identification? I answered in the affirmative, and in
less time than it takes to tell it, the ancient, irreplaceable, historic key to the front door of Scone Palace was pushed under
my hotel room door, in said plain brown envelope. The situation had been saved, and the key to the front door of Scone
Palace was soon restored to its rightful owners.

Do I know the identity of the souvenir hunters (for there
were more than one)? Yes, I do. And now, 30-plus years
later, am I ready to name names? I suppose if this were a
tell-all tome I could. And if I were to reveal the identity of
the phone caller seeking clarification as to no recriminations,

etc., it might serve to produce some educated guesses as to the culprits. But then, I did promise that their identity would be forever protected.

And as that famous curler, Gertrude Stein, would say, a promise is a promise is a promise.

There are two postscripts to the yarn. The first came in November 1996, 21 years after our media soiree at Scone Palace, when England renounced its claim to *Lia Fail*, and the famous Stone of Scone was driven north, this time with considerable fanfare, to find a new resting place in Edinburgh. By 2001, Scotland had its own Parliament. The second PS came during the 2006 Scott Tournament of Hearts in London, Ontario, when a member of an earlier media bunch known as "The Zoo" enquired as to the identity of the culprits. I repeated my 1975 promise, but was then asked if I would, at least, exonerate The Zoo from any responsibility, and I'm happy to say the absconders of the key did not include any of that motley bunch.

When he wasn't buying souvenirs in Perth, 1975, Bob Willson was filing reports for CBC Radio. Photo by Michael Burns

THE MARMALADE MAN

As the media trooped off the bus and entered Scone Palace, they passed a small table displaying souvenirs for sale; it was part of the regular Scone Palace tours for visitors. Included among the souvenirs were small jars of marmalade, which had labels pronouncing that the marmalade had been made by the Countess of Mansfield.

I think it was Bob Willson of CBC Radio who, while perusing the label, voiced in his perfect diction the somewhat cynical media comment "Made by the Countess of Mansfield...hah...I don't think so!"

"I did so make it," said the lady behind the table, slightly flustered.

"I'll take a half dozen," quickly replied our hero.

Chapter Twenty-two

ŞEREFÉ AND THE SUAVE CONCIERGE

I WANT YOU TO KNOW THAT BY 1978 I NO LONGER CONSIDERED MYSELF a rookie. I had for 10 years been ensconced in my dream job as executive director of the Air Canada Silver Broom. Thanks to the airline, I'd been able to travel to many of the watering holes of Scotland, Scandinavia and the rest of Europe. Thanks to the Brier and Lassie (which would soon become the Tournament of Hearts), I'd already managed every Canadian province and soon would be able to include the Northwest and Yukon territories too.

In short, I'd been around.

And then, in 1978, there I was sitting in a bar in Bern with Detlev Bandi, at that time Air Canada's public relations manager for Switzerland. We had spent most of the day meeting with various committees responsible for the 1979 Broom, listening to their plans for the next world gathering, offering the odd suggestion or (better still, from their viewpoint) indicating how the airline could enhance their ideas. The meetings had started at 9:00 a.m. and it was now about 5:00 p.m. When I say the meetings had begun at 9:00 a.m., that's exactly what I mean. The Swiss are famous for their punctuality. The trains run precisely on time. And when a Swiss meeting is called for 9:00 a.m., you'd better be ready to start the moment the big hand hits the top of the clock. There had been a break for lunch, of course, but otherwise we had been in the same hotel meeting room for most of the day.

Detlev Bandi and a Canadian piper in Bern, 1979. Photo by Michael Burns

By 5:00 p.m., all of us, Swiss and Canadian visitors alike, were ready for something that wasn't on the agenda, namely a light pick-me-up before dinner. I don't know where everyone else went, but Detlev and I headed outside for some fresh air. Four or five turns later, we found ourselves in a part of Bern we had not visited before. We were outside a bar and restaurant, and it wasn't too hard to convince ourselves that perhaps a five o'clock bracer might be in order.

The bar was one of those hollow squares that probably kept three or four bartenders busy during the rush hours. But this was a downtime in the pub-crawling business. There was only one barmaid on duty as we sat on the high stools along one side of the square. We were the only ones on that side. There were two chaps at the near corner to the left of us, a couple off to the right of us, and a lone woman across from us on the opposite side.

We placed our order, clinked glasses, muttered "Cheers" and set in to talk of the details of the day. We were in a world of our own; we didn't even mention how nice-looking was the lady on the far side.

After a while we felt the need for a refill, so asked the barmaid for "the same, again." She complied. Up to this point, it was a scene common to thousands of *estaminets* anywhere in the world. As we clinked glasses again and uttered the time-honoured "cheers," off to my left came a sweet voice. "*Şerefé*" said the voice; it sounded like "share-uh-fay."

"*Şerefé*?" I queried, discovering that the voice belonged to the damsel from the opposite side, who had since deposited herself close to the pair on our left.

"Yes," she said, "*şerefé*. In my country we say *şerefé*, where you say 'cheers.'"

"In that case," said I, with an approving nod from Detlev, "you must allow us to buy you a drink so we can say *şerefé* to you." It was, I'm sure you will agree, the least we could do. The polite thing to do.

"Oh, but I couldn't," she said, with a beguiling smile. "You see," she added, "I have to watch my voice. I'm the singer here for the after-dinner entertainment. Thank you, but no thanks."

Might I remind you that Detlev and I were not a pair of rubes just in from the boonies. No sir, we were world travellers, we'd been around. So in a conspiratorial manner, we asked, "What time is your first set?"

"Oh, not till nine o'clock or so," she replied.

"Nine o'clock?" we scoffed. "That's more than three hours away—surely one small drink would do no harm. After all, we've added *şerefé* to our international list of toasts. We can already say *santé, skål, kampai, prost, na zdrowie, cin cin* and *slainte*. You must allow us to say *şerefé* to you."

We could see that the force of our brilliant repartee was working. There was a short pause, and then, ever so demurely, she replied, "Well, yes, since you put it that way, I suppose I could have just a small drink."

Delighted that our suave, men-of-the-world demeanour had been recognized, we summoned the barmaid, and indicated that our new-found friend would like, perhaps, a small libation.

Before you could say *şerefé*, cheers, or whatever, the cork was out of a large bottle of champagne and a small glass of bubbly was poured for the lady. The accompanying bill was quickly proffered to us.

I do not wish to indicate the exact amount of the tab. It was, of course, for the entire bottle. Suffice it to say it approached the size of the national debt of many a developing nation. It was also of a size that could only be included on an expense account if your name was Conrad Black, before his troubles. It would certainly not have been accepted by the airline, and we didn't even try.

Also suffice it to say that we quickly realized that the lady in question, like the two of us, had also been around. I suspect she was an expert angler, for she had carefully cast a fly into a still, silent pool. And two trout had risen to the bait. Too late we recognized that we had been hooked, reeled in, and gutted but good. Too late we discovered that *şerefé* was a Turkish salute. We never discovered, although we suspected, that the bubbly bill included a decent amount for both barmaid and şerefé-sweetie. But we did not—and I add this emphatically—we did not accede to her request to buy her a meal (which might have cost the equivalent of a meal for every member of her entire family back home).

I did mention, did I not, that Detlev and I were experienced travellers, suave urbanites, men of the world? And not, *definitely not*, rookies.

We never saw her again. Still, the champagne (for all we knew, it may have been, probably was, ginger ale!) and the monstrous tab we paid was worth it; both of us have dined out on that story for, lo, these many years.

And you will understand, I'm sure, that the next time I'm with you, comfortably ensconced in a neighbourhood watering hole or at a table in your curling club, I just might raise my glass in your direction and propose that old Turkish toast ... *şerefé*.

You could also say that the experience was a bubbly, refreshing start to the 1979 Silver Broom. Remember that this was the second time we had come to Bern for a Broom, the first having been in 1974. That visit is the subject of this next story, which I never would have heard about, had not the participants (with a blush and a giggle) told me the details. I call it the Summit of Suave.

You may recall that, a number of years ago, an

TO YOUR HEALTH ...
SANTÉ. SKÅL. KAMPAI.

Now that you've mastered the pronunciation of *şerefé*, you can work on the Scottish *slainte*, or *slainte mhath*! David Smith, the sheriff of Ayr and indefatigable historian of all things Scottish and all things curling, answered my request for the correct spelling and pronunciation as follows:

"*Slainte* is the correct spelling [for the Scots toast]. Gaelic orthography is very difficult. Because of changes in pronunciation over many years, some letters and some groups of letters are not pronounced as one would expect, or are not pronounced at all. *Slainte* is pronounced *Slanchy*. The word for good—*math* (pronounced *mah*)—becomes *mhath*, pronounced *vah*, when it qualifies *slainte*.

"So the whole expression is *Slainte mhath*, or *Slanchy vah*!"

Şerefé!

amorous couple in the SkyDome Hotel in Toronto made international news when they cavorted (how's that for a euphemism?) in their hotel room, which looked out onto the American League diamond where the Toronto Blue Jays were trying to win a baseball game. I can't recall who the Jays were playing, or whether they won or lost. And most other baseball fans are in the same boat, I imagine. But most of the 45,000-plus fans present that evening, I suspect, can remember every detail of the loving pair, in their hotel room, with curtains wide open, bathed in the light of the baseball field.

So you can understand why it is that the details of a similar incident from the '79 Bern Broom remain etched, ever so clearly, in my memory. You will also understand, I'm sure, why I do not wish to name names.

The story involves a Silver Broom regular and his companion who had come to the first Bern event five years earlier. Shortly after the Swiss capital received its second nomination to host the world event, I received a phone call from our hero, who indicated that he and his friend had so enjoyed Bern in '74 that they wished to return in '79. "And would it be possible," he asked coyly, "to have the same hotel room we had in 1974?"

I told him I could make the necessary arrangements.

Shortly after their arrival, I ran into the couple and casually asked if the arrangements were to their liking. They told me everything was fabulous. And then, with a bit of hesitation, the gentleman also mentioned how impressed they were with the concierge—the suave concierge—at their hotel.

Now if you've ever stayed at a fine hotel you probably know just how important a good concierge can be. You probably also know how suave a good concierge can be; in fact, "suave" was probably invented to describe a top-class concierge. They are the fount of all local knowledge.

Nothing fazes them. My friend was impressed with this particular concierge.

"He's good, is he?" I queried, more out of politeness than anything else.

"Good? Let me tell you how good he is," came the reply. "We had just arrived from the overseas flight to Zurich, followed by the bus ride to Bern." (Bern does not have an international airport.) "We went up to our room, the one you had arranged for us," he continued, "and thought we would just lie down for a few minutes to...rest up. Some time later our phone rang and it was the concierge.

"After introducing himself, he announced that Bern was the capital city of Switzerland, with a long history and many fascinating points of interest. He went on to mention the bear pit, the large clock in the old city and some of the fine restaurants nearby. 'I also have a suggestion to offer,' he added, 'which might enhance your enjoyment of our city. As a matter of fact, the suggestion is not mine, but that of the office manager from across the street. It seems he is having a little trouble getting his employees to concentrate on their work. Might I suggest, sir, that you draw your drapes?'"

Chapter Twenty-three

THE ENVELOPE, PLEASE

CURLING, LIKE OTHER SPORTS, HAS ITS ROSTER OF AWARDS, ALL OF them vital to their constituency. The only ones where I had any involvement (in their creation) were those at the international level. In almost all of those cases, they mirrored similar awards at the national level. For example, players at the Brier vote among themselves to decide the winner of the Ross Harstone Award, and in the same fashion, players at the Scott Tournament of Hearts vote for the winner of the Marj Mitchell Award. Both awards honour the player who, in the opinion of the other competitors, best combines sportsmanship and playing ability.

Ross Harstone was a diminutive Hamiltonian with a booming voice and was one of the early Brier trustees. Marj Mitchell of Regina was Canada's first women's world champion (1980) who died of cancer at age 35. In addition, there are other awards, at the national level, for outstanding executives, volunteers, MVPs, shot-of-the-week, and more. But the two key awards are the Harstone and the Mitchell.

At the world level, players vote for the Collie Campbell Memorial Award (men) and the Frances Brodie Award (women), the counterparts to the Harstone and Mitchell awards. Both the Campbell and the Brodie awards honour the players, selected annually by their peers, as the most sportsmanlike, most talented players at the championship event. A third award—the Elmer Freytag Award—honours builders of the game.

The world awards take their names from three of the giants of international curling. Collie Campbell—Brigadier the Hon. Colin A. Campbell, to give him his proper rank, title, name and respect—had an incredible influence on curling, not only in Canada, but also across the entire curling world.

In an astonishing career, he was a Brier skip in the thirties, president of the Dominion Curling Association (forerunner to the Canadian Curling Association) in 1947, second president of the International Curling Federation from 1969 until his death in 1978. He had been a cabinet minister in the Ontario government under the premiership of Mitchell Hepburn, and during World War II was a brigadier in the Canadian army. He was a natural politician, whose ability to reconcile diverse opinions and interests was of the highest order.

Frances Brodie was the instigator and chair of the first World Ladies Championship in Perth, 1979, and a key figure in the development of the women's world championship. But she was much more than an organizer; she was an outstanding curler in her own right, having won "The Scottish," the unofficial women's championship, five times. The Brodie Award didn't come onto the scene until the start of the dual championships in Milwaukee, in 1989.

Elmer Freytag was a wealthy Chicago lawyer whose life away from the law was centred on the curling rink. When the ICF came into being, the United States Curling Association nominated Freytag as its senior representative, and he brought his keen, analytical mind to the job. He also brought a dedication to, and an abiding love for, the game. For many years, Elmer, more than any other, lobbied to change the ICF from a committee of the RCCC (at its inception) into the independent governing body of international curling, first known as the ICF, now known as the WCF.

One of the joys of watching Elmer in the committee room came from his competence in his profession. As a consummate lawyer, he could debate a case or position persuasively and passionately, with logic and clarity; but win or lose, he didn't carry a case over into other areas of life. He might argue against your position but he never battled you personally. He started lobbying for an independent ICF almost from its inception but didn't let his initial failure dissuade him, make him bitter or stop him. Eventually he was successful. And when the ICF did become a truly independent body, he didn't gloat or say "I told you so."

In 1985, when Air Canada retired as sponsor of the world championship, the award became the joint responsibility of Hexagon International and the ICF. But the federation did not rate it high on their list of priorities and in 1990, at their meetings in Västerås, Sweden, the ICF representatives (many of whom neither knew, remembered, nor understood Elmer's contributions) decided to retire the Freytag award. But some of us who had been involved with Elmer thought the 1990 move was, not to put too fine a point on it, a disgraceful disservice not only to international curling but also to the memory of one of the key ICF architects. We began some polite lobbying, then added some hints that our group was prepared to play hardball. If the ICF did not maintain the Freytag tradition, we suggested, others would. The lobbying paid off, and the award still continues, now known as the Freytag World Award.

There are, of course, many other similar awards throughout curling, all of them important, but since I never had first-hand experience with them, they are not included here. There is, however, one other award I should mention. It lasted exactly one year, was created by an unplanned fluke, and the only reason I mention it here is because it was such enormous fun.

It was called the Backward E Award. It came into being in 1982, was presented monthly during the run-up to the 1983 Silver Broom in Regina, and then was retired to the trash can of curling history.

But let Laurie Artiss, chair of the Regina Silver Broom that year (as he was in 1973 and of the Brier in 1976) tell the story. "It's an example of the planning and smarts of the Regina team."

"I guess you could say," writes Artiss, "that the award owes its birth to the closing ceremonies at the 1982 Silver Broom in Garmisch-Partenkirchen. We had ruled out the standard short speech full of platitudes, and in its place our promotions chair, Tom Lukiwski, came up with a whiz-bang idea: We'd have some of our people do a snappy flash-card routine as both thank you for '82 and plug for '83.

"So we had 30 large, 24" × 36" (61 cm × 91 cm) cards made up, each with one letter on it, blue letter on one side, red letter on t'other. The one side spelled out WUNDERBAR GAR-MISCH-PARTENKIRCHEN, while the other side spelled out SEE YOU IN '83 FOR REGINA ENCORE! The exclamation mark was necessary to utilize the same 32 cards.

"Lukiwski selected the card-carriers and rehearsed them like an orchestra conductor. It was 1–2–3–up, and then seconds later, 1–2–3–flip. After several rehearsals, all were satisfied the crowd would be impressed. So would the TV folks, who were alerted and ready.

"On cue, up snapped the red message congratulating Garmisch-Partenkirchen. From the capacity crowd came an appreciative 'Ahhh....' Then came the quick flip to the blue Regina message, and an even more pronounced 'Ahhh...' followed by a light titter that grew to a giggle as the crowd got a better look at the signage.

"The second-last card," continued Artiss, "was an E on both sides, one red, one blue. Obviously the pressure of the moment got to the holder. Instead of flipping the card, he rotated it, and in so doing, changed the direction of the E, but not the colour. Where everyone else now had a blue letter, he was still holding the red side, with a backward E.

Regina's flash-card routine wowed 'em in Garmisch-Partenkirchen in 1982, and thanks to an unidentified (to protect the guilty) committee member, prompted establishment of "The Backward E" award. Photo courtesy of Laura Argue

"Down on the ice," continues Artiss, "I didn't know whether to laugh or cry. The mayor of Regina (who was with me) asked 'Who the hell is that yo-yo up there?' He may not have said 'yo-yo.' That night at the closing party I had at least six people come up to me to congratulate us on our master touch. They thought it had been done on purpose!

"From that point on, it wasn't hard to capitalize on the Backward E. It became our monthly award for goof-ups...and it wasn't subtle. As we progressed from planning to the actual event, the recipient of each month's major screw-up was given a colourful (red, white and blue) original Montreal Expo baseball cap, with the prominent Expo E reversed."

When Laura Argue (one of the Regina committee VPS) had her film of the '82 event developed, there was the shot of the

Backward E in all its glory, captured by a friend to whom she had given the camera (since Laura was one of the card carriers). That photo was duplicated and used as the committee Christmas card and sent all over the world!

Artiss completes the story when asked if that was the end of it all. "Not quite," he answers. "Another committee VP, Keith Critchley, who owned a printing firm, and who got the job of printing the Christmas card, did a nice job with the 4" × 6" full-colour card. He also delivered several cartons of stock-size envelopes...all in the 3" × 5" size! That month's award didn't even require a vote!"

Artiss even added a PS to the Backward E yarn. "There was probably only one miscarriage of justice and one undeserving recipient of that award," he writes. "At the committee's windup party, I was called to the stage and received a cap. Not with one, not two, but three Backward Es!"

"Undeserving," he says. Sure, Laurie, sure.

Will there be other international awards? I hope so; curling needs to recognize its pioneers, its innovators and its heroes. My own suggestion for a new award would be for some kind of recognition of the happiest fan. You know, the curling supporter you would most want to have alongside you on a trip to a world championship, or to the Brier or the Hearts— the fun person who makes you feel better just by being present. And I can think of a goodly number of people I would be happy to nominate for that award. Indeed, my first choice would be Sam Richardson, of the 1959–63 Scotch Cup winners. If you've read his authorized biography, *Say It Again, Sam!* by Arnie Tiefenbach, you'll know why. Also, it would, in a particularly neat way, tie the past to the present.

Chapter Twenty-four

INNOVATIONS AND THEIR INNOVATORS

WELL, THEY MAY HAVE BEEN CONSIDERED INNOVATIONS WHEN THEY were introduced, but nowadays they are considered as standard—and integral—elements of curling. Early major innovations include the Free Guard Zone rule (hello there, Russ Howard), the centre line (ah there, Laurie Artiss), even such an issue as the width of a sheet of ice (Sven Eklund of Sweden was instrumental in that one) and (ahem) time clocks. I have been accused, on occasion, of engineering some of these changes, and while I might plead guilty in some cases—usually as an accessory after the fact—most times the changes were made with considerable input from others. The Free Guard Zone and time clocks each rate separate chapters, while some of the lesser innovations are covered here and in the next chapter.

THE "EYE ON THE HOG"

for the record, i had nothing to do with the "eye on the hog," although I happened to be an observer of the gizmo in its early stages and heartily applaud its Saskatoon roots and development. The hog line sensor, for me, is the innovation that has helped save the sanity of both long-sliding curlers and hog line judges. That's the upside, and there is no downside, unless you consider putting a few hog line officials out of work a downside. The "Eye on the Hog" replaces those hog line officials with an electronic sensor. Sure, it sounds simple, but getting it right, and getting it into the game, was been anything but.

Over the course of many years' attendance at, and coverage of, the Brier, the worlds and other big-time events, I became well aware of some of the epithets that had been unloaded on the poor hog line official. There, on a cold chair out on the ice, he or she had to sit, looking neither left nor right, with a walkie-talkie ready to call an infraction. In the early days of the Silver Broom, I placed the officials in the stands, where they were not quite so conspicuous. But eventually we decided to maintain the same protocol as that of the Canadian Curling Association. It should be noted that there were safeguards attached to the position to avoid errors. In the first place, there were officials at either side of the playing surface. It wasn't enough for one of them to detect an infraction; both had to agree.

The conversation would normally go something like this. Official on one side of the arena: "Hog line, ice C, red rocks." Official on other side: "Confirmed." Or "Denied," if that official did not agree with the call. If there was agreement that the hog line had indeed been breached, the head official would then indicate this to the official at ice level, and the rock would be removed from play.

For a number of years I had been involved at the worlds, and even one time at the European championships in Sweden, with the selection of hog line officials, and I can vouch for the fact that the hog line job is not one that any sane individual would request. Either the stone-faced official was too timid to ever call an infraction or he or she was the exact opposite, a bounty hunter who revelled in the job. If you were ever going to advertise for hog liners, you might want to ensure that "masochist" was somewhere in the ad. Installing safeguards to ensure that hog line calls were accurate and appropriate was extremely difficult. So when the Startco Sensor came along, all kinds of people, including me, applauded its introduction and subsequent acceptance.

The weakness in the subjective system was with the official. To say it is a difficult call to make is an understatement. If, in the delivery of the stone, the curler holds onto the handle well past the hog line, it's easy. But detecting the exact moment the handle is "clearly released," as stated in the rules, is very difficult, and over the years had led to harsh words and suggestions that eye tests might be useful for some officials, or that there were some whose maternal origin was in question.

The defining hog line moment came at the 2001 World Championships in Lausanne, Switzerland, and involved Randy Ferbey, the six-time Brier champion and Canadian skip with the long-sliding, silky-smooth delivery. Admittedly, Ferbey flirts with the hog line, but so do a considerable phalanx of players. (According to my files, no less than 47 hog line violations were called at the 1986 Brier.)

In Lausanne, playing a semifinal against Andreas Schwaller of Switzerland, Ferbey was called for breaking the hog line rule, not once, not twice, but three times by the resident Swiss official. To say Randy was livid is putting it mildly. I hasten to add that Andi Schwaller was not involved in any of these shenanigans; he is one of the better Swiss curlers to play at the world level, and doesn't need any kind of surreptitious help from Swiss cheerleaders who might also be employed as officials. However, it seemed passing strange that most of the other hog line calls in that event were only in games involving Swiss teams. Those calls were, probably, merely coincidental, but they also turned out to be the catalyst in the development of an objective system of detecting hog line infractions.

Among those musing on this was Neil Houston, a world champion curler himself, in 1986, who subsequently worked for the CCA. As Neil told me, "There's a lot of technology available, some of it in other sports, and I thought maybe some of it could be adapted and developed for curling. When Kevin Ackerman, a former Saskatchewan junior curling champ, approached me with a project that he and his engineering-student team were planning as part of their postgrad process, we (the CCA) provided funding and there was actually a prototype tested at the Ford worlds in Winnipeg [in 2003]." There were still some bugs to be worked out, and when the Ackerman team began to run out of time, their professor called in Garry Paulson and his boffins to see what they could do.

In the autumn of 2002 I was in Saskatoon, doing what's known as "the book flog," promoting my 2002 book, *Canada Curls*, and I had some extra time, so Bill Lewis, a long-time Brier media buddy, drove me out to the suburbs to meet Paulson, who was president of Startco Engineering Ltd. Paulson had founded Startco while still a graduate student at the University of Saskatchewan. While pursuing a doctoral degree, he had developed a digital, solid-state starter that became an essential element in the transport of ore by conveyor belt in Saskatchewan's potash mines. It wasn't as easy as it sounds, for some conveyor belts were over a mile in length and required an extremely smooth, gradual and efficient start. The firm grew from that small beginning, and when I visited Paulson there were over 40 engineers in the firm, tackling all sorts of intriguing challenges.

A number of them were curlers (isn't everyone in Saskatoon a curler?), and what they created is now a standard item in the major Canadian and world championships. Their "Eye on the Hog" has removed one of the major irritants in big-time curling, namely the myopic hog line judge.

How does it work? The sensor uses a long magnetic strip, similar to a fridge magnet, set across and under the ice surface at the hog line. Small, wafer-shaped batteries inside the plastic handle of the stone provide enough power for the sensor's operation. A special coating on the handle completes the circuit. If the curler's hand is still touching the handle when the stone passes over the hog line's magnetic strip, it is a rules violation, and a small red light on the handle signals the infraction. If no infraction, a green light indicates a legal delivery. Curlers love it and accept it, for it is unbiased, objective, foolproof.

In Saskatoon, Bill and I watched as a prototype was previewed for us. One of Paulson's engineers, Travis Klassen, was a pretty good curler with a long slide, and when he delivered rock after rock, we were impressed. We asked Travis to try to release the stone just before the line, or right at the line, or just over. We hovered right at the hog line and tried to call an infraction, based on the visual, but even so we couldn't agree if an infraction had been committed. The sensor proved infallible.

The CCA put the sensor into use at the first Continental Cup in Regina in November 2003. And everybody concerned—officials, curlers, observers—liked it. The CCA bought the necessary equipment for the following season and has used it ever since. The WCF, however, demurred and came up with all sorts of reasons why they should wait to be convinced—arguments that, frankly, I found specious and silly. The real reason, I felt, was political; they did not want to be seen to be following Canada's lead. The following year, when the WCF saw the Startco system in operation, they were eager to climb aboard the sensor train and purchased a full set of handles. Today, hog line brouhahas are fast-receding memories.

Not all new ideas worked as well as the Startco sensor. The history of the hack shows that. (That's "hack" as in "foothold from which to deliver the rock," not "hack" as in the title of this book.)

Crampit curling in New Zealand. Photo courtesy of *Canadian Curling News*

THE HACK

at the world level, the hack was an early challenge, starting with the Scotch Cup. One of the contentious items when the Richardsons first journeyed to Scotland was whether to use the Canadian hack, the Scottish hack, or the crampit. Let me explain.

The crampit is a metre-long piece of metal set on top of the ice. It has a raised ridge at the back end, and if you are a right-handed shooter, you put your right foot sideways against the ridge to anchor your body, while the left foot is set toward the front of the crampit, pointing down the ice. The stone is swung from this stationary position, in pendulum fashion, and is delivered without any slide at all.

In addition to the crampit, Scotland had at least two varieties of hack that I recall. One was an angled, rubber-fronted piece of wood akin to the Canadian hack except that it sat on top of the ice and had pins at the corners that fitted into holes in the ice, anchoring the device. The other, and smaller, hack was an H-shaped piece of metal that looked like a large belt buckle. There were pins at the top and bottom of the uprights of the H, while the crossbar of the H was raised about an inch off the ice. You set your foot against the crossbar when delivering the stone.

There was always a feeling of insecurity with either of these footholds for, as often as not, a curler with a high backswing might kick the hack out of those holes in the ice and could unexpectedly end up in a distinctly embarrassing position. When Ken Watson, Jock Waugh and Norman Tod got the Scotch Cup underway, they reached agreement that the Canadian teams could use the (sunken) Canadian hack, while the Scots could use the (surface) Scottish hack, although I recall that one of the Scots (Willie Young, I believe) used the crampit. Eventually Brier competitor Marco Ferraro of Montreal came up with the current, excellent hack that is now in universal use.

One idea I considered was installing the hacks so the stone could be swung between them and delivered on the centre line, as dictated by the rules. Instead of setting the hacks with the inside edge three inches (7.6 cm) from the centre line, perhaps they should be set six inches (15.2 cm) apart. That would leave a 12-inch (30.4-cm) distance between the hacks, about the diameter of the stone, and the granite could then be delivered on the centre line. I seem to recall some private experimentation, in which I discovered it was a terrible idea. It was quickly discarded, and no one was told. So forget you ever heard about it!

Chapter Twenty-five
MORE INNOVATIONS

IN MOST CASES, SMALL INNOVATIONS WERE MERE ADJUSTMENTS TO MEET the needs of the day. Still, they did help in the development of big-time curling. One such adjustment involved the standard 12-inch diameter "button" that was fine at the club but in an arena proved to be too small for spectators to see. There was nothing in the rules that said the button had to be 12 inches (30.4 cm); the rules mentioned only that the outer ring should be 12 feet (3.6 metres) in diameter. So we expanded the world championship button to 18 inches (45.7 cm) in diameter, and found it not only easier for spectators to see, but also easier to display the Air Canada logo in the ice. That concept is now used in title tilts everywhere.

The same thing was done with the hog lines. Instead of a thin line, as in the club, each hog line was widened so that it was visible even to fans high up in the nosebleed section of the arena.

Back in 1971 I lobbied the International Curling Federation to look at standardizing the rules, to which they agreed. I thought it would be easy to find common ground on most rules, including the one about the width of a sheet of ice. Naïvely, I suggested the ICF agree to the dimension in the Canadian rules: 14 feet, 2 inches (4.3 m). Sven Eklund of Sweden, later to become president of the ICF, explained why that was a non-starter, and it was an explanation that made eminent sense.

"Suppose there is a stone barely biting the 12-foot ring at the tee line," said Sven. "Under Canadian rules, there is only one way to remove that stone: from the 'inside out.' If you try and remove it 'outside-in' you would hit the sideboards first. We in Sweden feel the stone should be available to either an in-turn or out-turn hit. That means there must be enough room *on either side of the stationary stone* for a take-out to miss it, with either turn. Thus there should be about 22–24 inches (56–60 cm) between the edge of the rings and the sideline or sideboard."

Sven's explanation made such sense that we quickly agreed the width for world

Sven Eklund, who was instrumental in establishing the width of a sheet of ice for international play. Photo by Michael Burns

competition should be 15 feet, 7 inches (4.75 m), which it has been since the early seventies.

When I first attended the Brier in 1960, the score sheets given to the media were different from the scoreboards on the ice. On the media bench we used the "baseball score sheet," while the boards on the ice were the same as the "Macdonald boards" found in most curling clubs (numbers along the centre score line, with end numbers hung above or below the score line—very confusing.) When it came time to begin the Silver Broom, it wasn't difficult to suggest that the new scoreboards (waiting to be constructed) should utilize the baseball design. That basic design continues today in all major competitions.

Those media score sheets from 1960 were about the size of "galley sheets," an old printing term meaning about 6 inches wide and a little over 13 inches in length (15 cm × 33 cm). The next year they were still 6 inches in width, but had been reduced to 9 inches (23 cm) in length. Because they were loose sheets, I kept misplacing mine, and by 1966, I had taken to bringing a three-ring binder to the Brier. I designed my own score sheets for use in the broadcasts Bill Good and I were doing for CBC radio.

In 1968, when the Silver Broom began, I printed up media score sheets, put them in three-ring binders, and was gratified to note that the Brier followed suit the next year. Those binders, much more developed today, are still in use.

SUBSTITUTES, ALTERNATES, REPLACEMENTS, FIFTH MEN

What to call them? Should they even be allowed? When I first got into the organizational side of the game, curling was held to be a four-player game. And before I scribble any further, let's eliminate the sexist notion that pervades when you call it a four-man game. Should they be called fifth men? Fifth women? Fifth players? Let's just say that all these terms are interchangeable, so if I use one gender name, and you prefer the other gender name, feel free to replace it. Okay? Okay.

In 1968, when the first Air Canada Silver Broom arrived in Pointe Claire, the concept of an "official fifth man" was introduced. Mind you, it was also agreed that using a replacement player would be the team's decision. Or they could elect to do without a fourth player. Don't forget, as I have outlined elsewhere, we only had a little over two months to get ready for that inaugural event, so you can imagine how much time we spent on this subject.

There was the suggestion, as at the Brier in those days, that we should have a roster of outstanding local shooters on hand who could fit into any team in the event of an injury. And that policy was in use at a variety of other bonspiels. But internationally, where language difficulties and national pride could pose a problem, a local curler with a different nationality was neither attractive nor acceptable.

Then there was the matter of cost. In the early days, the sponsor agreed to fly the four competing players, plus the president of each country's curling association, to the championship. To add a fifth player would increase that budget item substantially, so it became an option for each team, initially at their expense. And so some of the teams either dropped the idea, or (and the American team comes to mind) nominated their president as the "fifth man." Joe LeVine was the USCA president that year (his story, about his Scandinavian genealogy, appears in Chapter 2). But Joe was in his late sixties, perhaps seventies, and as far as US skip Bud Somerville was concerned, was not wanted if it meant he had to play should one of the US team come down with the collywobbles. They liked Joe, respected Joe, were glad to have Joe along as USCA president, but they definitely did not want Joe as a shooter should one of them come up lame.

Between then and now, of course, there have been a variety of additions to "the team roster." A substitute, alternate, replacement, fifth player—call it what you will—was relatively easily

JOHNNY WAYNE CHECKS OUT ANOTHER INNOVATIVE IDEA

There was one gimmick I tried in the mid-sixties when asked to organize the Tournament of Champions at Maple Leaf Gardens in Toronto. I reasoned there was too much emphasis put on the skip of the team; nobody knew the names of the other players. So we added the names of the four players on each team across the scoreboard, top and bottom. That way, all four shooters got equal time in the identity game. One day, prior to the start of a game, Johnny Wayne, of Wayne and Shuster fame, and a great sports fan, was down at ice level, when he looked at our revised scoreboard. It showed Hersh Lerner's lineup of Bob Lemecha at third and the Dudar twins, Allan and Bob, on the front end.

"That'd make a great song," said the famous comedian, and he trotted out the Stephen Foster oldie, "The Camptown Races." "Lerner's team has Lemecha, Dudar, Dudar." The team names on the scoreboard disappeared shortly after, proving once again the truth of one of curling's oldest themes: never let progress stand in the way of tradition.

accepted as a bona fide team member. Then came the coach. The physiotherapist. The sport psychologist. The massage therapist. The team leader. The national coach. All of these are now accepted as members of a competing team at the Brier, the Hearts, the Worlds, the Olympics. But it wasn't always so. Curling used to involve four players and no more.

I recall a time when our small group of Air Canada organizers could have used a shrink. Just ask Tony Schoen, then a key member of the airline's PR staff. In 1984 Tony had to become an amateur shrink and accompany a curler from the championship site in Duluth to the player's European home and then turn right around and fly back to Canada. I should add that getting the said psychotic player out of the host city involved Tony's wife, Edith, persuading the curler to come out from under his hotel bed and get into a cab with Tony and Edith for the two-hour drive to the nearest Air Canada gateway, which was Thunder Bay. In Thunder Bay he had to be taken to the hospital, where he was restrained and sedated, until it was time for his flight to Toronto and thence to a European city, where his family was supposed to be waiting. The flight arrived on time, but the family didn't show until two hours later, and only then could Tony contemplate his return flight to Canada, only to discover that (you guessed it) his bags were missing! And so was his watch. The bags were quickly located, but, to this day, Tony is waiting for his psychotic friend to return the watch, the Swiss-designed, 14-karat gold watch with the Silver Broom logo, which the disturbed player coveted and which became the talisman that kept him quiet for the trip.

Speaking of timepieces brings me to the subject of time clocks (sneaky segue eh?), which is a cue to start the countdown to the next chapter.

Chapter Twenty-six

GOT THE TIME?

Douglas Maxwell, you have been charged with knowing more about time clocks in curling than the average water buffalo. How do you plead?
Guilty as charged, Yer Honour.

Explain, then, for the court, all that you know about time clocks...er, no, on second thought, I don't think we have that much time. Just give us the background to time clocks.
I'll try, Yer Worship. What exactly do you wish to know?

Well, for a start, when were the first time clocks used?
Time clocks were first introduced in 1989 in Milwaukee, at the first combined world championships for men and women. No, I take that back—they were first used in the inaugural TSN Skins Game in 1986.

I take it from your hesitance, Mr. Maxwell, that there may be some further explanation you wish to offer?
You're absolutely right, Yer Excellency. May I ask you to bear with me as I sketch a little background for you? Back around 1983, I was becoming increasingly concerned—as were a number of others—with the length of time it was taking some teams to play a 10-end game. It wasn't that some players were slow...

But they were?

Well, yes, Yer Grace, they were. It wasn't so much a case of some skips dithering over strategy as it was a case of some teams deliberately stalling in an attempt to "psych out" the opposition. No matter the reason, there was concern on how best to control the length-of-game situation. I do recall some games that lasted well over three, almost four hours! In addition ...

All right, I understand you. Go on. About the time clocks, please.

Indeed, Yer Beadleship. The CCA floated a plan whereby it would allot a specified time for each player to put his or her stone in play: a short time for a lead, and increasing time for the rest of the team, until the skip would have significant time. The trouble with that plan was, if each player took the allotted time, no more, no less, in every end of the game, the game could, theoretically, last four hours, perhaps forever, whichever came first!

Please, no frivolity, you're under oath!

Sorry m'Lord.

Please continue. You mentioned the CCA. What about the ICF?

The ICF, Good Sir, was considering a "time-wasting" rule, which said that if, in the opinion of the chief umpire, a player was taking too long to put the stone into play, the umpire could instruct him or her to play the shot within 30 seconds or lose the stone.

That sounds a bit fuzzy, a bit subjective, doesn't it?

You're quite right, Excellency. We thought it would be difficult to control, and it would put huge pressure on the head umpire.

What happened next?

Well m'Lord, I can't recall the exact day when I said to myself "we're not really interested in how long it will take for an individual player to play a shot; what we really want to know is how long it will take to play a game, a normal game." Who cares if a player takes five or ten minutes to deliver the stone? If a 10-end game is finished in two and a half hours, isn't that what we want? With that as the benchmark concept, the rest followed automatically.

I'm not sure I follow you.

Well, Yer Holiness, it's like this. In Canada we reckon an average 10-end game should go about two and a half hours. That is, if there are no extended conferences or suchlike.

Is that timing true worldwide?

No. In Scotland, an average 10-end game is usually completed in two hours.

Pray continue.

Let me return to that theoretical game, Yer Wise One. If it takes two and a half hours to play a full game, then, theoretically, each side should only take one and a quarter hours to play their stones, and a game would then be over, except for an extra end. That was the starting point of the theory.

So how did reality stack up against the theory? And how did you test reality?

I began my research at the European championships in Grindelwald, Switzerland, December of 1983. I was there because of my Silver Broom duties. I started to use two stopwatches to record each team's game time. When I explained to a bystander what I was doing, he suggested maybe I should try a chess clock, as it would simplify matters.

And did it?

Yer Majesty, it did. Over the next three years, I hauled out a chess clock to time Silver Broom games, Brier games, club games, bonspiel events and so on. I didn't tell the teams what I was doing; I merely noted the times. So after recording three full years' research results, I was amazed to find that, on the average, most "normal" games were completed in far less time than the theoretical 75 minutes allotted to each team.

And that's when you developed the time clock concept?

Not exactly, Yer Justiceship. Although I felt I was getting somewhere, I wanted to check my thoughts with others, so I wrote to a number of friends all over the curling world, setting out the background, my research results and the concept of time clocks. I asked if they could poke any holes in my theory and was gratified to hear that most of them thought the idea had merit.

So that's when you put the theory into practice?

No, Mr. Arbitrator. The next move was to try the idea in a competition, a sort of dry run. Since Jim Thompson and I were the instigators of the Skins, it wasn't hard to get Jim's agreement to use time clocks in the very first Skins Game series, in 1986, in Newmarket, Ontario.

Jim Thompson?

Mr. Thompson was an old friend from my CBC days, Yer Worship, and at that time a vice-president at TSN.

Thank you. Please continue.

Out of that test came the conviction that 75 minutes per team was sufficient time for a team to play a normal game. But in the Skins Game, we decided to put the teams under artificial pressure, and in subsequent years we cut their time limit, first to 70 minutes and then 67 minutes. From our Skins experience we became convinced that 75 minutes per team was a reasonable time for a team to play a game. In fact, we discovered that even with the pressure-cooker Skins Game competition, teams still managed to finish the game with time on the clock

What happened next?

I'm glad you asked, Yer Honour. That was in the Skins Game, but what I was really interested in was how long a world championship game might take. After all, what we wanted was some mechanism that would guarantee a game would finish in a predictable time frame. And in an age of television, Yer Holiness, where it's necessary to estimate when a game will be completed, such information is vital.

I understand. But if you set limits, you must also set a penalty. So what is the penalty if a team goes over its allotted time?

For a while, I couldn't figure that out, Yer Grace. Take away a shot? Penalize the team a point? Something else? It was Kaytaro Sugahara, a New York curler and curling fan, who came up with the penalty. "Why not do the same as in chess?" suggested Kay. "If you run out of time, you lose the game. It's simple, direct. And with such a penalty, it's bound to keep a team focused on what has to be done."

So that's what you did?

Kay was right, Good Sire. Since the introduction of the time clock I've heard of (or been involved in) only one or two games in which a team has run out of time. Although Sugahara's basic premise has been tweaked a bit—the concept of a 60-second time out was added—basically it was a sound concept. There was another benefit to the time clocks. It removed the temptation for one team member to stall in an attempt to "psych out" an opponent.

In other words, such a tactic would only hurt the stallor, not the stallee?
Yer Reverence, I couldn't have said it better myself.

Now, you said time clocks were not introduced into world competition until 1989?
That's right.

Why 1989? Can you explain that?
Sire, I can. It happened at the Milwaukee World Championships because, for the first time in world play, the event involved both men and women. Because the combined championship hadn't been indicated in the original bidding specifications, Milwaukee's successful bid was based on only a week of competition, as in earlier years. The problem in 1989, when it became a competition for both genders, was that the organizers found they could not obtain the arena for any additional days, so on a couple of days, four draws per day would be needed. Obviously, if even one game ran overtime, it could delay the ice preparation and the practice time for each succeeding draw. Even if we started at 8:00 a.m., we could be finishing games well after midnight.

And you didn't want that.
No one wanted that. At one of our pre-event meetings, it was obvious we would have to control the length of games in some way. The ICF said they would look after it, but when asked how, they were woefully short of ideas. So with the TSN Skins experience, and my three years of research as backup, it wasn't too hard to convince everybody to try time clocks. They worked (as promised) and the rest, as they say, is history.

This may seem an odd question, but have you ever reconsidered the concept?

Funny you should ask, Yer Clemency. As a matter of fact I have. A number of curlers have pointed out—and I agree with them—we shouldn't be clocking the playing time of a team. Once the rock has left a curler's hand, there's nothing that can be done to speed it up or slow it down. No, say the critics, what we really should be timing is the period between shots, the time when the strategy conferences take place. That's the time that can be controlled, say the critics, and that's the time we should be clocking.

Please continue.

Let me put it another way, Yer Eminence. Right now, every team's time consists of "rock time" and "talk time." "Rock time" is the time a stone takes going down the ice. There is little a curler can do to influence that time. As every curler knows, a draw is a draw is a draw, and is slower than a takeout. "Talk time" is the time it takes for a team to make up its mind what shot to play. That's the time for strategy conferences, to decide where to go after the game, or to comment on the ancestry of the timekeeper. And it's talk time we should be using, not rock time, because that's the time a team can control.

So why is that system not being used now? Nationally or internationally.

I suspect it's because it's difficult to change something that appears to be working well.

If it ain't broke, don't fix it?

Exactly, Kind Sir. Besides I'm out of the loop now so I leave it to others to make changes. I'm just an observer now, a curling hack.

So I understand. Thank you, Mr. Maxwell. If I had to summarize all this, I'd say that time clocks are your legacy to the game?

Oh, Yer Grandness, Yer Perceptiveness, thank you, thank you. You might say that, but I couldn't possibly do so.

Chapter Twenty-seven

THE BEST WAY TO DECIDE
A CHAMPION

I WONDER IF THERE REALLY IS A BEST WAY TO DECIDE A WINNER AT the world level? Or at the Brier? Or the Tournament of Hearts? Or even Podunk Junction's annual bonspiel?

I'm not being facetious about this. I recall, back in 1982, working on a treatise that set out the many varieties of curling draws that could be used to decide a winner. Having developed a world curling championship round robin draw and playoff system (three-team, four-team variety) and never quite getting it exactly to my satisfaction, I had developed an inordinate interest in the many varieties of competitions. So when Labatt Breweries, then sponsor of the Brier, asked me to produce a booklet that might be of help to club drawmasters, bonspiel organizers and others, how could I refuse?

But I wasn't about to do this on my own. I recruited some of the best bonspiel minds in the country and the result was a 48-page effort that, when I look at it today, still works pretty well. Together with Doug Scrymgeour of Winnipeg (then the drawmaster for the Manitoba Bonspiel, the biggest in the world), Bill Schnarr of Cobden, Ontario (veteran curler and maker of square draws) and Tom Caldwell of Toronto (club manager and developer of a variety of club draws, involving any number of teams playing on any number of sheets of ice), we put together just about every kind of known competition schedule. At least that was so when we wrote it. We titled it, with great originality, the *Labatt Curling Draw Book*.

The key sentence I composed then, and it is as accurate today as it was when I wrote it, reads like this: "*There is no such thing as a perfect system of declaring a champion. If there was, someone would have discovered it long ago and we would all be using that system today.*"

A number of years later, another great curling friend, Jack Lynch of St. Bruno, Quebec, told me about a playoff scenario known as the Page Playoff System (or the Page System, or just the Page). If ever I get to update that 1982 booklet, the Page System will have to be added. I have no idea where the name originated, but I do recall Jack telling me he had come across it at a Pan American Games baseball event, and he thought it might work in curling. By 1995 he had convinced the CCA to adopt the Page System at the Brier. While some teams were ambivalent about its advantages, others were not.

Let me take a few minutes to talk about Jack Lynch. I first met Jack through the Olympics. In 1972, when I was appointed Chef de Communications for the Canadian Olympic team in Munich, Jack was the long-time technical director of the Canadian Olympic Association (now the Canadian Olympic Committee), and lived in St. Bruno, in the Eastern Townships of Quebec. Although it was the Summer Olympics we were involved in, I knew that Jack was a pretty good curler and curling writer, so we had some interesting conversations. Suffice it to say we became good friends. He had an encyclopedic knowledge of all sports and proved invaluable to the ICF when it was wooing the IOC to have curling recognized as a medal sport, but that's another story.

Why did the CCA, and more recently the WCF, adopt the Page System? What makes it advantageous?

For one thing, it confers a benefit on the top team or, more accurately, the top two teams at the conclusion of the preliminary round robin series. Secondly, it builds to a wonderful championship climax. It permits an exact timetable for television, a not inconsiderable benefit. And in Canada at least, it has become an accepted part of championship play.

Here's how it works: Let's call the top four teams at the end of the round robin numbers 1, 2, 3 and 4. (If I've lost you at this point, perhaps you should shift to another chapter.)

The first playoff game pits #3 against #4, with the loser being eliminated. The winner moves to the semifinal. The next playoff game is between #1 and #2. The winner moves to the final, and the loser drops into the semifinal (against the winner of the 3–4 game). In this way, the loser of the 1–2 game earns a second chance. Put mathematically, the formula for the semifinal reads (W 3–4) vs (L 1–2). The winner of the semifinal then moves to the final to play the winner of the 1–2 game.

There's a further reward for the top team in that not only does it have choice of stones in any of its playoff games, it also has the hammer in the opening end in any of its playoff games. So there is a powerful incentive to finish first in the round robin standings. And if you're awarding gold, silver and bronze medals, it also automatically confers a medal on either of the top two teams. However, therein lies a drawback, if you wish to recall the Ford worlds in April 2005 in Victoria, BC, when the WCF, in my opinion, messed up the six-way tie for first place. It was—ouch!—a different story there. For the first time in history, the final standings after the round robin series showed not one, not two, not even three, four or five, but *six* (count 'em, six) teams tied for the top, each with a record of eight wins and three losses.

Stop for a moment and consider that result. It's amazing, and someone smarter than me will no doubt have figured out the odds of that happening even once. Or of it ever happening again.

In all the years of the Brier, since its beginning in 1927, there have been only nine occasions when there was a two-way tie at the top of the standings. Four times there was a three-way tie for first, but only once, in 1993, was there a four-way tie at the end of the round robin. A five-way tie? Never! A six-way tie? Are you kidding?

At the world level, in 1990, there were four teams tied for first place after the round robin. And there have been three-way and two-way ties. I also recall a five-way tie for second place, in 1982, but never a six-way tie for anything. Never, nowhere, nohow, nosiree.

Were the tall foreheads of the WCF prepared for this? Sadly, the answer is no, they were not. Any other year, before the advent of the Page System, there were tie-breaking formulas ready for any eventuality, including a six-way tie. But, unfortunately, the world body had neglected to think about tiebreaking formulas for the Page System. The CCA had Page System tiebreaking formulas available, but somehow they had escaped the attention of the WCF.

There is a flaw to the Page System, as there is in any of the other championship systems. Suppose, just suppose, the top team has gone through the round robin series undefeated, wins the 1–2 game, but then loses the final, marking that team's first loss. Where's the second chance then? The answer is "tough luck; in this case, there ain't no second chance." It all comes down to that old truism of championship play: no matter what system you use, if you want to be a champion, the one game you must win is the final one.

The Page worked very well in Canada for 10 years. So it's not surprising that the CCA was able to cite this decade of success when it convinced the WCF to adopt the system for the 2005 world championships in Paisley, Scotland, for the women, and in Victoria for the men.

In Paisley it worked like a charm. Sweden (11–0) and the USA (10–1) were well clear of the rest of the field as the two top teams. Canada was in third place (8–3), and Norway took fourth after a tie-breaking win over Russia. The Page System worked according to theory in Paisley, where the unbeaten leader, Sweden, lost to the United States in the 1–2 game. Norway ousted Canada in the 3–4 game, to qualify for the semifinal against Sweden. The Swedes took advantage of that second chance and defeated Norway in the semifinal. That left Norway with the bronze medal, and gave Sweden another chance against the USA foursome in the final. This time Sweden made sure of the win as Anette Norberg downed Cassie Johnson for the 2005 title.

Let me take you on a slight detour here, but still along the path to enlightenment for understanding the title of this chapter.

Back toward the end of Clif Thompson's sojourn as president of the world body (he served from 1982–85), he asked Laurie Artiss and me to come up with a complete set of tie-breaking charts covering every possible situation that might occur at the conclusion of the Silver Broom preliminary round robin series. Which we did. It took some considerable time to do so and involved much discussion of possibilities and competition philosophies. Our charts were subsequently debated by the ICF, and eventually approved, with final agreement reached in time for the charts to be included in the ICF Handbook of 1985. All told, we identified something like 65 different scenarios that could happen, and we provided tie-breaking formulas that involved, at the most, three additional rounds of play before identifying the final four teams that would meet in the championship playoffs.

There was some debate when we presented our tie-breaking options. Stanley Flostrand of Norway, good friend, persuasive and convincing, argued that the fairest way to handle a six-way tie (or five-, four- or even three-way tie) was to play a further round robin. Laurie and I countered his argument with one of our own. "Look," we said, "the fairest way would be for one team to win all its games, and then there would be no doubt which was best! But when you wind up in a tie at the top, you forfeit the right to fairness. What we need in that case is a way to move, as quickly as possible, through tie-breakers, to the playoffs. After all, we're hemmed in by TV times, hotel reservations, plane reservations and such."

We also formulated a basic rule that was readily agreed by all, namely: "*no team tied for a place in the playoffs may be eliminated in any other way than by losing an extra game.*" Okay, so maybe we could have offered better wording, but it was, we felt, perfectly clear to all countries, especially those whose mother tongue was not English.

When it came to deciding the ranking for tie-breaking games, we suggested the record of games between the tied teams be used. If that didn't work, we thought the decision could be made by lot—a draw out of the hat. Later, it was agreed to use skill (a pre-event draw to the button) instead of the "by lot" bit.

All this was developed for the playoff system then in use, namely a four-team playoff where #1 met #4 in one semifinal, with #2 vs #3 in the other semi. If that system had been in effect in 2005, there would have been a formula for a first-place, six-team tie-breaker series. But the Page System, with its medal benefit attached to the two top teams, negated that kind of tie-breaking series

So how was it decided? The quick answer is "poorly," as you will discover in the following chapter.

Is there a best way to decide a champion? If you want my opinion, there are some ways that are better than others, but there is no best way. If there were, someone would have discovered it long ago and we would all be using that system today.

Or have I already said that?

Chapter Twenty-eight

THE PERILS OF PAULINE

REMEMBER WHEN THE SATURDAY MORNING MOVIES (10 CENTS AT THE neighbourhood Bijou) offered some variation on *The Perils of Pauline?* There she was, blond tresses blowing in the wind, tied to the tracks, the sinister villain (boo, hiss) lurking somewhere off camera, while the thundering train approached ever closer, CLOSER, CLOSER.

Okay, now substitute "the Page Playoff System" for "Pauline" in the title, and suddenly we are in the near past. We're in Victoria, the 2005 Ford World Men's Championship. But here there is no swashbuckling hero, no mustachioed villain, only the confusion that comes from a seemingly small difference between the Page System in Canada and the Page System just introduced at the world level.

Perhaps I should issue a warning right here. Those of you who find the intracacies of competition draws boring, unfathomable or mind-numbing—or any combination of the three—may want to skip ahead to the next chapter. You will probably remain in a much better mood. Those of you, however, who revel in such arcane matters—and the politics of world curling—read on.

In the pre-2005 playoff system for the worlds, it really didn't matter if you finished first or fourth; you were in the playoffs and about the only benefit received for finishing clearly ahead of another was choice of stones and last rock advantage in your playoff game.

In the Page System, as we have seen in the previous chapter, there is another difference, and added benefits are conferred on the top two teams: a second chance if you should lose your first playoff game, and a sure medal, no matter what. It's a major incentive to play well, and it is a difference that, the first time it showed at the world level, caused all kinds of trouble.

I mentioned previously how Laurie Artiss and I had sweated out some 65 different scenarios that we codified in the ICF tie-breaking charts, and how there would be no more than three tie-breaking rounds of play to determine a world champion. And how we had stated our axiom that *"no team tied for a place in the playoffs may be eliminated in any other way than by losing an extra game."* The corollary to that axiom is simple: to win a medal you must win a game for that medal. You shouldn't be given a bronze medal simply for losing the Page 1–2 game and then losing the semifinal game.

In Canada, the Page System is intent only on declaring a winner. Finishing second, third or fourth means little (like kissing your sister, as the saying goes). At the world level, however, there are medals to be won, along with potential funding for the following year; so while winning gold is important, so too is winning silver or bronze. And here, as set out above, "winning" is the operative word.

Some opinionated types (and I include myself as one) think the world Page System should be amended slightly so the bronze medal is won rather than given to the loser of the semifinal. A slight change in format would be all that is necessary, and could be worked into the schedule quite easily. Give the bronze medal to the winner of a game between the loser of the 3–4 battle and the loser of the semifinal. All agreed that this principle maintains parity with the axiom above, please raise your hands. Thank you. The notion is carried.

One other thing. Let me repeat a foundation phrase mentioned in the previous chapter. It is this: *there is no such thing as a perfect way to decide a winner. If there were, someone would have discovered it years ago, and we'd all be using it today.* Bear that in mind as we survey Victoria's secret.

Perhaps this would be a good time to remind you what actually happened in that fair city. Because while another six-way tie is still possible, the odds of it happening again are very, very long. And also because the real story of Victoria has never been told till now.

When it appeared that the 2005 world standings could wind up with some kind of deadlock, Bill Robertson, the head official, was prepared. Prior to the start of the final draw, the experienced and knowledgeable Robertson had turned to Brian (Mouse) Cassidy, the CCA's head statistician and computer whiz, for help. He asked Cassidy to fire up his computer and have it spit out all the possible combinations of deadlocks Robertson might have to face. It turned out there were 18 different scenarios, covering all manner of ties following the final round of play.

One of those 18 showed a six-way tie, and that is, of course, what Victoria provided. Each of the six teams had eight wins and three losses. Alphabetically they were: Canada, Finland, Germany, Norway, Scotland and the USA.

When the next test was applied—how each tied team fared against the other five—three teams (Scotland, Germany and Norway) showed three wins and two losses each, while the other three (Canada, Finland and USA) finished at 2–3. Within the top trio, Scotland had a 2–0 record, Germany was 1–1 and Norway was 0–2. It wasn't hard to rank Scotland as #1, Germany #2 and Norway #3.

Among the bottom group, each team had a 1–1 record against the other two. Even so, it wasn't difficult to determine the bottom trio rankings. Before the start of the Victoria games, each team had participated in a skills competition, in which all four players had thrown one stone, closest to

Roy Sinclair, WCF president 2000–06. Photo courtesy of *Canadian Curling News*

the button, with the cumulative distance ranked against that of the other teams. Using those results, Canada was ranked #4, Finland #5 and the United States #6.

The first hint of trouble arose in naming the top three nations, for in announcing Scotland and Germany as the top two (in the Page System) it was tantamount to handing those two some colour of medal. There are those who suggest that with three teams tied for the top, something must be done to reduce the three to two. By putting Scotland and Germany into the top two spots (and medals), Norway (with the same 3–2 W-L mark) was potentially, and as matters developed, left out of the medals.

Remember the earlier Artiss–Maxwell axiom? The one that said *"no team tied for a place in the playoffs may be eliminated in any other way than by losing an extra game?"* Replace the word "playoffs'" with "medals" and you can see why many people in Victoria felt that, while Scotland and Germany were digging for medals in the WCF mine, Norway was getting the shaft.

How to arrange the tie-breakers is what became Victoria's secret, but not for long. Did the WCF have a set of tie-breaking formulas for the Page System? No. Was there a set of formulas available anywhere? Yes. The CCA had worked out all the necessary details some years earlier. Under the CCA-charted scenario, the bottom three teams (1–1) would have battled it out to determine which was #4, and after that the Page System could proceed.

Robertson was preparing to use the CCA charts when Roy Sinclair, WCF president, overruled him and told him to use the existing, pre-Page tie-breaking charts! Why? I dunno. Ask Roy. Some simply assumed that he was blustering his way through the WCF's negligence in not having worked out a set of Page System tie-breaking formulas, or obtained the CCA set Robertson was about to use. Others opined that it was his normal modus operandi.

It was easy to decide that Scotland would meet Germany in the Page 1–2 game. What was difficult, and some would say unconscionable, was the decision to drop the Norwegians out of their #3 ranking and instead lump them in with the bottom trio, where, according to the old WCF charts Norway would play the sixth-ranked USA team for third place, while Canada would play Finland for fourth place. The two winners would then meet in the Page 3–4 game, with the winner moving to the semifinal where it would be assured of a medal.

In those tie-breakers, Norway beat the United States (10–5), and Canada defeated Finland (9–5) to set up the Page System 3–4 game. In the 1–2 game Scotland beat Germany (8–7), and that dropped Germany into the Page semifinal. Canada's Randy Ferbey won the Page 3–4 game, beating Norway's Pål Trulsen (7–6) to qualify for the semifinal against Germany's Andy Kapp. In the semifinal, Canada downed Germany (8–6) leaving the team from Füssen with the bronze medal.

It was difficult to reconcile Germany's bronze medal (gained via two losses) without their having to play Norway, as in our earlier notion. In the final Canada took gold by beating Scotland's David Murdoch (11–4). It was Ferbey's third world title and gold medal, and Murdoch's first silver. Murdoch returned to Lowell, Massachusetts, in 2006, where he won the gold medal, Scotland's fourth world title.

As complicated as the 2005 playoffs already were, television provided an added dimension of concern.

We'll never know the extent to which the CBC was involved in all the playoff details; no one is prepared to provide such information. Bear in mind that the following paragraphs are a product of my thoughts and imagination, unfettered by facts. I could be quite wide of the mark, except that I have a lifetime of TV experience, and I think I can guess, reasonably accurately, the conversations that probably took place between the WCF and the CBC. At the very least, television would want to know, as far in advance as possible, what the playoff schedule was in order to make their own preparations.

There were two key areas of television production concern. The first was the feed to television networks around the world. Outside Canada, most networks were providing their viewers with a truncated version, probably on a "tape-delay" basis, so the time element of tie-breakers was of little importance.

The second concern was the broadcasting in Canada, where the playoffs would be shown live, and the three-hour time difference between Victoria and the CBC's major viewing market in Eastern Canada was of paramount importance. For example a 9:00 a.m. game in Victoria would mean a noon start in the East; an evening start in Victoria would mean a late-night game in the East.

Also bear in mind that 2005 was a year of unparalleled difficulties for the CBC's curling coverage. Earlier the national network had outbid TSN for the right to cover curling's "Season of Champions," and was just finishing year one of a four-year pact (rumoured to be worth $10 million.) But curling fans, miffed at the loss of TSN coverage, had already discovered many of the games had been arbitrarily shunted off the CBC's main network onto its new digital network, Country Canada, a specialty pay service, available only to a small number of viewers, and The Score, another cable channel.

Curling fans from one side of the country to the other were less than happy with the Mother Corp.'s coverage. So it is entirely understandable that the CBC would not be enthused about a schedule that made their life even more difficult, particularly if any of the Canada games should be scheduled at a "difficult" time, which would require them to either clear the national network or shift coverage to Country Canada or The Score.

But hey, all the above is in the past, and what does it matter today? The short answer is: it doesn't. But perhaps you can understand, and empathize with, the poor head official, trying to do his best to rationalize the concerns of the teams, the spectators, the television troops, the scheduling purists ... and all the other cooks simmering the playoff stew.

Chapter Twenty-nine

THE PATH TO THE TOP OF MOUNT OLYMPUS

THE FIRST THING YOU SHOULD KNOW ABOUT THE OLYMPICS IS THIS: nothing is ever as it seems. The second thing you should know about the Olympics is this: it's 75 percent political, 25 percent athletic. And the third thing you should know about the Olympics is this: go back to number one.

Is "the Olympic Family" a nest of vipers; thugs, thieves and thespians, or is it one big happy gathering of five-ring enthusiasts? Are the athletes superbly gifted, charismatic competitors, or are they steroid-driven stars? Is the International Olympic Committee composed of rogues and rascals, or are they men and women of impeccable credentials who value sport for sport's sake?

My Olympic experience is actually quite limited, so my impressions may not count for much. Still I have to say that the vast majority of Olympic competitors I have encountered are strongly principled, magnificent athletes who believe firmly in the Olympic credo. Most of the athletes are not household names; few make the "News at 11" headlines. And of those who do, the vast majority have worked hard to bring honour to themselves and their country.

If you wish to read about the seamy side of the games, let me suggest all or any of three books, involving the investigative work of Andrew Jennings: *The Lords of the Rings*, a follow-up book entitled *The New Lords of the Rings* and *The Great Olympic Swindle*. Jennings describes in some depth the ills of the IOC, not the athletes. For athletes the Olympic Games hold a magnetism that is palpable, a magnetism that has only lately come to curling. Think Pinerolo, Brad Gushue, the team's gold medals.

Part of what follows comes from my own experiences at the Olympic Games and has nothing to do with curling. Yet my experiences became the catalyst for some of my curling efforts. I worked as chef de communications at three Olympics, on behalf of the Canadian Olympic Association, and my efforts of those 12 years helped refine my thoughts about curling.

My first Olympics was in 1972, the Summer Games of Munich, forever sadly remembered for the massacre of Israeli athletes in the Olympic Village. That was also the year of the first Russia–Canada summit series of hockey, a series that was played at the same time as the Munich Games. As far as most Canadians were concerned, hockey was more important than the Olympics, a fact I had to downplay when explaining to German officials why so many of Canada's top sports journalists chose to pull out of Munich before the games began. In most cases their cancellation was "due to illness" or "a change in direction at their paper" or the like, and had nothing to do with hockey (ahem). I sure didn't want to get into a debate centred on "you mean a two-country hockey series is more important than the gathering of the greatest athletes in the world?"

I remember vividly the devastation felt by the host Germans who had been told the 1972 Games were designed to showcase Germany's re-entry into global society some 25 years after the end of World War II. I recall, with great affection, how a small group of German curlers helped me immeasurably to do my job for my country, in their country.

But it was the massacre that was, and is, the defining moment of the 1972 Summer Games. When I arrived in Munich the young men of the security force were wearing pastel-coloured outfits that had been designed to promote peaceful, comfortable, soothing feelings to all. The day after the massacre, pastel was out and in its place was the camouflaged battledress of paratroops (for that's what they were).

One of my most vivid memories of Munich, however, is of the splendid and wonderfully colourful opening ceremonies. They were a kaleidoscope of swirl and excitement that had taken years to prepare. The opening parade of teams (it took them well over an hour to enter the stadium) had been worked out with exquisite precision. The Munich committee knew exactly how many members would be marching in each national team. They worked out, to the second, the length of time it would take each team to cover the distance from their stadium entry to their clearing of the salute area. The entry music for each nation (based on a folk song of that country) had been arranged in march tempo, timed exactly (from entry to salute area) and pre-recorded. It was hard to tell it had been recorded because the special orchestra, seated on high at one end of the stadium, appeared to be playing without a pause throughout the hour-long entry of nations. It was a dazzling theatrical presentation of seamless music, as one national folk tune segued automatically to the next, and it still brings goosebumps just thinking of it.

It changed forever my idea of what opening ceremonies should be.

In curling I had meekly accepted that the traditional opening of the Brier had always been, would always be, the same: bagpipes leading in the teams, too many eminently forgettable speeches, an opening rock down the centre sheet, and then "Okay boys, let's get at it." Well, not always bagpipes. In 1947 the teams were led in by an official playing the harmonica!

I couldn't do much about the Brier but, by God, I could, and did, challenge many Silver Broom committees to come up with something new and better. And in many cases they did, including that time in Winnipeg in 1978, when they even managed a ceremonial pow-wow fire at centre ice! Don't ask.

Back in 1924, when curling first entered the Winter Games in Chamonix, France, only three countries showed up for the outdoor competition. Canada and the United States did not. The three countries who did appear were the host French, a squad from Sweden, and a team from Britain (for which read Scotland). The neighbouring Swiss withdrew at the last moment.

Each game of the three-team round robin was 18 ends in length, and the Brits (who beat the Swedes 38–7 and the French 46–4) were easy gold medal winners. For the record, Sweden won silver by downing France 18–10. The winless hosts had to settle for bronze. How about that? Fail to win a game, and gain a bronze! (Shades of the Ford worlds in 2005.)

It wasn't until 2006, some 80 years later, however, that the IOC recognized the British triumph as the first gold medal in curling and corrected their records accordingly. If the IOC was willing, in 2006, to recognize the curling of 1924 as a bona fide medal event, perhaps they might care to do the same for the 1932 competition in Lake Placid, where curling recorded its second appearance? On second thought, they might not, since the only teams participating in that sylvan setting in upstate New York were four rinks from Canada, and four from the United States. It's difficult to see how that event could be construed as being a full medal event without representation from any other nation. In 1932, the world was still in the grips of the Great Depression, and if a curler couldn't fund the trip to the Adirondacks on his own, fuhgeddaboudit.

Of the eight teams that showed up, four were from Canada (Manitoba, Northern Ontario, Ontario and Quebec) and four from the States (Connecticut, New York, Michigan and Massachusetts). Each Canadian team played each American foursome, but not each other. Of the 16 games played, Canada won 12, with Manitoba as the only unbeaten team. It wasn't hard to recognize the Winnipeg quartet, skipped by William Burns, as the gold medallists.

After 1932, Olympic curling remained a distant dream until the formation of the International Curling Federation in 1966. In its early handbooks, the ICF listed among its objects the following:

To negotiate with the [International] Olympic Committee with a view to the game of Curling being granted recognition as a sport to be included in the Olympic Winter Games. In the event of such recognition, to act as the channel of organization and administration between the Olympic Committee and the countries represented by the Members of the Federation.

If there was any such action taken, it was a well-kept secret, and in truth most ICF members felt that "their" world championship, the Silver Broom, took precedence over Olympic aspirations. By the time the 1985 ICF Handbook was published, the Olympic objective had quietly disappeared.

Four years after Munich, in 1976, I journeyed to the Winter Olympics in Innsbruck, Austria. On this occasion, we were well aware that the '76 Summer Olympics were scheduled for Montreal in just a few months' time. It would be Canada's first opportunity to host an Olympics, and the entire country was enamoured of the prospect of an Olympics that "could no more lose money than a man could have a baby," Mayor Jean Drapeau's boast that is still remembered by Montreal taxpayers.

In Innsbruck, on behalf of all of us present for the COA,

I was anxious to "get it right." We knew the rest of the world would turn to us for information about Montreal, so we thought long and hard about how we could rise above the ordinary and show Canada in a favourable light. Out of our concern came a number of ideas that turned out to be "firsts" in the five-ring community, but which were standard at the Silver Broom. For example it wasn't hard to propose an Olympic version of the Silver Broom's daily news bulletin, "The Eye-Opener." We called it (with perfect bilingualism) "Journal Canada."

Almost a year in advance of the '76 Winter Games, along with the COA's chef de mission who was also my good CBC friend Don Goodwin, I visited Innsbruck on a survey and found an empty storefront location in the main downtown area. It would be ideal for the creation of a "Canada House," destined in our minds to be a gathering place for Canadian athletes, some of whom were not yet out of their teens. Parents of the competitors would also be welcome, along with other Canadian supporters, media and officials. More than that, though, we felt it could become a point of interest for visitors from other countries, whose officials, athletes and media might want to hear what Montreal might offer a half-year hence. I'm told that "Journal Canada" and Canada House (Canada Lodge at the Winter Games) have become standard features ever since.

Thanks to the efforts of Air Canada curling friends Hal Cameron and Tony Schoen, we were able to arrange the delivery of a variety of Canadian daily newspapers, not so much so the athletes could read about their Tyrolean exploits, but so they could keep up to date on the NHL results, which, as you might suspect, could not readily be found in the local papers.

We were also able to arrange for some Canadian beef, beer and other food specialties as a means of letting team

After dressing the Mountie mannequin, the temptation for a "silly bugger" moment was too much. Note the buckles, on the inside of the boots—a definite RCMP no-no. Photo by Michael Burns

members and visitors know that people at home were behind them. It was in Innsbruck where I learned how to shave British Columbia smoked salmon into those paper-thin offerings! It was also in Innsbruck where I experienced one small moment of Olympic benison that never made it to the media. Because we in the media often dwell on the sensational, on big stories, let me relate this small tale of Olympic joy.

I managed to score a rinkside ticket to the final hockey playoff between Russia and Czechoslovakia. You may recall that, in those days, the cold war overtones were everpresent, and there was little love lost between the Soviets and their satellite, or between East and West, separated by the Iron Curtain. Hockey became a metaphor for the battle between them and us. So I was somewhat surprised to see one of the Russian players, at the end of the game, skate over to the sideboards and lift his stick over the glass and give it to a strapping young chap with the distinctive logo of the US Olympic team on his jacket.

As luck would have it, the recipient got onto the same bus as I did, clutching his souvenir. In the ensuing conversation, I learned he had met the Russian in the Athletes' Village, and discovered that both were jazz fans. Earlier, the American had given his communist counterpart some jazz records from home. The Soviet hockey stick had now completed the pact between the two. Olympic friendship had trumped cold war rhetoric.

It was also in Innsbruck where I learned the intricacies of dressing a male mannequin in an RCMP uniform. We put the Mountie model in the storefront window of Canada House as identification of our location and as an attention-getter for the local population. One of the first people through the door was a gentleman who identified himself as a member of the RCMP on overseas service at a Canadian Embassy, who gently chided me for my fashion mistake.

"Those spurs on the Mountie," he said, "are wrong."

"They look okay to me," I said, and explained that the only Mountie dress code I knew had been gleaned from watching Dave Broadfoot as Sergeant Renfrew (with his faithful dog, Nome) on the CBC's "Royal Canadian Air Farce."

"The buckles go on the outside of the boots," he explained patiently, suggesting I consider the consequences of standing at attention with the buckles on the inside, where they could lock together and cause an undignified pratfall!

While there was no curling in Innsbruck, there were a few indications of a sport similar in nature: *Eisstockschiessen*. You may remember that name from Chapter 6. Seeing a couple of *Eisstocks* reminded me that perhaps there was some lingering element of, and appreciation for, curling in earlier Winter Games, and perhaps curling could build on that in its quest to achieve Olympic status. But if there was *Eisstockschiessen*, nowhere could I find any indication of curling: no stones, no brooms, no brushes, no posters, no photos. I concluded that the quest to get curling back into the Olympics was a long shot at best.

Chapter Thirty

CURLING GOES FOR GOLD

IT WOULD BE ANOTHER FIVE YEARS AFTER THE INNSBRUCK WINTER Games before curling's Olympic flame would be kindled again. In 1981 Calgary was named host city for the 1988 Winter Olympics, and it excited one Calgary curler in particular. Ray Kingsmith was a long-time executive with the Southern Alberta Curling Association and a sometime media reporter who would go on to become the 1983–84 president of the Canadian Curling Association. On a crisp December day in 1982, Kingsmith, along with Warren Hansen, met with Brian Murphy, vice-president of sports for the Calgary Olympic Organizing Committee. Hansen, from Vancouver, had been one of Hec Gervais' Brier winners in 1974 and had become a contract employee of the CCA. The two friends had but one aim: to achieve demonstration-sport status for curling at the Calgary Games, considered a first step to inclusion as a full medal sport.

But getting curling onto the Olympic timetable, even as a demonstration sport, was no slam dunk.

Murphy told the pair that six sports were being considered as demonstration events but only three would be anointed. The choices were freestyle skiing, short-track speed skating, ski orienteering, dog-sled racing, ballroom dancing and curling. Eight months later, Kingsmith and Hansen made a formal presentation to the Calgary executive board, an occasion Hansen later recalled as "one of the more anxious moments in my life." It didn't take Calgary long to decide that curling, short-track speed skating and freestyle skiing would be the favoured three.

Ray Kingsmith and Warren Hansen were instrumental in adding curling as a demonstration sport at the 1988 Calgary Winter Olympics. At an earlier Silver Broom, they won the
media curling event, The Brass Whisk: (l–r) Terry Begin, Kingsmith, Air Canada flight attendants Maridee Coulter and Janice Ballanger, and Hansen. Photo by Michael Burns

After the Calgary decision, Kingsmith was named chief
organizer of the '88 curling event, to be held in Calgary's
Max Bell Centre, a friendly location with seating for just
over 2,000.

The feeling among most curlers before the start of the '88
Games, was that it would only be a matter of time before
the IOC would recognize curling as an ideal addition to the
Winter Olympics. After all, it was a winter sport, and what
sport better embodied Olympic ideals than curling? Okay, so
we were all naïve. We also surmised that with Vancouver's
Linda Moore skipping the Canadian women and Calgary's
Ed Lukowich leading the men, there would be a sold-out
arena, and in all likelihood, a pair of gold medals to help
cement curling's image.

Most of us, however, failed to recognize the Olympic axioms outlined in the previous chapter: Nothing is ever as it seems and the Olympics are 75 percent political, 25 percent athletic. It seems we were concentrating on the 25 percent, while ignoring the 75 percent.

Action began on two fronts: organizing and lobbying. The international lobbying effort, sadly, was diffused and unco-ordinated. In hindsight, one of the unfortunate aspects for the granite set was that we were bedazzled by the fact the Max Bell Centre sold out before any other Olympic venue. It was only when the games began and there were hardly any fans in the seats that we began to ask what had happened. Well, here's what happened.

Several large national and international corporations, as Olympic sponsors, had quickly bought up all the tickets they could find. Not just curling ducats, but also those for skiing, hockey, figure skating, speed skating, you name it. Then when special clients, or visitors, or employees arrived, they found their friendly corporation had a lovely supply of complimentary tickets for the various events.

Now if you happened to be a visitor who had never heard of the demonstration sport of brooms and stones, which ticket would you pick first: skiing, hockey, figure skating... or curling? Right. Which explains why so many unclaimed curling tickets were left on the "help yourself" table. There was another explanation offered by Larry Wood, a good friend of Kingsmith, and for many years the curling columnist (later sports editor) of the *Calgary Herald*.

"Although we knew the entire event had been sold out well in advance," Wood wrote me, "much later it turned out a batch of ducats had been completely mislaid." The demo show was a good one, but those members of the IOC who knew nothing of the game or, for that matter winter and snow, were never convinced.

Of course a number of Calgarians had bought tickets early and were in their seats for every draw, but the rest of Calgary was told, when they tried to buy tickets, sorry, the arena's all sold-out. And when they lined up outside the arena, hoping for some of the few rush seats that might be available, they were still told "sorry, no tickets available." When they discovered the arena was mostly empty, they were understandably miffed.

It wasn't till after a few puzzling early draws that it dawned on Kingsmith and his fellow volunteers what was happening, and they took immediate steps to rectify the situation. But, as far as the IOC was concerned, the damage had been done.

"That ticket snafu," summarized Wood, "left many IOC pooh-bahs peering down long schnozzes at the rock-tossing, arching bushy eyebrows and harumphing loudly. Nor was that the only disappointment resulting from curling's first demo inclusion since the dark ages," he continued. "Two weeks before the games began, Kingsmith was diagnosed with lung cancer. He died three months after the conclusion of the Calgary Olympics."

While Linda Moore's squad (Lindsay Sparkes, Debbie Jones-Walker, Penny Ryan and Patti Vande) won gold, Ed Lukowich's foursome (John Ferguson, Neil Houston, Brent Syme and Wayne Hart) lost their semifinal to Norway's eventual gold winner, Eigil Ramsfjell, a loss that gave the Canadians an automatic bronze. But the two golds so confidently predicted earlier failed to materialize.

Also failing to materialize was curling's great hope of becoming a medal sport. Instead it remained a demonstration sport for the '92 Winter Games in Albertville, France. Those 1992 games were spread over some 13 nearby mountain towns and villages, with curling scheduled for the small community of Pralognan la Vanoise. This was seen to be beneficial to curling's cause, for not only would it be close to Juan Antonio Samaranch's home in nearby Lausanne, but also the tall foreheads of the WCF were certain they could, under such ideal conditions, and in a European setting, demonstrate curling's allure.

They were wrong.

During the week of the eight-team event, everything that *could* go wrong, did. The local organization could only be described, charitably, as somewhere between execrable and non-existent. As one Canadian observer, with impeccable credentials, told me, "most *club* bonspiels in Canada are run with better organization and expertise."

The biggest single drawback was the ice. Two of the four sheets in the arena were unplayable and had to be scrapped from the schedule. The revised order of games became a nightmare. Roy Sinclair, the WCF's head official, was roundly criticized for his inability to reschedule the games equally on the other two sheets of ice. A series of last-minute, flip-flop decisions had several teams scratching their heads in wonderment. Perhaps the worst example of scheduling involved the Canadian men, led by Kevin Martin, who had to play nine of their ten games on the same sheet of ice, and mostly with the same rocks!

But there was more to it than organizational errors. At the time, conservationists in the Austrian, Swiss and French Alps were up in arms, claiming, with considerable backup data, that the uncontrolled expansion of ski sites in all three Alpine nations was causing irreparable harm to the ecosystem. They pointed out that some of Europe's greatest rivers—the Rhine, the Po, the Rhone—begin their journeys in the Alps. According to the International Centre for Alpine Environment, the uncontrolled development of ski resorts threatens to destroy a third of the Alpine woodlands by 2050.

There were other causes for concern. More highways had been built, and the pollution from the added cars caused acid rain that attacked the trees, causing them to lose leaves and needles. As a result the sunlight, which could now reach the ground, encouraged the growth of grasses—grasses that choked out the mosses that had acted as reservoirs of moisture. The soil thus became harder and less able to absorb rainfall. There was also added pollution from the increase in use of detergents because of all the new hotels and inns. In the winter the denuded slopes were unable to stop avalanches. In short, for many natives of the region, the Winter Games were more a curse than a blessing.

What was supposed to have been an economic boon proved otherwise: 4 of the 13 Olympic communities around Albertville declared bankruptcy following the '92 Games.

It wasn't hard to see why the locals weren't entirely enthused about Olympic curling. While they had some sympathy for skiing, which was the foundation of their livelihood, they had little understanding or feeling for curling, which was, after all, not even a medal—or a European—sport.

The protests often turned ugly. The ice situation, for example, has always been a mystery to me. How could a brand-new arena, built to curling specifications, fail so miserably to provide decent ice? As mentioned, two of the four sheets were unplayable, and when Kevin Martin, an accomplished ice-maker, offered to help, the offer was refused, partly because the host French neither wanted nor trusted an outsider working on the ice and partly because the WCF did not want to endure the PR fallout that would inevitably erupt if one of the competing curlers were to "improve" the ice. As things turned out, Martin was doubly lucky his offer was spurned, for it turns out he could have done nothing. The real reason for the rotten ice would not become known till 2005, some 13 years later. That was when I finally discovered the answer and at last had a scoop! To the best of my knowledge, you're hearing the real story here for the first time.

While in Victoria for the 2005 Ford World Men's Championship, I set up my tape recorder for a series of one-on-one interviews with a number of curling honchos. In a lengthy conversation with Gunther Hummelt, by then a past president of the WCF, I discovered the answer to the mystery of the rotten ice of 1992.

"What about the ice problems in Pralognan, Gunther?"

"The main problem was caused by terrorists," said Gunther.

"I beg your pardon? Terrorists, as in al Qaeda?" (While Gunther's command of English is outstanding, it is sometimes wise to confirm his choice of words.)

"No, no, not like al Qaeda. I mean eco-terrorists." He then proceeded to tell me how "the eco-terrorists" worked to sabotage curling's efforts of '92. Using both words and sketches, Hummelt told how some anti-Olympic "tree-huggers" had shoved small pine or hemlock cones into the coolant pipes as they lay on the ground waiting to be installed in the new arena. As a result, with the blockage in the pipes, two of the four sheets became unplayable. No one, at least no one in an official capacity, it seemed, had either the curling or organizational savvy to make the two-sheet competition work. If ever an event bumbled its way from start to finish, 1992 was it. Pitfalls? There was a new one every day, it seemed.

Those pitfalls in Pralognan seemed to indicate, to some, that curling's chance of being named a medal sport had lost momentum. Those who had been concentrating on the athletic side of the Olympics, the 25 percent portion, were desolate. They forgot about the 75 percent portion, the political part. Their focus should have been the opposite, for in July 1992, in Barcelona, the IOC dropped the demo idea and voted to add curling as a medal sport in the Winter Olympics!

Finally, curling had ceased being a wannabe and had become a full member of the Olympic Family.

Chapter Thirty-one

THE POLITICS OF OLYMPIC INCLUSION

TRYING TO IDENTIFY THE KEY MOVERS AND SHAKERS WHO WORKED TO get curling into Olympic's Golden Lodge as a medal sport is like trying to get directions from an egg beater. Ask the question of identification in Canada or the United States, and you'll be given some North American names. In Scotland, Scandinavia and other European outposts (where the Olympic Games are still thought of as a Euro franchise) the answers are different. In Asian countries, other names are bandied about.

In my opinion, there were four men who were key to gaining medal status for curling in the Winter Olympics: Gunther Hummelt, Franz Tanner, Jack Lynch and Kaytaro Sugahara, from Austria, Switzerland, Canada and the United States respectively. To my mind, they were the heavyweights in the politicking that saw curling finally gain medal status in July of 1992.

So how, then, *did* curling become an Olympic medal sport? The quick answer is that it wasn't easy. When the International Curling Federation was first formed in 1966, it included Olympic recognition as one of its objectives, but that was mere lip service. In fact, the first meeting between the ICF and the International Olympic Committee, where the cause of curling as a full medal sport was advanced, took place in Lausanne, Switzerland, in December 1984.

The European championships were being held in nearby Morzine, France, and in addition to the ICF's regular semi-annual gathering, the federation

Gunther Hummelt, Franz Tanner and Kaytaro Sugahara. *Photos by Michael Burns.* Jack Lynch. Photo courtesy of *Canadian Curling News*

was holding a special meeting to ratify the sponsorship proposal from Hexagon Curling International. Late in the week, ICF president Clif Thompson, of Stroud, Ontario, invited CCA representative Mike Chernoff and me to accompany him to Lausanne for a meeting that had been arranged by Franz Tanner, good friend and fellow Lausanne citizen of IOC president Juan Antonio Samaranch.

Little came of that meeting, which was polite but restrained. Shaking hands with Samaranch was, I recall, like grasping a trout that had been landed a half-hour earlier—cold and limp. The meeting was short and perfunctory, and we guessed Samaranch had scheduled it simply to please Tanner. We left the IOC headquarters at Chateau de Vidy, discouraged and pessimistic.

The next year, when Thompson completed his term as ICF president, he turned over his Olympic files to the incoming president, Philip Dawson of Scotland. It appeared that the Aberdeen lawyer then embarked on his own personal mission to speak for curling, with the emphasis on "personal," for to my knowledge he never asked anyone else to assist in the task.

In '84, the organizing efforts for the Calgary Winter Games of 1988 were gaining momentum, with curling's efforts being quarterbacked by Ray Kingsmith of Calgary and Vancouver's Warren Hansen. They soon discovered that the ICF's appreciation of the politicking required to obtain formal Olympic recognition for curling ranged somewhere between little and none. There was no cohesive or concerted planning evident; whatever action being taken was amateurish and ill-informed. There was, for example, the little matter of an international sports governing body needing to have a minimum of 25 member nations from three continents, a basic fact that had, till then, escaped the ICF's attention.

In addition, curling had to battle, almost surreptitiously, the six existing and entrenched Winter Olympic sports groups—skiing, hockey, figure skating, speed skating, bobsled and luge—which were funded mainly from the television rights money negotiated by the IOC. Those hundreds of millions of TV dollars were shared, firstly, by the IOC, then the host community and finally the international sports bodies. The latter's share was then divvied up, in varying amounts, among the six winter sport governing bodies. While each one professed an interest in curling, they realized that if the new sport became a medal sport, their share of the money pie would be sliced seven ways instead of six. You might add a new event within a given sport (think snowboarding or aerials as a part of skiing), and that wouldn't affect the division of the money pie. But add a new sport, curling, and it could change each other sport's finances dramatically.

Two key moments in the drive for medal recognition came in 1990 and 1991. In '90, Gunther Hummelt was elected president of the ICF, and in '91 he championed a seemingly innocuous name change from the International Curling Federation to the World Curling Federation. In that way, Hummelt removed any confusion with other ICF's (International Canoeing Federation or International Chess Federation, for example).

By 1992, Hummelt began to preside over an expansion of the federation's membership to obtain the requisite minimum of 25 nations from three continents. New curling hotbeds appeared out of nowhere, clamouring to become WCF members. One day it was Belgium, the next Andorra. Mexico joined the federation, and when it was discovered that there were a half-dozen curling enthusiasts in the US Virgin Islands, a curling association there was quickly formed and recruited to WCF membership. Rumours abounded that some of the new WCF members even had their yearly dues paid by the president, but they were just rumours. If true, we never found out for certain, and besides—no one cared.

Once he cleared the numbers hurdle, Hummelt then set out to exercise his considerable charm and political wiles to gain admission to "the Olympic Family." One of his early allies was Jack Lynch, from St. Bruno, in the Eastern Townships of Quebec. Jack had been the longtime technical director of the Canadian Olympic Association, whose knowledge of, and contacts among, the world's key Olympic players was legendary. Nor did it hurt that Lynch was well respected by Canada's ranking IOC member, Dick Pound of Montreal.

Although Jack and I had both worked for the Canadian Olympic Association at earlier summer and winter Olympics, and although we often talked curling, he knew I was a journalist and so kept many of his involvements to himself even until the last days of his life. His specialty was to advise Hummelt on the intricacies of Olympic politics, who the key players were and to offer his opinion when asked.

Franz Tanner lived in Lausanne, headquarters city of the IOC. He had been instrumental in helping establish a short-lived bonspiel in Lausanne, where the champion's cup was the politically named "Trophy of the President of the IOC," and was presented by Samaranch. Jean Paul Bidaud, the organizing chair, had invited me to come to Lausanne as drawmaster for the 'spiel, so both Jean Paul and I were well aware of Tanner's desire to recruit Samaranch as a curling fan.

Tanner was more than a curling fan, however. He was a top-level curler, who had, in 1980, won the Swiss championship and arrived at the Silver Broom in Moncton as second on the team that included son Jürg at skip, along with Patrick Lörtscher and Jürg Hornisberger. Franz, a fitness buff, easily kept pace with his three young teammates, and when they came to London the following year, they won the Air Canada Silver Broom, beating the United States' Bob Nichols foursome by one of the lowest scores in curling history, 2–1. In 1982 (Garmisch-Partenkirchen) Tanner returned a third time, to finish in a five-way tie for second place. That was the year Al Hackner won the first of his two world crowns (the other coming in 1985). I still cherish the huge Swiss cowbell, with its wide collar and inscribed plaque, presented to me by the Tanner team as a memento of the London Broom of 1981.

So Tanner wore his reputation as a world-class curler when he came to speak to Samaranch about the potential of curling as an Olympic sport. Equally important, he enjoyed the confidence of Gunther Hummelt. In 2002, in recognition of his many contributions to international curling, Tanner was given the World Curling Freytag Award.

With curling listed as a demonstration sport in Albertville, 1992, the IOC dispatched an official observer, Fernando Bello of Portugal, to Pralognan la Vanoise, site of the curling competition. More important were the visits of President Juan Antonio Samaranch, and the Swiss vice-chair of the powerful Programme Commission, Marc Hodler. It probably didn't hurt that Hodler was there when his countryman, Urs Dick, sidelined Canada's Kevin Martin in the semis, and then went on to grab the gold against Norway's Tormod Andreassen.

Hodler was a big wheel in the IOC. President of both the International Ski Federation and the Association of Olympic Winter Sports Federations, he was also a member of the IOC executive board and a key member of the Programme Commission's winter sports subcommittee. When he returned for the men's final, he was accompanied not only by Samaranch, but also by the organizing committee's co-president (and famed skier) Jean-Claude Killy, plus IOC sports director, Gilbert Felli. They met with Hummelt over lunch and, while no decisions were reached, Hummelt said later he was optimistic that medal status would be granted "sooner rather than later."

A formal decision, however, would follow the IOC's timetable. The Programme Commission met the following month, followed later by a meeting of the winter sports subcommittee, which had to deal with what many saw as a petulant anti-curling opinion from Canadian skier Ken Read. The next meeting of the IOC executive board was scheduled for Monaco in May, so that would be the earliest a decision could be announced. Then again, the decision could be delayed…and was, until after the Barcelona Summer Games. When the announcement finally came, on July 21, 1992, that curling had been accepted as a full-fledged medal sport, no one could deny that the triumph belonged primarily to Austria's Gunther Hummelt. He had achieved curling's entry into the lodge, with significant help from three other curlers: Tanner, Lynch and Sugahara.

At the same time, the IOC elected to move the Winter Olympics into a four-year rotation, separate from the Summer Olympics, starting in 1998. In this way, there would be Olympic fervour every two years instead of every four. Lillehammer, Norway, originally cast as host for 1996, now had an additional two years to prepare, and although the Norwegians indicated they would be happy to include curling on their calendar, as a demonstration sport, the IOC nixed the idea. When Nagano, host city for 1998, asked that curling be included as a medal sport in their games, the answer was yes. How that seemingly simple decision came about is another example of Olympic politics at work, and you are probably reading it here for the first time ever. The name of my fourth nominee in gaining Olympic medal recognition, Kay Sugahara, looms large in this part of the story.

Kay Sugahara had a number of attributes of interest to Hummelt and Tanner. He had invaluable corporate connections in both the United States and Japan. He was chair of Hexagon International Curling, at that time sponsor of the men's world championship, and in that role had developed a close relationship with Hummelt and Tanner.

He had come to know Tanner in the preparations for the Lausanne world championship of '88. "I had many opportunities to have dinner with him (and his son, Jürg)," he wrote me, "and came to know of his very close relationship with Samaranch. He would use my frequent visits to Lausanne as an excuse for a meeting, or a meal...to push curling. It was through these meetings that I came to be included in the official party at the Calgary Olympics in 1988. There the Japanese delegation learned of my access (and presumed closeness) to Samaranch.

"Tanner acted as the catalyst to ease the way for Hummelt to develop a close relationship with Samaranch and the other nodes of Olympic power," wrote Sugahara. "Franz's part should not be minimized as he had been quietly talking to the Olympic power players for many years before the push for curling became a media event," he continued.

Sugahara also told me that in 1988, the ICF had been so neglectful of basic PR that they hadn't even invited Samaranch to the world championship being held in his Olympic home town. "In Lausanne, I asked President

Samaranch if he had plans to attend any of the draws that week and was surprised when he said no one had even asked him. I invited him, of course, and that was why he even showed up at the finals."

Sugahara's influence was also key to Olympic aspirations in Japan. "In the late eighties," he pointed out, "I had asked Ray Turnbull to do a series of schools around Hokkaido and northern Honshu. One of the schools was in Karuizawa. We were holding one of those classes when I was asked to meet with a delegation of about eight people from the Nagano Bidding Committee (for 1998). Somebody had seen me hanging around the headquarters hotel in Calgary [in 1988] and since I would speak familiarly with Samaranch in the bar, the Nagano people thought I was buddy-buddy with him.

"At that time, Nagano was in a panic since they had already spent about $5 million and were not favoured to win [the hosting bid]. They wanted my advice on what they might do to improve their position. Luckily (and coincidentally) on the long plane ride from New York to Tokyo, I had read a feature in *The New York Times* on what Atlanta had done to get the 1996 Summer Games. I regurgitated a lot of that stuff (with embellishments), threw in a few new wrinkles and, lo and behold, Nagano won.

"They put me on an honor committee of three (with the Governor of Nagano Prefecture, and the then richest guy in the world who had had to resign, in typical Japanese fashion, as president of the Japanese Olympic Committee due to some irregularity committed by an underling). They also asked me to sit on the main platform during the opening ceremonies. But...I said I'd watch from my hotel room...and only go to the opening of the curling in Karuizawa.

"In a typical Japanese-ism, they 'owed' me, and they were finally able to 'escape their indenture' when I sent word it would be appreciated if Nagano agreed to hold curling even though they were under no contractual obligation to do so. I wasn't too worried about that, having already sounded out the mayor of Karuizawa, who was dying to hold some Olympic event in his city."

There is no need to recount here the heroics of the 1998 curling in Karuizawa, in particular, the gold medal brilliance of Sandra Schmirler and her team from Regina (Jan Betker, Joan McCusker, Marcia Gudereit and Atina Ford). Both Guy Scholz and Perry Lefko have told the Schmirler story beautifully in separate books.

For Canada, the golden brilliance of the Schmirler foursome was complemented by the silver garnered by Mike Harris and his Toronto team of Richard Hart, Collin Mitchell, George Karrys and Paul Savage. Earlier, all signs had pointed to a double gold for Canada, but the flu bug laid skip Mike Harris low in the finals, and he played probably the worst game of his entire career. With a raging temperature of 104°F, Mike could only muster a 25 percent game, certainly not enough to guarantee gold. This should not, however, be construed as a total excuse for Mike and his squad, for his Swiss opponent (good friend and

VOTING PATTERN ALTERED

An unintended result of Gunther Hummelt's drive to move the WCF membership to 25 countries, and thus make it eligible for Olympic recognition, is the diminished clout exercised by the ICF's original Big Three: Scotland, Canada and the United States. The federation's early minimum membership requirements—number of curlers, number of sheets of ice within each country, length of curling season, bonspiel or championship participation—were quietly jettisoned as new curling countries were added to WCF membership. The new nations, many of them members in name only, were given voting privileges at the annual meeting, a move that watered down the earlier sway of Scottish, Canadian and American associations. It was a move that has never been adjusted, although the membership of the WCF has now expanded to include 46 countries, most of whom are making excellent efforts to promote the sport in their land. However, "Rep by Pop" is a figment of the imagination in the world of curling in the 21st century.

ex-Silver Broom champion) Patrick Hürlimann, played wonderfully well. Any other time, it would have been a classic tussle, but in 1998, it wasn't even close.

There was another aspect of the 1998 Games that played into curling's favour. Poor snow conditions caused several of the ski events, due for full TV coverage, to be postponed. Fortunately for curling, the prime time coverage was switched from the ski hills to the curling arena in Karuizawa, so a wide audience quickly discovered the granite game's appeal on the small screen. The IOC noted that appeal with the award of a special medal to the CBC for its outstanding coverage of curling.

The pattern of boffo television from 1998 held true for the 2002 Winter Games in Salt Lake City, where once again, viewers at home, particularly in the United States, discovered the pleasures of the game through the intimacies of the TV tube. It was the same in Britain, where an unheard-of audience of over six million stayed awake into the small hours of the morning to watch Rhona Martin's Great Britain team win a gold medal with their last stone against Luzia Ebnother's Swiss side.

Originally, curling had been accepted as a medal sport on a contingent basis. Today curling is recognized as a vital part of the Olympic winter calendar, thanks mainly to efforts of four skips named Hummelt, Tanner, Lynch and Sugahara.

Chapter Thirty-two

THE MONCTON 100, A.K.A. THE HOWARD RULE

THE YEAR WAS 1989 AND I, ALONG WITH 151,538 OTHER FANS, WAS comfortably ensconced in Saskatchewan Place, the brand-new, 8,900-plus-seat arena that was home that year to the Labatt Brier. The stands were packed—the Brier in Saskatoon is an automatic sellout—but instead of cheers reverberating from on high, there were cries of "bor-rr-ring." Understandable, too. It was embarrassing. Here we were, watching the cream of Canadian curling, and what were we seeing? Team A: throw up a front stone. Team B: peel it. Team A: throw up another front stone. Team B: peel it. Team A; throw up yet another, and so on, ad infinitum. The teams might have been throwing up front stones; the fans just wanted to throw up.

The problem was best illustrated in the seventh draw. Although Rick Folk was there representing British Columbia, the Saskatchewan fans were still behind him as their former hometown hero. In the seventh round he was up against Alberta's Pat Ryan, and in a drab encounter, Ryan won with a final score of 3–1 that saw ends three to eight blanked. Did I say "drab"? How about dreadfully dull? Or, yep, bor-rr-ing.

The Brier schedule that year showed a total of 68 games, including play-offs. That means 680 ends, of which 124 (18 percent) were blanked. More than 50 percent of the games were conceded early, usually because Team A was ahead of Team B by two or three points, and B saw little chance of catching up. Instead of watching 680 ends of play we only saw 634, due to early concessions. Those 124 blank ends climbed from 18 percent (above) to 19.5 percent of actual ends played. Were there any big counts? Twice we saw a score of five points, and there were just four four-counts. Boring? Well, I guess.

In case you were wondering, Ryan of Alberta won his second straight Canadian crown. Folk was runner-up, while Russ Howard of Ontario finished third.

Curling fans were not surprised that Russ Howard, he of the legendary sweeping calls, lost his voice. He dashed to an electronics store to grab a wireless microphone and ear-pieces so he could relay sweeping signals to his team. The CCA hurriedly called a meeting and decided to outlaw the idea, claiming it could hamper their own wireless equipment. I only add this to establish that Howard was, and is, a curling innovator. He was also one of the key curlers we wished to invite to Moncton for a splashy cashspiel that by now had been dubbed The Moncton 100.

Among the spectators at that event was my friend Bud Gerth, a mover and shaker in Moncton. Bud had been co-chair with Dr. Ralph DeWare, of the eminently successful 1980 Silver Broom and at this point was involved in making The Moncton 100 the kickoff event for the city's centennial year, 1990.

The idea had sprung from the fertile mind of Don Canning, the city's director of marketing and promotion. His proposal for a bonspiel to begin their Centennial year had been accepted by city council and Gerth had been conscripted to work out the details in concert with other Moncton enthusiasts, many of whom I knew from the 1980 Silver Broom.

Bud had called me with an intriguing proposition. He wanted to know what I thought of putting on a bonspiel as the kickoff to their centennial year. And if I did think it was a good idea, would I be interested in becoming the director of competition? And, oh yes, did I have any ideas that might make The Moncton 100, for that would be the name of the 'spiel, more compelling?

What an opportunity! This would be a one-shot event. We could do what we liked to make it memorable. All ideas were welcome, even if, at first glance, they seemed zany. It wasn't long before we settled on some basics. If we were going to get national attention, we'd need to put up big money. A quarter of a million dollars would do. That $250,000 was far and away the most money any bonspiel had ever offered up to then. And still is even today, over 15 years later. We'd need sponsors of course, good sponsors, national sponsors. Dream no small dreams was our mantra.

We decided to go for 16 teams, the best to be found anywhere, and we'd play a double-knockout competition. Start on a Thursday and wrap it up by Sunday. Invite a couple of women's teams. We'd need a team or two from Atlantic Canada to help stimulate ticket sales. Why not put up prize money for every game, money that would escalate for each succeeding draw?

How about a singles competition, an update on the old Scots points game, in which each player could win money by playing some standard shots: draw, raise, takeout, draw through the port, hit and roll? This competition would later become known as a Hot Shots event, and I always wished I had thought of that name!

The Moncton sales folks got busy and quickly produced two major sponsors: Air Canada and Labatt Breweries. The City of Moncton was an obvious contributor, both financially and with contributions in kind. After all, this was scheduled to be the kickoff for their year-long centennial celebrations, and their enthusiasm was contagious. Admission was inexpensive (we wanted a full house): top ducats for the four days of play cost just $39, and if you couldn't

Two of Canada's world winners competed in The Moncton 100, alongside male curlers. Thunder Bay's Heather Houston (l) won the Women's World Championship in 1989, while Linda Moore, the 1985 world winner, was also gold medallist at the 1988 Calgary Winter Olympics, when curling was a demonstration sport. Photo courtesy of *Canadian Curling News*

make every draw, you could get a walk-up ticket for only $5 or $7 tops! In addition to those three sources of revenue, sponsors for each team were recruited.

Each team would pay an entry fee of $1,000. Their transportation to Moncton would be covered, courtesy of Air Canada, and their hotel rooms would be complimentary. Even if you were eliminated by losing your first two games, you'd take home $1,500 for those two games. Hey, you couldn't lose. Besides, if you had been in Moncton for the Silver Broom in 1980, or for the Brier in 1985, or had ever attended the annual Monctonian Bonspiel, you knew how hospitable and friendly Moncton could be.

Who should be invited? In order to meet the "international" part of the event, it was decided to ask four European teams: Eigil Ramsfjell of Norway (1988 Olympic gold medallist in Calgary, and same-year winner of the world title in Lausanne); Switzerland's Patrick Hürlimann (runner-up to Pat Ryan at the worlds in Milwaukee, 1989); Sweden's youthful Thomas Norgren and Scotland's brothers team of David and Peter Smith, David and Mike Hay.

There was some internal debate about adding two top

women's teams to the mix, but the debate was ended when two of the most popular women's teams of the day were contacted. Linda Moore's gold medal team from the Calgary Olympics and Heather Houston's Thunder Bay squad, which won the world women's title in 1989, were both happy to attend.

The two "local" teams invited were skipped by Lorne Henderson of Newfoundland, who had tied for third place at the 1989 Brier, and Jack MacDuff, who had moved to Moncton after winning Newfoundland's first (and only) Brier in 1976.

Among the eight Canadian teams would be the top three finishers at the '89 Brier, plus such other Brier biggies and champions as Ed Lukowich, Ed Werenich, Al Hackner and Orest Meleschuk. The final entry, the big money-winner of the day, was Saskatchewan's Arnold Anderson.

We had also decided to introduce a couple of other elements to the competition. Time clocks (which had been used in the Skins Game since 1986 and introduced at the 1989 World Championships in Milwaukee) would be used, complete with time outs allowed. Teams could use either brush or broom, with a one-end notice of intention to switch, and there would be two draws closest to the button. The first, involving all four team members, would take place prior to the start of the games, with cumulative distance used to determine last rock advantage in the playoffs. In addition, one member of each team, nominated by the committee, would throw closest to the button before each game to determine hammer advantage in the first end.

So there we were, Bud and I, in Saskatoon, ready to recruit the top trio as soon as the Brier was over. Pat Ryan, the winner, and runner-up Rick Folk said yes, as did Russ Howard, who had finished third. And we asked each of the three if they could suggest a competitive wrinkle that would

Russ Howard won two world championships: the first in Vancouver, 1987; the second in Geneva, 1993. In between those major moments, Howard was the catalyst for one of the most important changes in curling, the Howard Rule (Moncton 1990), later re-named the Free Guard Zone rule. In 2006, he became the oldest Canadian Olympian when he joined the Brad Gushue team for the Torino Winter Games. Photo by Michael Burns

help set The Moncton 100 apart as special.

"Why not do what we do when we practise?" said Russ Howard. "We try to make our practices more meaningful, and at the same time, fun."

"How" I asked.

He told me they didn't allow any hitting until the leads had finished their play. As long as the lead's stones were between the hog line and the tee line, they couldn't be removed until it was the second's turn to play.

Suddenly we had the antidote to bor-rr-ing. If there were up to four stones in play anywhere between the hog line and tee line, we wouldn't need to be concerned about blank ends or the deadly peel game. Bud and I liked the idea immediately.

The other teams were agreeable too, and as we watched the 'spiel progress, it was obvious that the peel game was becoming less important, while aggressive skills were coming to the fore. More importantly, when we surveyed the paying customers, we discovered that over 90 percent liked the new concept.

The players liked it too, or at least most of the shooters did. A note left for me at my hotel read, in part:

"We honestly believe everyone involved in the event—players, organizers, sponsors, and volunteers, were a part of something special, something new.... The 1992 World Championship will be played using a version of the rules introduced here in Moncton—and it will be a major improvement to the fan appeal of our game. Thanks for your hard work, and for your vision."

ED WERENICH, JOHN KAWAJA AND TEAM

One person who was unsure if it was a good idea was Ed Steeves, a two-time Moncton Brier competitor, 1970 Ross Harstone Award winner, and the 1990 president of the CCA. His reluctance may have contributed to a rather cool reception from Canadian officialdom.

One person who did like the concept, which soon became known as the Moncton Rule or Howard Rule, was Eigil Ramsfjell, the three-time world winner (1979, 1984, 1988) and gold medallist at the 1988 Calgary Olympics. At the time, the heavy thinkers of the ICF were working to have curling recognized as a full Olympic medal sport, but were scared that when high-ranking Olympic nabobs came to watch curling in France, they would be subjected to the deadly peel game, blank end piled on blank end, and hear "bor-rr-ing" or however it might be voiced en français. So, at Eigil's suggestion, they latched onto the Howard Rule as a means of putting more rocks in play. But (and this is only my opinion, and will be denounced by Euro curlers) knowing how Eurocentric the Olympics is, they didn't wish to have it appear as a Canadian idea so they altered the rule slightly to mandate no removal of stones by lead players, *but only for stones in front of the rings.* Nor did they wish to have any mention of Howard or Moncton, so they called it the Free Guard Zone.

The ICF may have liked the new rule, but there was considerable debate among a wider contingent of Canadian curlers about its merits. When the CCA finally did agree to the FGZ rule, they opted for a three-rock version rather than the four-rock world wording.

I still cling to the belief that curling would be better with Howard's original thought, where stones in front of the tee line would be kept inviolate until the seconds come to play. That way, there might be more of the rings in use than currently, since the FGZ rule forces play into the centre of the house, into the four-foot ring. Will we see Russ's original idea come into force any time soon? Don't hold your breath on that one.

The Moncton 100 was a smash success (well, I may be biased). It was then, and is still today, the richest-ever cashspiel in the history of curling. And it certainly put Moncton on the curling map.

It is also interesting to note that another member of that Moncton 100 committee, Lorne Mitton, went on to become a CCA president (1994) and later Mayor of Moncton. In 2006, at

SHAKE HANDS

When I first started to cover curling in Toronto, one of the local shotmakers was Annis Stukus. If you're of a certain age, you will remember Stuke, not so much as a curler as a football coach and field goal specialist, first with the Toronto Argonauts, later with the Edmonton Eskimos and finally with the BC Lions. He disdained the usual football padding and usually kicked field goals and converts with minimal padding. He didn't even bother to remove his watch while kicking. Stuke was a colourful guy who also doubled as a sports writer in each of his football homes.

Colourful? It spilled over to the curling rink. He told me once he always followed the proper etiquette of curling. After the game, of course, he shook hands with the opposition, "and then," he continued, "I shake hands with my teammates. I tell 'em 'I might as well shake hands with everyone who was against me!'"

the annual meeting of the WCF in Lowell, Massachusetts, Les Harrison, also from Moncton, became president of the World Federation, only the third Canadian so honoured.

And to top it off, seven years later, in 1998, Russ and Wendy Howard and their children, Steven and Ashley, moved East from Penetanguishene, Ontario, to...where?

Why, Moncton, of course

Here's a thought. The 2007 men's world championship is slated for Edmonton, meaning the 2009 world event will be held in Eastern Canada. But 2009 is a special world championship year, for it marks the 50th anniversary of the first Scotch Cup in 1959. Back then it was a two-country event held in Scotland. Why not, say Monctonians, celebrate the World Curling Championship golden anniversary in Canada and what better location than the city where the WCF president resides, where the man responsible for the Free Guard Zone rule (and a 2006 gold medal Olympian) resides, where both the Silver Broom and the Brier have played to packed houses. Where would that be? Why, Moncton, of course.

Chapter Thirty-three

THE BACKYARD APPROACH

"DREAM NO SMALL DREAMS" MIGHT WELL HAVE BEEN THE MOTTO OF a bunch of curling friends at the East York Curling Club back in the late sixties, early seventies. In 1968 the club, a member of the Toronto Curling Association, decided to hold a junior bonspiel and each year thereafter tried to expand and improve it. I don't know if it was Jimmy Brown, or Dave Prentice, or Stan Wadlow or Willis Blair who first called me to ask if perhaps I could help corral a clutch of juniors from outside the country. I said I'd try and, frankly, I had no other option. Jimmy Brown, with his rich Scottish burr, took to calling me every day to check my willingness and progress. His conversations became the Scottish equivalent to the Chinese water torture. Mind you, I was all in favour of the idea anyway, so I called Scotland. After receiving a polite rebuff from Robin Welsh, secretary of the Royal Caledonian Curling Club, I called the ever-reliable Chuck Hay in Perth. Could he send over a youthful quartet and we, meaning the East York organizers, would look after them? The event, I said, was known as the East York Masters, and the group had ambitious plans. As usual, Chuck came through, and East York had its "international" label.

By 1972 the 'spiel boasted teams from Scotland, Sweden, United States, Quebec and Manitoba, and I was delighted when they named me honorary chair of the event.

If that's all there was to the event, it wouldn't be in this book. But the following year, they made a major move.

And this is where I bow out, and let my long-time Brier bench mate, Bob Picken, take over. Pick is a triple-threat media maven. He is quite comfortable as a top-flight broadcaster, or film writer, or a newspaper journo. He has also been a committee chair for the CCA, a national appointee to the ICF, and is highly respected throughout the curling world. In Canada he is also in the Canadian Curling Hall of Fame. Perhaps you can see why from the following story.

I WAS COOKING HAMBURGERS ON MY BACK-yard barbecue on a warm summer day in 1973, when a man came walking up my driveway. He introduced himself as David Prentice, said he was passing through Winnipeg on the way back home to East York, Ontario, after a Western business trip.

Prentice had heard I was a newly elected Canadian representative to the International Curling Federation.

Bob Picken—curling broadcaster, long-time Canadian rep on the International Curling Federation, chair of the international committee of the CCA for eight years, member of the Canadian Curling Hall of Fame. Photo by Michael Burns

"We heard you talking about junior curling on CBC Radio, and our committee in East York believes you might be interested in helping our pitch to the ICF," he suggested.

Prentice accepted my offer of a beer and burger, sat down and proceeded to tell me all about the junior men's bonspiel the East York organizers had started four years earlier.

"We now have a major title sponsor," revealed Prentice. "Uniroyal, the tire people, are providing the funding. Everybody involved thinks we have the makings of a world junior championship, and we intend to apply for endorsement from the ICF. Will you help us?"

For somebody who had guided junior curling for several years on the council of the Manitoba Curling Association, the proposal had instant appeal. On the other hand, knowing something about the politics of the ICF, I wasn't at all certain how they could best proceed. In the months that followed I learned that ICF sanction was not going to come easily. Two other Canadian ICF reps were lukewarm to the proposal due to their close ties to Scotland, where the governing Royal Caledonian Curling Club was opposed. Although many curlers in Scotland were in favour, RCCC officials thought another world competition would detract from the existing men's world championship, the Air Canada Silver Broom.

I contacted Bob Sutherland, Uniroyal's advertising and promotions manager, who was more than a little dismayed by the negative reaction in Scotland but wasn't about to drop the proposal. I assured him I had a couple of allies in two American ICF reps, Elmer Freytag and L.C. "Tink" Kreutzig, who could lobby in positive fashion with the European delegations.

Doug Maxwell, who had encouraged me to stand for the ICF position, also provided a boost from his Silver Broom executive director's position, advising that Air Canada was in favour of the event. (Subsequently, he and Sutherland flew to Edinburgh to advise the RCCC of Uniroyal's interest, and Air Canada's endorsement, of the competition.)

I remember writing letters and making phone calls to ICF reps I knew in other countries, and along with Freytag and Kreutzig, twisted a number of arms in smoke-filled rooms in advance of the federation meetings in Bern, Switzerland, in April 1974.

When the issue came before the ICF assembly, Kreutzig moved its adoption and I was pleased to second it. Freytag, a gifted attorney and devoted curler, spoke in favour with his

Two of the Canadian giants of world curling: (l) Clif Thompson, ICF president 1982–85, and (r) Bob Sutherland, who masterminded the Uniroyal World Junior Championship 1975–90. Photo courtesy of *Canadian Curling News*

usual superb eloquence. The Royal Club reps responded in opposition, but I recall their startled looks when they realized nobody else shared their reservations.

Only Scotland voted against the motion to sanction the Uniroyal as the world junior curling championship, but after losing the vote, quickly asked to change their votes to make the adoption unanimous.

The inaugural Uniroyal Championship was staged at its birthplace, the East York Curling Club, in the spring of 1975. Nine countries participated: Canada, Scotland, the United States, Switzerland, France, Italy, Norway, Sweden and

West Germany. Jan Ullsten skipped his Swedish team to the first title.

There were many other milestones over the succeeding years. The entry was enlarged to 10 countries when Denmark was added in 1976. In '77, in Quebec City, the Uniroyal was televised for the first time, by the CBC in Canada and PBS in the United States.

In the first two decades, the event was staged in exotic sites like Aviemore in Scotland, Grindelwald in Switzerland (twice), Megève in France, Füssen and Oberstdorf in Germany, and in 1987, in a gorgeous springtime setting in Victoria, BC. It also was held in Sofia, Bulgaria, in 1994, which had to be one of the grubbiest places the curling fraternity ever was required to visit.

The female gender entered the picture in 1988. A European Junior Ladies Championship had been held for five years, and the ICF agreed to absorb the euros and sanction a world junior ladies championship. It was launched in Chamonix, France, with nine countries: Sweden, Denmark, Norway, Scotland, Germany, Switzerland, Canada, United States and France. Julie Sutton's team from Canada was the first champion.

After a corporate merger, Uniroyal Goodrich Canada Inc. assumed the sponsorship of both events, and in 1989 the ICF combined them into the World Junior Curling Championships. That agreement was in place for two years, and the joint contract terminated with the 1990 edition in Portage la Prairie, Manitoba. Since then, the ICF has operated the dual championships with local sponsorship.

Canada dominated the podium for more than three decades, winning 14 times between 1975 and 2005. Canadians Paul Gowsell and John Morris are the only skips to win twice, but notables like Peter Lindholm of Sweden and Tom Brewster of Scotland, Olympians Brad Gushue of Canada and Ralph Stöckli of Switzerland have ruled the junior men's world.

While serving as CCA international chair in the late 1970s, I had the responsibility of managing Paul Gowsell's teams in the Uniroyals at Aviemore in 1976 and Grindelwald in '78. He skipped two different teams to world crowns (Neil Houston, Glen Jackson and Kelly Stearne in 1976; John Ferguson, Doug MacFarlane, and Stearne in '78), and I would describe my association with them as an "interesting experience."

Gowsell was a brilliant shotmaker, one of the best I have ever seen. He was audacious, confident, intimidating to opponents and inspiring for his teammates. The more difficult the shot, the more he was apt to try to make it. He screamed and hollered at his mates, demanding—and getting—their best possible performances.

The Calgary product wore his hair long and unruly, and he didn't like to shave. He made headlines with his on-ice demeanour, and if he was highly colourful to young compatriots he also was called wild, undisciplined, and a rebel to authority by many. But wherever he played, he drew the fans in droves.

I don't know why, but Paul and I were simpatico. When in Grindelwald, I saw him carrying a case of beer down the middle of the main drag. On another occasion one of his buddies (not a player) was spotted wearing Gowsell's Team Canada blazer. I confronted him, told him if he wanted a beer I'd get it for him and not to make a spectacle of himself. I also said he was the only Canadian athlete entitled to wear that blazer. He reacted favourably to both admonishments.

On the other hand, he would not be pushed around. After winning his second Uniroyal title in Grindelwald, CBC television moguls wanted him to return to Canada immediately to participate in their annual curling series. Paul and his girlfriend had planned to go on a holiday to Yugoslavia and had booked their travel and hotel reservations.

"I don't want to do the CBC thing," he told me. "It would be good for your career, and good promotion for curling," I replied. "But it's your decision, Paul, there's no pressure here from the CCA."

He found a way out, demanding round trip expenses to Canada and back to Europe. The CBC refused, and Gowsell happily headed off to Yugoslavia.

After the Gowsell years, I expected to have much tamer Canadian personnel to supervise at the next Uniroyal, to be held in Moose Jaw in 1979. I was wrong.

The CCA junior chair at the time, Cec Watt, called me after Darren Fish's Edmonton team won the Canadian junior title in Charlottetown. "I think you're going to have problems with that team," he advised. "They don't get along, they've had fights along the way, and I hope you can get them in line."

At the time, it was the Canadian champion from the previous season that went to the Uniroyal. When I was in Edmonton (for the CBC) to cover the '78 Commonwealth Games, I met the team, discussed its previous behaviour, and laid down some rules of conduct that the CCA expected the four players to follow. I thought we had understanding and acceptance. But early the next season, we took the Fish quartet into Moose Jaw for a practice and orientation session. Only a few hours after going over the expected code of behaviour again, an internal disagreement led to the trashing of a hotel room. The skip went missing, but we found him the next morning hiding in another part of the hotel.

Now what? The chair of the Moose Jaw organizing committee and local officials were justifiably upset and requested we suspend the team and replace it with the Canadian runners-up from Nova Scotia as our world junior entry. After consulting with Cec Watt and my international vice-chair Laurie Artiss, CCA president Clif Thompson and I flew into Edmonton to meet the players and decide on a course of action.

The result was the suspension of the team's lead, Barry Barker. A replacement, Randy Ursulak (the second player's brother), was added for the Uniroyal. Right decision? It was done reluctantly, for it denied a young man his chance to curl in a world championship, and I have done much soul-searching in the years since then.

On the other hand, Barry's brother, Lorne, who played third on the team, told me later the suspension may have been a turning point in Barry's life, that he realized he was on a wrong pathway, and it changed his outlook and attitude.

How did the Fish team do in Moose Jaw? Not bad. Lorne Barker and Randy Ursulak were all-stars, while Fish and Murray Ursulak also curled impressively. The team finished first (8–1) in the round robin, but lost in the semifinals to Andrew McQuistin of Scotland, who in turn was beaten for the world junior title by Don Barcome Jr. of the United States. To their credit, Fish and company bounced back to beat Norway for the bronze medal, but perhaps more significantly, the team was a credit to Canada both on and off the ice.

And that may be the real legacy of the Uniroyal. In the words of Bob Sutherland, a truly dynamic executive director from 1975 to 1990, "these young people from different cultures are learning to relate to each other, and I believe we're building character and sportsmanship."

Chapter Thirty-four

THE CONCESSION
PROTOCOL

SOMETIMES, JUST WHEN YOU THINK YOU HAVE AN IDEA OR CONCEPT that is so simple any fool can accept it, reality sets in and you find that putting the idea into practice might not be quite as easy as you think. This comes to mind with the issue of conceding a game that has every indication of being irretrievably lost. For the past couple of decades, maybe more, there has been little concern over conceding a game. But 'twas not always so, trust me. Allow me to elaborate.

Example #1: I recall the very first Air Canada Silver Broom in Pointe Claire, Quebec, 1968. Unlike the Brier, which had no playoffs then, it had been determined that the Silver Broom would feature playoffs, a three-team affair. Chuck Hay of Scotland had gone unbeaten in the round robin and was awaiting the winner of the semifinal between Canada's Ron Northcott and Bud Somerville of the United States.

At the halfway mark of the 12-end semifinal, Canada held an 8–2 advantage, and when Northcott stole four more points in the seventh end, it made the score 12–2. The game had turned into a rout. Somerville checked with his teammates, off came the curling gloves, and the US foursome conceded the game to their northern neighbours.

Almost as quickly Jack Bowen of Air Canada came up to me, angrily demanding that I inform the teams they couldn't concede the game and they had to go back on the ice and play the full 12 ends. I was standing at the media bench, so this encounter took place in public, and to this day I still recall how the veteran CBC sportscaster Bill Good came to my rescue. Before I could even begin to discuss the situation with my irate colleague, Good growled at him "Doug knows what he's doing; I suggest you leave him alone!"

When I discussed the matter with Jack later, privately, I learned that his concern had nothing to do with the game but everything to do with the paying customers who were, he said, being cheated out of their admission price. As it was, no customers complained, and I suspect most of them, being curling fans, agreed with the early departure. Once you've won, there's nothing to be gained by heaping humiliation on the opposition, especially if they don't wish to continue. Besides, what sanction do you apply to a playoff team that is losing and wants to withdraw? There is none, at least none that makes sense.

If I'd had the gift of prophecy back then, I might have invoked a later situation, in 1982, to my irate friend. It was an instance when playing to the bitter end was not only dumb, but also publicly embarrassing. Call it Example #2.

It happened at the European championships of 1982. I was present on behalf of Air Canada and was also sending back a story on the event. Scotland was playing Sweden in a semi-final. The Scots, skipped by Mike Hay, were well ahead on the scoreboard and headed to the final when they graciously accepted the gloves-off congratulations of the Swedes. Both teams headed to the dressing room, but hardly had time to sit down before umpire Jim Whiteford came storming into the room and officially advised both teams to get back on the ice and finish the game. Dutifully both teams did as told and trooped back onto the ice. And, yes, they did finish the remaining ends of the game ... at warp-speed fashion. Every remaining end was blanked, as both teams whistled shot after shot through the rings. Then, having properly observed Whiteford's injunction, they shook hands again and headed back to the dressing room with exactly the same score as when the gloves first came off. I recall it made a laughing stock of Whiteford, and there were some Euro observers who were a mite upset, but in reality it was another example of petty officialdom being trumped by common sense.

While I favour allowing an early concession, I know there are some observers who do not and who cite examples of too-early departures as making a mockery of the concession protocol. In some cases I have to admit they are right. In fact I was involved in one such occasion, although the bonspiel was anything but a big-time event. It was a bonspiel in name, but not one of fame.

The competition was the annual Newsmen's Bonspiel, and it took place in Calgary. Now the Newsmen's is not a high-calibre competition, as is indicated, perhaps, by the other name given to the event: the Boozemen's Nonspiel. But I digress. Enter Example #3. And I'm sure you will understand that naming names at this juncture not only would add very little to the yarn, but also might turn out to be injurious to my health.

Having lost the previous afternoon, our team checked the draw sheet and noted that our next game was scheduled for early the next morning. *Very* early the next morning. Our skip (I wish I could remember his name) celebrated long and hard that night and bemoaned the fact we had to play on the early draw. However, it was imperative that we show up, for a default would have been unthinkable. (Well, actually, it was quite thinkable, but you get my drift.)

We stumbled out onto the ice, won the toss and the opposition lead threw his first stone into the rings. Our bleary-eyed skip looked at it long and hard and then turned to his opposite number and whipped off his glove. "We can't beat that," he declared. "We concede!" I have to admit it was good for a laugh, and we did play a few more ends before one side or the other (can't remember) did concede defeat, and both teams retired to the lounge for our morning tea and muffins. But it does illustrate that the concession protocol is not always honoured in its intended and purest form.

The matter of conceding a game before all the scheduled ends have been played has always bedevilled organizers and badgers. In the early days of the Brier, teams had to play the full schedule of ends regardless of the score. The rationale (as told to me years later) was that in a round robin schedule without a playoff your "contract" is to play 12 ends against every team, no shortcuts, no conceding a game; to concede would give an advantage to one team over the others. If that is a valid observation, my suggestion would be that perhaps "the contract" in a round robin series should include a ban on extra ends, so that games are either won, lost or tied, in regulation time. Relax—it's not a major suggestion.

So when, and how, did the Brier change its system? That was the question I was asked recently by a journalistic confrere, Alex Roberts of Halifax. I could not recall anyone as the sole arbiter of the concession rule, I responded, but my recollection is that it was a committee decision made by the CCA and the Brier trustees. I do know that many of us in the media argued it was silly and unfair for a team to have to play all 12 ends of a game when it was obvious that the game had been lost. Why continue a contest that was, say, 14–2 after 10 ends and have it finish at 16–3? This was particularly true for the three-game Brier day, Thursday, in which a team that, by the luck of the draw, had to play every end of three 12-end games that day! It was even more onerous for that team if their last game, scheduled for that evening, was against a team that had drawn a bye somewhere on Thursday. And in the days before time clocks, that three-game

Conceding a game early was not a concern of chief umpire Ray Turnbull (l) at the 1983 European Curling Championships in Västerås, Sweden. Nor was it a problem for his assistant, Doug Maxwell (r). Photo courtesy of *Canadian Curling News*

day often became a 14-hour marathon, hard on players, fans...and media alike.

When we meddling media queried Brier or CCA officials about the lack of a concession protocol, the answer always was that it was "necessary for the Brier records!!!" Which most of us thought was a crock. I also recall some of us suggesting that even in cricket, that most "gentlemanly of games," a side could "declare" once they had run up what they considered a suitable score. Our argument always failed. We should have saved our breath to cool our coffee.

I recall thinking that if logic couldn't sway curling's politicos, perhaps research could. So I did my own analysis, by looking at previous Briers. I knew that the CCA and Brier trustees were debating both the concession protocol and the shortening of games from 12 to 10 ends. So I looked at all the scores of all the games in the earlier Briers (some 30 to 45 years' worth), noting who was leading after 10 ends, who was tied after 10, and whether, or how, the game changed in the final two ends of play. After eliminating tie scores (after 10), it quickly became evident that most games (I think it was in the 85–95 percent range) wound up with the leader-after-10 winning the game. Seldom did a losing team turn the game around in the final two ends. And this was particularly true if the leading team had a commanding advantage. (Remember, this was before the Free Guard Zone rule came into being.)

Curlers who looked at my research agreed with the argument "Why play another half hour or more, when both sides are just going through the motions and want to get off the ice? Why not allow the losing team, if it wishes, to concede the game in polite fashion?"

In the first Garmisch-Partenkirchen Silver Broom of 1972, I was able to convince the International Curling Federation to shorten the games to 10 ends. No one complained, least of all the players. Five years later, the CCA followed suit at the Montreal Brier, and 10-end games became the new normal.

As for the concession protocol, at the Brier, it wasn't until 1973 that teams were allowed to shake hands early. However, at the Broom, and later the Brier, there was always "an understanding" that in the playoffs, where TV was a concern, no team would concede a game until eight ends had been completed.

How early in a game should one team be allowed to whip off the gloves and proffer a handshake of victory congratulations? Perhaps you might want to make that a point of discussion at your next meeting of the neighbourhood curling judiciary. Just don't assume that it will be an easy debate.

Chapter Thirty-five

THE SWEDISH SOLUTION

THE YEAR WAS 1977, AND THE SILVER BROOM ARRIVED IN SWEDEN FOR THE first time. Karlstad, a thriving city set on the shores of Lake Vänern, midway between Stockholm and Oslo, was the host city. Sweden's first world curling championship (but not its last) came to Karlstad largely because of the vision, tenacity, enthusiasm and intensity of one man: Lennart Hemmingson.

Lennart, a curling enthusiast to match any I have ever met, was possessed of a marvellous combination of attributes that made the 1977 Broom a favourite of mine. A very successful businessman, he had surrounded himself with a coterie of curling friends who felt as strongly about the game as he did. Together they formed a magnificent team. Lennart was the spark plug, a man who simply refused to let problems daunt him. He exemplified the World War II motto of the US Army Corps of Engineers, "The difficult we do immediately; the impossible takes a little longer."

An example of his drive and vision was the Grand Transatlantic Match. Indeed, the GTM is Lennart's lasting contribution to the fun side of world championships.

Early in our meetings for the 1977 world event, Lennart proposed that Karlstad should organize a match for the visiting spectators that would take its inspiration from the famous Grand Match in Scotland. While the Scots play the Grand Match as North against South, Lennart suggested we organize the GTM as East against West, Europe against North America. I liked the idea and encouraged him to make it happen.

Jokingly, I made one other stipulation about the GTM: it should actually take place. Maybe you know that the Grand Match in Scotland, when it was held outdoors, was sometimes called "the greatest non-event in curling," for it could only be held when there was at least six inches of hard ice on one of the Scottish lochs. And that didn't happen too often. The last time, in fact, was on February 7, 1979. Nevertheless, the Scots organizers made detailed plans every year, only to cancel the match when the ice failed to reach the desired thickness.

More recently the Grand Match moved indoors and is now a regular attraction on the Scottish curling calendar. With climate change now upon us, it was probably a smart move, but I suspect it's not the same as when the match was held outdoors. When I used that "greatest non-event" phrase one time in Scotland, one of the Scots present took me behind the proverbial woodshed and administered a verbal spanking. I guess it was okay for a Scot to call it that, but not for someone who only had a Scots name and who lived an Atlantic away from the heather.

Lennart's GTM idea sounded great. But where could it be held? There was not likely to be any outdoor ice in late March in Sweden sufficient to handle a thousand or so curlers. No worry, said Lennart, we've got just the spot: the local bandy field. And it has artificial ice.

Bandy? It's a game that's a cross between soccer and hockey. Bandy aficionados won't like that thumbnail description, but never mind—it's the easiest way I can explain it. The game is played on ice, with a ball and a curved stick, like a hockey stick. The field is soccer size (indeed, it is a soccer field in the summer) with soccer-size nets. Teams of 11 skate all over the icy field chasing the ball and trying to put it into the opposition's net. The Swedes are among the best bandy players in the world, along with the Russians, and so Lennart knew he had a site for his GTM.

We won't worry about the length of the curling ice, he said.

The first GTM was held on a bandy field in Karlstad, Sweden in 1977, where (in a bid for the front page of the local paper) a topless curler braved the cold. Photo by Michael Burns

We'll put the sheets across the field, from sideline to sideline, and truth to tell it worked out just fine.

Oh, the ice wasn't the immaculately manicured kind we have come to expect in our indoor clubs, but it was playable, it was outdoors, it was curling as it was originally played and it was fun. Lennart had scoured all of Sweden for sufficient stones. His planning was so good that the GTM continues to this day, in almost the same fashion as when he first proposed the idea. Except that today, with the addition of Asian teams and spectators, it has morphed into the Grand Transoceanic Match, but still the GTM.

In 1977 there was a special Swedish breakfast before the GTM began and special Swedish entertainment after each game. So many visitors and spectators signed up to play that year that several shifts had to be scheduled. Lennart's planning, like all his efforts, was meticulous. He produced a special proclamation from "King Frost," who appeared in a horse-drawn sleigh. And there were other features that his churning mind produced. I seem to recall small drams of aquavit, but that may have been another time. I do remember one particular moment that was definitely not of Lennart's doing.

Concerned that we were not getting sufficient curling coverage in the local newspaper, we were searching for some way to hit its front page. "Get one of the flight attendants to curl topless, and you'd be guaranteed the front page," was one suggestion, quickly vetoed, though not by us—by the flight attendants. But the idea continued to percolate, until Mike Burns and I cooked up a caper that we thought might do the trick. It was a bright, cold, nippy day on the bandy field. I told Mike I would strip to the waist and would slide out on my tummy (no snide remarks, please) and he'd better get the shot the first time 'cause I wasn't about to repeat the manoeuvre; it was too damn cold. I did and he did and yes, we did make the front page. What some guys will do to promote a cause!

Perhaps the best example of Lennart's problem-solving ability was his solution to a situation that threatened the promotion of the Winnipeg Silver Broom, set for the following year.

Vic Palmer, chairman of the 1978 Broom, had worked with his 'Peg cohorts to host a mammoth promotional party in Karlstad, slated to start at 10:30 a.m., at the large Sandgrund Restaurant, in order to have everybody at the arena in time for the afternoon games. The problem was that the serving of alcoholic beverages before noon in Sweden was strictly prohibited by law. And when it comes to the law about alcohol in Sweden, there can be no exceptions. None.

What to do?

Lennart was equal to the task. Without going into all the ins and outs of the situation, suffice it to say that he called in some IOUs from his political friends and somehow arranged

At the opening ceremonies of the Karlstad Silver Broom, Sweden's King Carl XVI Gustaf delivered the first stone and then welcomed competitors, including (l–r) Canada's Jim Ursel, Art Lobel and Don Aitken. Photo by Michael Burns

to have the Swedish Parliament declare the Sandgrund Restaurant as Canadian territory for a part of that day. So, just before the start of the reception, the Canadian flag was run up the flagpole in front of the restaurant to signal we were now on Canadian soil. We all saluted (I can't recall if we sang "O Canada") and with Canada's laws then in force, it was legal to serve a welcoming libation to visitors!

So when I salute Karlstad and its citizens for a great Silver Broom, that salute is aimed squarely at Lennart Hemmingson and the other members of his hardworking committee.

For them, the icing on the cake came when their King, Carl XVI Gustaf, officially opened the Silver Broom (he even delivered a stone on TV) and their national champion, Ragnar Kamp, closed it with a homeside victory (over Jim Ursel of Canada).

That set the example for the good burghers of Gävle, who hosted the world championships in 2004. Not only was it the last worlds where both men and women curlers gathered as one (and that's another story), but it was also where Peja Lindholm won his third world title in front of his fellow Swedes, just as Kamp had won the 1977 world title.

Chapter Thirty-six

THE SHOPSY 'SPIEL AND OTHERS OF THAT ILK

OF ALL THE CHAMPIONSHIPS I HAVE BEEN INVOLVED IN, THE SHOPSY is the one that lingers ever-so-affectionately in my memory. I can understand if you say you've never heard of the Shopsy, since it only lived for a couple of years. But while alive it was nothing but fun.

So what was the Shopsy? It surfaced back in 1967, and its not-very-elegant, prosaic name was the World Heavyweight Curling Championship. "Shopsy" refers to Sam Shopsowitz, a giant of a food giant, whose Shopsy's Deli Foods was a staple of downtown Spadina Avenue in Toronto. Sam was a sports buff who loved all facets of athletics in Hogtown, be it football, hockey, baseball, you name it, so of course he came into contact with athletes, and other like-minded chaps, including a number of the city's journalists. He also entertained many international stage and film stars who descended on Toronto from time to time. In short, he was one of the Big Smoke's Big Schmoozers, and one of Toronto's best-known citizens.

One of his media buddies was Paul Rimstead who toiled for the now defunct *Telegram* and subsequently *The Toronto Sun*. Rimmer was a writer who could easily have been lifted straight out of the cast of Damon Runyon's "Guys and Dolls." I can't remember how, why or when Rimstead called me and said that his pal, Shopsy, had liked his (Rimstead's) idea of a heavyweight curling event, and what did I think of the idea, and more importantly, could I make it work. I didn't ask, but I could guess, at what time of night (or early morning) the concept had morphed from an idle thought into a Great Idea. I can't recall the exact words of our conversation, but I think it went something like this:

"Okay, Doug, whaddya think of the idea?"

"Kooky, but fun."

"Can it be made to work?"

"Definitely!!"

In a very short time we had worked out the details. To be eligible to play in the World Heavyweight Championship, a.k.a. The Shopsy, a team had to weigh in at a minimum of half a ton avoirdupois—1,000 pounds—and no individual player could compete unless he (or she) could tip the scales at a measly 225 pounds. Don't ask for this in metric; we weren't even thinking in kilos at that time. And while I say that nobody, male or female, could play if less than 225 pounds, you will readily understand why we neither expected, nor attracted, any curlers of the female persuasion to the entry list!

We arranged for one of those huge cattle scales to be set up so all four players could stand together for the official weigh-in. Frankly we weren't worried too much if a foursome was a pound under or a hundred over the half-ton mark.

The championship did not have a lengthy shelf life. I seem to recall that Shopsy Foods was sold a few years after the start of the 'spiel, and of course the new owners (and their unimaginative, straitlaced, bean-counting ad agency) were more bottom-liners than hog-liners. They certainly weren't curlers!

But before the event went belly-up, there were some extraordinary moments. The banquet was a culinary masterpiece, as Shopsy turned out a groaning table that was magnificent. The piece de resistance, as I recall, was a series of turkeys that had been pre-sliced and then reassembled, in turkey form, so all a diner had to do was lift off a slice

"I COULD HAVE SWORN THAT WAS A HAGGIS"

Cartoon by John Dunnett, courtesy of *Canadian Curling News*

or two. Perhaps three or four ... or more.

Another delicacy that first year was a large haggis, brought over from Scotland by Chuck Hay, whom I inveigled into attending, along with Hector Gervais of Edmonton, as two of our celebrity curlers. Today, of course, it would be next to impossible to get a haggis into the country. Someone in Customs and Revenue would surely object to a food product coming in without a two-year wait or three-year inspection. Naturally, the haggis was one of the hits at the banquet, as was its Scottish courier.

But, you ask, how did we get it through customs? Well, in those more innocent days, all we needed was some insider PR help with officialdom, some mid-level effort, and presto, the haggis arrived and was quickly whisked through. The only thing we had neglected to do, of course, was to alert Chuck to our efforts. So he was somewhat nonplussed upon his arrival in Toronto. Some years later he recalled the moment.

"I was concerned about the haggis," wrote Chuck, "so decided to gamble and not declare it. To my horror, Sam was with the customs man and greeted me with 'Where's the haggis? Don't tell me you didn't bring one!' I muttered something, opened my suitcase and produced this enormous haggis. The customs officer said 'So you had nothing to declare?' But he said it with a smile, even as I was sweating some, thinking what a Toronto jail might be like, how long

I would be incarcerated, etc. Then Sam said, 'C'mon lads, let's have a photograph.' So all of us, including the customs guys, gathered round the haggis, and the photo was taken."

The same sort of problem surfaced when Hay returned home to Scotland. The main difference there, however, was the lack of Shopsy intervention to get him through UK customs. Chuck remembers that time vividly too.

"On departing, Sam presented Hector and me with a Hickory Smoked Turkey packed in dry ice and a complete set of super pots and pans. This was to be another customs problem in Scotland but somehow I got lucky. This time, I declared everything. The customs officer got very excited about my gifts, and I thought this was going to cost me a packet, so I suggested if there was to be a hefty penalty I would just leave them behind, but the guy said 'you can't do that, your wife would kill you!' After some debate with his fellow officers he said, 'I have to charge you…how about 10 shillings (about a dollar or two in today's money).' What a relief!"

You'd be surprised how many heavyweight curlers there are at your friendly neighbourhood curling club. Or in the ranks of CFL footballers. Or among police departments and Armed Forces. I particularly remember when Tom "The Emperor" Jones and Norm Bosworth showed up for the weigh-in. Old time football fans will remember Jones as one of the legendary linemen of the old Ottawa Rough Riders. This was in the BS days of football (Before Steroids), and Tom must have been a good six foot, umpteen inches in height and into the upper 200s in weight. Norm? At that time he was president of Canada Dry Ginger Ale, and certainly didn't look like a heavyweight. But his weight was distributed over some six foot, eight inches of height (at least that's what my memory says), and he could have come in at 185 pounds for all we cared, if it assured us of his participation. Did I mention that he made the weight…and that there was also a goodly supply of Canada Dry product on hand? (Or had you already guessed that?)

Some of the curlers looked like they might have trouble bending over in the hack, but on the ice they displayed a surprising agility and élan. I think there were a couple of shooters who tipped the scales around 400 pounds: think of Dumbo...with a slider.

Did Sam play in the event? I've already said he was a sports buff, and he had no trouble making the weight; perhaps that gives you a hint as to the answer. To the best of my knowledge, Shopsy had never thrown a curling stone in his life. But he got a few members of the Sportsman's League to give him a crash course in the game and said he was ready. It is also my recollection that he thought perhaps he should throw a few practice stones before the event. A couple turned into maybe 20 or 30! It is also my recollection that he played on a team that included Chuck and Hector and famed footballer Jackie Parker and perhaps one or two others. Again Chuck came to my rescue with his memory of events. I should also mention that both Chuck Hay and Hec Gervais were among the lightest and most svelte of all those present!

"Sam was so stiff, after throwing all those rocks, that he could hardly move," said Chuck. "He skipped a few ends, in his own style, before retiring—still sore and stiff. In the second end, with Hector in the hack, he (Hec) asked me to inquire of Sam what it meant when he held the broom shoulder high and parallel to the ice. Sam's reply was 'he can play any part of the broom he likes,' which Hector did with great results."

The Shopsy Spiel was held a few months after the Israeli–Egypt Six Day War. "Most of the teams appeared in fancy dress for the opening game," Hay recalled, "and to everyone's horror our opponents took the ice dressed as Arabs. Sam, being Sam, thought it was very funny and was not the least upset. When their gaffe was pointed out, our opponents were quite upset and wanted to leave the ice and change, but Sam said it was not necessary, he was not the least bit bothered."

"Sam," Chuck continued, "did not want us to win any more than two games as he did not want to be involved any further as sponsor (that is, get any closer to the prize table). Besides he wanted Hector and me to man the hospitality room and look after his guests. One of the guests I remember was Johnny Wayne of Wayne and Shuster.

"Sam had arranged for Danny Kaye, his lifelong friend, to present the prizes, but Kaye was unable to fly in when his plane developed a fault. It was a superb weekend, and I remember CFRB morning man Wally Crouter summing it up on his radio show the day I flew home. He said, 'It was a great day for Toronto as two stout gentlemen are now leaving town. One is Hector Gervais from Edmonton and the other is Chuck Hay from Scotland, who were competing in the Shopsy Bonspiel.' He said he had been in their company all weekend and was glad they were going as he could not take any more of their lifestyle!"

"I have never seen so many huge men," Chuck recalled. "They all played the game in great spirit and were all such a friendly bunch. It was a great event and it's a pity it did not continue." To which I say, amen Brother Hay, amen.

One other fun-stained event that did live on for many years is outlined here, in general detail only.

THE NEWSMEN'S BONSPIEL

Most other bonspiels have little historical material for the avid storyteller to research, The Newsmen's Bonspiel (a.k.a. The Boozeman's Nonspiel) has plenty. Probably because most of the competitors were sportswriters, broadcasters or PR wordsmiths who could, and often did, record details of the competition, usually on asbestos paper, but seldom, if ever, in detail suitable for family publications.

This bonspiel was the brainchild of Cam McKenzie, sports editor of the *Saskatoon Star Phoenix*, who figured, back in 1959, since most of the writers of the day were also curlers, why not gather over a weekend for a few games and general frivolity. It wasn't hard to find a sponsor (a major brewery) and, in addition, there were other firms who helped (including one year, as I recall, when a funeral home provided a casket as a prize).

One year, one of the bonspiel mainstays, Cactus Jack Wells, recalled (in print) that, while the bonspiel was mainly a Western Canada affair, there were occasional effete Easterners who ventured west, including a rink that appeared for its opening game in top hat, white tie and tails. Other famous media names who attended at one time or another included Peter Mansbridge and Lloyd Robertson. Laurie Artiss honed his organizational skills by chairing the 1964 gathering in Brandon, and did it so well that he was dragooned, after moving to Regina, to chair the Brier of 1976, plus the Silver Brooms of 1973 and '83. I was only able to attend the bonspiel for a couple of semesters, and I have already mentioned, in Chapter 34, a memorable occasion when my skip conceded a game—or tried to—after the opening stone of a morning game. My memory goes blank after that, but if you wish further details you could contact Al Hutchinson or any other curling writer of the past 50 years because my lips are sealed.

Speaking of curling writers, or curlers who used to attend the big events and write on the side, I should mention that for each of the 18 Silver Broom years, we arranged an annual media event known as The Brass Whisk. This was before the combined men's and women's championships, when each day usually had only two draws scheduled, so the Brass Whisk could be played in the morning, when there were no championship games scheduled. It drew its name from the original trophy, handcrafted by Terry Denny of Air Canada's public affairs department. I surmise that the "handcrafting" took place late at night a few days before its inauguration in 1968. With an admirable design sense—and zero budget—Terry put a round leather baggage tag onto an old, gilt-sprayed whisk, and then mounted it onto a chunk of plywood (hastily, and obviously, hacked from a larger piece), and placed the entire item majestically onto an Air Canada desk display stand. There was room on the plywood for a series of plaques showing the names of the winners. The Brass Whisk might not have been quite on a level with the Silver Broom, but it nevertheless ranks in my memory as one of the better international events of them all.

OTHER CURLING EVENTS

Among some of the other "special" curling events I recall, is the World Lefthanders Championship, in Oakville, Ontario. And you would be surprised—well, maybe you wouldn't—how many of Canada's top curlers, male and female, are lefties. The southpaw event was invented, organized and tubthumped by John Bryant, who was also the one who first mooted the idea of Hamilton hosting a world championship at Copps Coliseum, but who passed away before the '96 event could take place. The fact that the world championship in Hamilton laid a financial egg (that's another story) could not be laid at John's feet, but he was more than willing to accept responsibility for the World Lefthanders Championship—a "sinister" (ahem) event, he would say—and whenever John called, it behooved you to write or broadcast something immediately about the southpaw shooters, or he would keep pleasantly pestering you till you did. John is no longer with us, but the World Lefthanders still rolls along.

I'm certain there are other curling events every bit as vital and as much fun as the ones I've mentioned, events that some of you either helped to develop or shaped into a local piece of history. But the ones above are the ones I recall, either as an organizer, promoter or participant. The one thing that unites the bonspiels of my memory, and the events of your memory, is the genuine love of the game and the camaraderie of the curlers involved. May it ever be so.

There is one other world championship I helped get off the ground, but you've already read Bob Picken's detailed account of that one—the Uniroyal—in Chapter 33.

Chapter Thirty-seven

STORM CLOUDS ON THE HORIZON

IN THE EARLY YEARS OF THE SILVER BROOM, THERE WERE FOUR KEY AIR Canada players. The late Jack Bowen got the event off the ground, but within two years, had turned over its stewardship to Don McLeod, who was vice-president of public affairs. Don became the principal architect of the event's success, and deserves every accolade that comes his way. When Don retired, Pierre Jerome succeeded him and added his inimitable imprint to the event. All three—Bowen, McLeod and Jerome—have now passed on; you'll have to take my word about their impact on the event.

The fourth key player was Claude Taylor, who succeeded Don as VP, public affairs. When he became president and CEO of Air Canada, the Silver Broom Steering Committee lost an outstanding executive, formidable ally and warm admirer. Taylor's successor was Michel Fournier. Those of us who loved the Silver Broom soon learned that Michel was not a sports buff. And of all the sports he disliked, curling was near the top of the list. That ennui showed in a variety of ways. Where McLeod, Jerome and Taylor had provided personal input to the Broom, Fournier allotted as little personal time as possible, nominating one or two of his minions to look after day-to-day matters. He also found it as difficult as his predecessors had found it easy to be present for the full week of the world championship.

Actually, it didn't matter that much. The Silver Broom steering committee (with stalwarts like Jerome, Hal Cameron, Tony Schoen, Terry Denny and

Art Tonkin, to name but a few) ran like a smoothly ticking watch and, for the most part, the event continued as it always had. But there were some glitches.

For example, in 1979 in Bern, Switzerland, Michel (attending his first championship) was tabbed to present the Air Canada Silver Broom trophy to the winners during the closing ceremonies. And with both the French and English Networks of the CBC providing coverage, the presentation was an important element of the sponsorship. Accordingly, I made arrangements with the CBC for key Air Canada executives to be interviewed at the fifth end break, with Michel, in particular, on the French network.

Unfortunately for all concerned—Air Canada, the CBC and the event—Michel failed to get to the arena in time for the mid-game interview. In fact, if the playoff game between Peter Attinger of Switzerland and Kristian Sørum of Norway had finished after eight ends, he might have missed the trophy presentation too. Don't ask me where he was; I don't know. I do know he had assured me he would be at the arena in ample time.

By the 1980 Moncton Silver Broom, I was sufficiently disturbed at ongoing developments that I submitted my resignation. Suffice it to say there were a number of matters of principle with which I disagreed, so I felt it better to remove myself than try to continue in a manner that would be anathema to me.

Later, when pressed to do so by a number of senior Air Canada executives, I withdrew the resignation on the understanding that the Silver Broom would continue with only minor changes. In 1981, in London, Ontario, the event went smoothly, thanks in the main to the efforts of chairman Dick Dolphin and his excellent committee. But 1981 turned out to be the lull before the storm.

1982 proved to be a watershed year for the Broom. Shortly

after Fournier arrived in Garmisch-Partenkirchen, he pulled out a piece of paper that appeared to have been hurriedly typed. It was not on Air Canada letterhead, so lacked the appearance of any authority. Neither Pierre Jerome, as chair of the steering committee, nor I, had seen the paper before, and Michel wanted to present it to an ICF meeting scheduled in the next half hour! The paper bore the heading "Conditions Under which Air Canada would continue to Sponsor the Silver Broom." Both Jerome and I felt the list of "conditions"—okay, call it an ultimatum—were clumsy, poorly-worded and ill-considered. We were unable to convince him to put it back in his pocket.

When Michel presented his paper to the ICF, it came as a bolt out of the blue. There had been no forewarning, no lobbying of key people, no quiet discussions with anyone, nothing. So it wasn't surprising that the ICF delegates were flabbergasted, flummoxed, fearful. When they found their collective voice, they suggested, through president Clif Thompson, that such a discussion should not take place while a world championship was going on. Why not, it was suggested, table the matter until the following June when a regular meeting was scheduled with the airline in Montreal? Agreed.

By the time of the June meeting, Fournier had had second thoughts and withdrew the paper and its contents entirely. But the harm had already been done. The ICF was now more than a little wary of his bona fides. He did suggest that the federation should take over the operation of the Silver Broom, with the airline putting up the sponsorship money, to which the ICF agreed. I gained the impression he thought this was one way he could dump me, but I could be mistaken. In any event, as soon as they agreed to the new deal, the ICF asked me to continue as before, and I was happy to do so.

Ken Meek, a middle-management PR man, became the Air Canada liaison. But his seeming insensitivity to the situation (he was merely following orders) soon surfaced, and problems began to arise at the 1983 event in Regina. However, thanks to the experience and enthusiasm of the Regina committee headed (again) by Laurie Artiss, the problems were contained. By now the ICF was totally immersed in the championship, and they began to experience first-hand some of the difficulties that had heretofore been hidden from them.

The whole thing came to a head the following year. When visitors arrived for the Silver Broom in Duluth, they found inflated hotel prices, for which they quickly blamed Touram, Air Canada's travel packaging firm. In all previous years, attractive hotel rates had been negotiated. Fans had come to expect fair treatment and were unhappy at what they perceived to be gouging, not by the hotels, but by the airline. In previous years, I had negotiated the hotel rates, on behalf of the airline, but did not do so in '84.

There were other problems. At two ICF meetings, Ken and his immediate superior, Lillian Rayson, were received politely, but coolly. At one of the meetings, the presidents of the competing nations were told that their courtesy travel, which had been in place since the start of the Silver Broom in 1968, would now be withdrawn. To say they were unhappy would be an understatement. At one of their internal meetings (which I was unable to attend), I learned later that the German delegate had summed up the new situation by talking about "Air Canada's salami solution — slice a bit off here, another bit there, and pretty soon..."

So the stage was set for something to happen, something that had been building since Michel's 1982 "piece of paper."

According to the sponsorship contract, either party to the pact had, after the completion of each year's event, a two-month "window" in which to advise the other party of its intention to discontinue the relationship. At a memorable meeting near the end of the Duluth event, the unimaginable happened: The ICF, led by treasurer Don McKay of the United States, gave Air Canada notice of its intention to withdraw from the contract in the two-month window.

An aside here: I know of only one other occasion when a governing body had, in effect, put a sponsor on notice. That was in 1967 when the Canadian Ladies Curling Association gave notice to Dominion Stores, sponsor of the Dominion Diamond D Ladies Canadian Championship, that they wished to withdraw from the sponsorship deal, following the '67 championship.

McKay, in addition to being a long-time rep of the United States Curling Association, was also a top-class New York lawyer. He was smart and had a knack, with his quiet manner, ready smile and quick humour, for defusing a tense situation. In explaining the ICF decision to Air Canada, he indicated that the federation was merely giving notice, to draw attention to the worsening situation. While the federation fully appreciated everything Air Canada had done for international curling, it was deeply concerned about a variety of items, which they felt could be dealt with at the usual summer meeting. However, McKay continued, there were two items in particular that the ICF felt were "non-negotiable." If they could be fixed, the "window" notice could easily be withdrawn.

Item number one was the Touram situation. It was critical, and something would have to be done about the perceived "gouging" of supporters. Item number two was a personnel matter: The ICF asked Air Canada to appoint another liaison to replace Ken Meek.

That was in April. By late May or early June, ICF president Clif Thompson began to receive hints that Fournier was going to stonewall both federation concerns. Fournier finally told Thompson, shortly in advance of the meetings, he was not prepared to discuss either of the ICF's non-negotiable requests.

Thompson, one of the most hard-working, congenial and knowledgeable presidents in the short history of the ICF, was shattered by this news. And truth to tell, so were the other members of the ICF executive. They could have accepted an assertion that these were difficult matters, and required further discussion. They could have lived with some political waffling or foot shuffling. But no, there was no indication at all of a willingness to even discuss the situation. As far as Fournier was concerned, those items would not be on the meeting agenda.

Some of the ICF executive felt that Michel was determined to use this as a pretext to scuttle the airline's sponsorship of the Silver Broom. Others felt that if they gave in on this rejection of their concern, the ICF would become nothing more than a toothless puppet and the event would be on a steep and slippery slope.

As executive director of the world championship and one who had already given close to 16 years of total effort to build the event into the finest curling championship in the world, I was devastated.

Was this the beginning of the end? Or, possibly, the end of the beginning?

Chapter Thirty-eight

THE DEPARTURE OF HEXAGON

THERE ARE PROBABLY MORE HALF-TRUTHS, NON-TRUTHS AND NEVER-were-truths surrounding the Hexagon years than any other period of world championship play. If you'd like my version of the Hexagon yarn, read on. In the interest of full disclosure, you should know I was one of the Hexagon six, so this is anything but an unbiased, impersonal account. Frankly, there aren't many chuckles in this chapter, but still what follows does contain some details that, until now, have never been told. So here's my version of "kiss and tell," except there aren't too many kisses.

In early June of 1984 the *Canadian Curling News* sponsored a promotional seminar in Brandon, Manitoba. As publisher and editor, I was there with the invited presenters, one of whom was Laurie Artiss, a key member of the International Curling Federation's executive committee, and one whose Silver Broom roots stretched back as far as mine. He had twice served as chair of an organizing committee (1973 and '83) and in 1976 had chaired the Regina Brier. He had helped rewrite the ICF rulebook, he had been a major player in the television negotiations involving the federation and TSN, and was one of the most astute international curling people around. No one doubted his great love of the game.

Also present were a pair of Dons—Lewis and Turner. Don Lewis, whose ice-making expertise had been a boon in the early days of the Silver Broom, had been more than icemaker as he made himself invaluable in a variety of ways. In later years he would go on to chair the 1992 Regina Brier and in 2001 to become president of the Canadian Curling Association. Don Turner, a retired farmer from Weyburn, Saskatchewan, was probably one of the most intense curling devotees I have ever met. He'd been one of Regina's key organizers in both 1973 and '83 (chair of International Day) and when he wasn't collecting curling memorabilia (now housed in the community-built Don Turner Curling Museum in Weyburn) he was an enthusiastic spectator.

After the seminar, Laurie, the two Dons and I were sitting around with our feet up when the conversation turned to the fragile world sponsorship situation. Out of that session grew the germ of an idea. While the ICF's opting-out notice had been given, in Duluth, basically as a defensive move, what would happen, we wondered, if Michel Fournier decided to call their hand? Did the federation have any other option but to fold? Before we left Brandon, we were on the phone to Scotland and New York to acquaint Chuck Hay and Kay Sugahara about our concerns and thoughts. What if we offered a plan to the ICF that would serve to stiffen their resolve?

Chuck Hay is, of course, one of the giants of world curling. Some of his accomplishments have already been covered, but to remind you... not only was he (at the time) Scotland's only world champion, it was his example that had revolutionized competitive curling in Scotland in the sixties. He had been a player in the final Scotch Cup, 1967, and in the first Silver Broom, 1968. He had been president of the Royal Caledonian Curling Club, a valued Scottish representative to the ICF, and the first Scots curler to be honoured by the Queen with an MBE (Member of the Order of the British Empire). Like Artiss, he had been chair of a Silver Broom organizing committee, 1975. He had also been a chief umpire for the event. Blunt-spoken he may be, but when he speaks, his

Laurie Artiss (l) and Ray Kingsmith (r) were key figures in the lead-up to the Hexagon years. Contributed photo

words have the ring of truth to them. Sincerity, intensity, wisdom and conviction are other words that come to mind.

I hadn't met Kay Sugahara until the 1981 Silver Broom in London, Ontario, but had quickly recognized his enthusiasm for curling. I also discovered he was one of the smartest men I have ever met—and certainly one with the means to indulge his passion. In 2006, the savvy organizers of the world men's curling championship in Lowell, Massachusetts, named him honourary president of the event, an honour richly deserved.

But back to 1984. It was Sugahara who helped straighten out our priorities. "There's no such thing as being half-pregnant," he said, or words to that effect, when we talked over our thoughts in a conference call. If we were to offer the ICF a viable alternative, he suggested, then it couldn't be just something to stiffen their resolve. We had to be prepared to put our money, our thoughts, our energy, where our mouths were.

We quickly saw the logic in Kay's observation, so with considerable enthusiasm we prepared a presentation for the federation with great attention to detail. It was imperative to keep our plans confidential; after all, if Air Canada did accede to the ICF's non-negotiable requests, then we would simply fade into the sunset. But if Fournier did decide to play hardball, we were prepared to offer the federation an alternative proposal.

To that end, Laurie (as a CCA official) was asked to advise the association of our thoughts, requesting their confidentiality, while I was delegated to tell the key ICF members.

Laurie did his job by telling the late Ray Kingsmith, then president of the CCA, of our plans. We'll never know how much Ray passed on to his executive, but Laurie had done his best. As ICF competition director, I was expected to be present for the summer meetings in Montreal, so when I suggested to President Clif Thompson (from Stroud, outside Toronto) that we might drive to Montreal together, I also told him of our thoughts. During the six-hour drive, we were able to discuss all aspects of our plan. I told Clif that the other five members of Hexagon (it was Sugahara who came up with the name) were flying into Montreal, and that all six of us would be available for whatever might ensue.

As we motored down Highway 401, I outlined the numerous ideas we had in mind. I had advised Thompson earlier of the Hexagon membership, and repeated that our background, experience and abilities were his guarantee of our commitment. I emphasized again that it was our intention to become involved only if Air Canada failed to offer some sort of solution to the federation's concerns. I reminded Clif that both of us had served on the CCA's five-man sponsor search committee in the late seventies, when Macdonald Tobacco had severed its 50-year support of the Brier and he had been CCA president. He readily recalled how we had overcome a variety of obstacles in signing Labatt Breweries as the new Brier sponsor. And we convinced ourselves that if Air Canada did decide to walk, we could find another sponsor.

In short, Clif (and the ICF) now had a Plan B option available, if Fournier decided to stonewall Plan A.

We waited in our hotel room while the ICF executive met with Fournier. Shortly after Fournier departed, Clif called to say Michel was not willing to even discuss either of the federation's two "non-negotiable" concerns, although he did agree to meet again the following morning. Thompson said the executive, discouraged and disappointed, was still on hand—would we come to the meeting room and acquaint them about the Hexagon proposal, including our offer to provide a minimum of a half million dollars in rights fees over the next five years. We were greeted warmly by the executive as we passed around our carefully prepared presentation.

There had been no suggestion of the usual Air Canada–ICF gathering for dinner that night, so we were invited to continue our conversation over steaks and wine. It is fair to say the executive members were both relieved and excited about the possibilities. In addition, they now saw they had a viable Plan B for their meeting with Fournier the next morning.

The next day Fournier said there had been no overnight change on the part of the airline. The ICF gained the strong impression (we were told later) that Michel's stonewalling was, in reality, his way of dumping a sponsorship that had worked well for Air Canada in the past, but which did not fit his idea of a corporate support vehicle. With nothing left to talk about, the meeting drew to a close.

We were invited to return and discuss the Hexagon proposal in line-by-line detail, and shortly after, the executive voted unanimously to accept our plan. We agreed to fund the world championship until a new sponsor could be found. We knew that might take time, but we were certain it could be done, and were certain the event could be maintained at the same high level as in the past.

When the Hexagon sponsorship was publicly announced in August, we were shocked at the reaction. Far from our offer being perceived as a suitable sponsor replacement, some saw it, and said so, as a bunch of carpetbaggers intent on lining their pockets. In particular, the CCA lined us up against the figurative wall, ready to offer us a blindfold and one last cigarette. Of the six, Laurie Artiss and I, in particular, were castigated, excoriated, clapped in verbal irons. It appeared that the CCA hierarchy had not been advised of Laurie's earlier conversation with Kingsmith, and in particular, Laurie was blasted as having a conflict of interest. The CCA, we quickly learned, would oppose Hexagon at the upcoming semi-annual meeting of the ICF in Morzine, France, site of the European championships in December, where our offer would be put forward for formal ratification.

Although we met quickly with the CCA directors to explain the situation, it soon became apparent they were not interested in explanations. The association named Ralph Boyd and Clyde Opaleychuk, the two most senior CCA directors, and International Committee Chair Mike Chernoff as their delegates to the meetings in Morzine, with instructions to put the hex on Hexagon.

In Morzine, the full ICF assembly heard our submission, plus two other sponsorship offers, one of which had been hastily engineered by the CCA. The other was a European offer that had appeared within the previous month or so. When it came time to vote, the Hexagon offer was overwhelmingly accepted and approved. Only Boyd and Opaleychuk voted against it. Mike Chernoff abstained, saying that while he would not disobey the CCA's earlier directive, he was unable, after hearing all three proposals, to vote for either of the other two.

The international curling community had snubbed the CCA, its largest member, a snub that led a dispirited Ralph Boyd, in his first attendance at an ICF meeting, to mention to one Scot that it was unbelievable that a bunch of "banana republic ICF members" would disregard the feelings of the federation's largest member. Unfortunately, the Scot to whom he said this was Willie Kemp, the long-time, well-known (and well-regarded) curling reporter for *The Scotsman* newspaper. For Willie, the comment must have seemed a heaven-sent headline quote. It was also an indication of how little either Boyd knew about the politics of the world curling community, or world curling media, and both Boyd and Opaleychuk were obviously surprised and chagrined to see the unfortunate "banana republic" quote hit the papers the following day! When I was fact-checking for this chapter, Bob Picken confirmed the "banana republic" comment. He wrote:

"I can certainly verify Ralph Boyd's comments to Willie, because he repeated them to me in a CBC radio interview I did with him from Morzine. When he made the comment 'banana republics of curling' I stopped my recording, and said 'Ralph, I'm taping this for the CBC network, are you sure you want to use those terms? He replied, 'Why not? Those people have a lot of nerve going against Canada's position.' I was dismayed, of course, but ran the interview."

An aside here: Sugahara later wrote to me that, in 1988, when he had stayed with Kingsmith during the Calgary Winter Olympics, he discovered that Ray had been surprised at the reaction of some of his CCA executive. Nor was there any reference to who (if any) of the CCA had been informed of the Hexagon proposal in advance.

In a subsequent (1986) speech in Portage la Prairie, Bob Picken (who by now had completed eight years as a CCA rep to the ICF) told his audience "it almost seems [there is] an ongoing vendetta, as the CCA management has bucked the Hexagon deal whenever it could." As we met with a variety of potential world sponsors, Picken's words about "persistent sniping at Hexagon" appeared prescient. Somehow or other, whenever we got to the point of detailed conversation with a potential sponsor, something happened to cool the climate. Rumours of association opposition continued to surface.

Finally, it appeared our sponsor search was successful. A large international firm appeared enthusiastic about the prospect of world curling sponsorship. Months of detailed discussion led to the preparation of a formal contract. But when Kay Sugahara and I met with the firm's vice-president to sign the contract, he said he had decided to back away from the deal. "I have a funny feeling in the pit of my stomach," he told us, "and I don't want to ignore that feeling!"

To say we were shocked would be a huge understatement. After all, we had spent many months working over each sentence of the contract. We had met with a number of his marketing and PR executives to plan details of the official sponsorship launch. There was no problem with budget. Everyone seemed pleased and excited over the future. To this day, we cannot explain the abrupt termination. We discovered it was his decision alone.

After 1986, the first year of Hexagon sponsorship (using our own money), Kay Sugahara bought out the shares of the other five members of Hexagon. Subsequently, in Vancouver, 1987, with little to show by way of sponsor success, he advised the ICF that Hexagon would bow out following the 1988 event in Lausanne. That day was one of the most disappointing days of my curling life, and I dare say for the other Hexagon members too.

THE SHOW & TELL TIN

It's only a small, round tin I picked up at a flea market; it measures a little over four inches in height, and about four and a quarter inches in diameter. I think I paid a dollar for it, mainly because the word "Brier" was there, in big red letters, and below it (on a leaf of tobacco) the words "Virginia Tobacco." Between those words was a small gold heart, same shape as the legendary purple heart of Brier fame. In an oval on the tin you can find Rex Wood's famous portrait of the Macdonald Lassie.

My Macdonald Tobacco "show & tell tin" was an essential part of my earlier speeches about "Sponsors I Have Known." Author photo

Sometimes when I'm invited to speak to a curling club banquet, I take my "show & tell" tin with me. It's my prop, and cue, to talk about "Sponsors I Have Known" and, in particular, how Macdonald Tobacco's support of the Brier became the template for all the other national championships that followed.

There have been a number of books written about the Brier. I even wrote one myself: *The First Fifty*. But it's not the Brier history I want to detail here, but rather the impact of the Brier, for to my mind the Macdonald Brier became the standard by which all succeeding championships were measured. Any sponsor who strays too far from the Brier blueprint does so at its own risk. You only have to recall the excesses of Dominion Stores Ltd., first sponsor of the Canadian Ladies Curling Championship, to realize that fact. Or to attend a Scott Tournament of Hearts today to understand why their 25th anniversary event in London, Ontario, in 2006, was such a signal success.

Curling has been blessed with many wonderful sponsors. But the reverse is also true: those wonderful sponsors have been blessed with curling as their vehicle, whether it be for reasons of public relations, or marketing, or both. I could go on for quite some time about this, and if you invite me to speak at your club sometime, I promise I'll bring my show & tell tin, and expand on this theme.

Chapter Thirty-nine

THE SKINS GAME

WHILE TROLLING THE INTERNET IN THE RUN-UP TO THE 2006 WINTER Olympics in Torino, I chanced upon a US story, telling of a television program (on NBC) called "ICE 2005." This was a two-day, four-hour telecast in December 2005 highlighting four of the "lesser" Olympic sports, all played on ice: bobsled, luge, skeleton and curling. And included in the curling segment was a Skins Game.

So why did this jump out at me? Because I was directly involved in the development of the Skins concept in 1986. And to have the Skins accepted as an integral part of curling some 20 years later was sweet indeed. Particularly when NBC estimated, based on "ICE 2004" that "ICE 2005" would draw at least 6.5 million viewers!

Let me, then, take you back to the days following the Kitchener-Waterloo Brier of 1986, won that year by Alberta's Ed Lukowich. In my game scribbles I find two main items. The first notes a total of 121 blank ends, while the second shows a total of 47 hog line violations, neither of which are the kind of stats destined to excite curling fans.

Jim Thompson and I were chatting about these and other Brier bits one day, and Jim quickly made me aware of his thoughts. Jim and I had been CBC buddies for many years, particularly during the various CBC curling series, me in front of the cameras, he as an executive behind them. Now he was a vice-president at The Sports Network (TSN) and was concerned about the direction the game seemed to be taking. "If curling continues in this direction," he told me, "we in TSN are going to have to take a second look at our coverage. It is simply too dull. What can we do to give curling a lift?"

Out of that conversation grew curling's version of the Skins Game. We borrowed shamelessly from golf's Skins Game to design a made-for-television event we thought might gain the approval of both players and viewers. Our "invention" turned out to be an instant success, starting with our first event in Newmarket, Ontario. That December, TSN put up $30,000 in prize money and invited four world champion rinks to get the event off the ground. We also asked the four to work out nuances in the rules, and Al Hackner, Rick Folk, Ed Lukowich and Ed Werenich all co-operated wonderfully. So much so, that the rules have hardly changed since that 1986 inaugural year.

More importantly, from a television viewpoint, the event consistently pulled in huge audience ratings and spawned interest around the world. Over the years, I sent out copies of the rules to clubs all across the country so they could stage their own in-house Skins Games. I crossed the Atlantic to help Scottish TV begin its version of the Skins. So perhaps you can understand why, when NBC elected to feature the Skins, I could feel a surge of pride. I only wish Jim could have been here to share in the enjoyment. But shortly after retiring as president of TSN, he took on a huge challenge as president of the Canadian Olympic Committee, only to die suddenly during a discussion in Vancouver about the Winter Games of 2010.

If I seem quite immodest about our claim to the Skins, I hasten to add that the popularity of the Skins Game was due not so much to Jim and me but to two essential elements: the sponsorship of McCain Foods (Canada), and the efforts of a large crew of outstanding people at TSN. In addition to Jim Thompson, there were such skilled and hard-working TV experts as Barry Duller, Keith Pelley, Richard Wells, Paul

Jim Thompson and the author, instigators of curling's Skins Game. Author photo

MacLean, Pete Buchanan, as well as the famous trio Vic Rauter, Linda Moore and Ray Turnbull. Plus of course a dedicated and talented clutch of camera operators, sound people and lighting technicians. And Shorty. Shorty Jenkins, the superb icemaker who produced an outstanding surface each year for the top curlers who put on the show.

But the Skins Game might well have expired early had it not been for the financial support of McCain Foods (Canada), and more particularly for the direction provided by Scoop Fredstrom. Scoop, of course, is not his square name, but it's the name he is known by in the curling world, in the PR firmament, and throughout the orbit of McCain companies, where he is director of public relations. The "Scoop" moniker was hung on him when he was a youthful reporter on one of his first jobs, and it stuck. Fredstrom became the key organizer and heavy thinker in all 16 years of Skins sponsorship by McCain. His direction illustrates perfectly how vital it is to have a sympathetic sponsor executive involved in an event. He also remembers exactly, with all the accuracy of a veteran journalist, how the TSN–McCain relationship began. Enough of my words, here's Scoop with his:

"One spring evening in 1989," he wrote me, "several members of McCain and TSN management were meeting at Toronto's Inn on the Park, among them Jim Thompson (by then president of TSN) and McCain VP marketing, Archie McLean. It was a convivial dinner, the principal topic being a possible (and major) ad buy by McCain in the relatively new Sports Network. I was there to try to get some exposure for the two new McCain SuperSpiels, one in Portage la Prairie (Manitoba), the other in our headquarters area of Florenceville and Grand Falls (New Brunswick). It turned out TSN was also looking for a sponsor for their TSN Skins Game—why not put the two SuperSpiel winners in the Skins? The discussion carried on, and finally, to reach a decision, McLean opted to flip a coin for the whole extended agreement, all or nothing. You could say that TSN won the flip (for I'm told that Jim kept that coin as a permanent souvenir), but you could also say that McCain was a winner too, for we built a 16-year Skins success story on that coin toss. It was great theatre, and the result was a handshake agreement that never needed a written contract."

Well, curlers know all about the importance of handshakes, but hold on here, the story is outrunning itself. Let's go back to 1986 (pre-McCain) and consider some of the challenges we faced in getting the Skins off the ground. For example, how many teams should be invited? And who? How much money should be put up for the event? Were there any other ideas that could be incorporated that would add some spice to the mix? How could we get away from the deadly peel game? Remember, this was before the advent of the Free Guard Zone.

All these questions and more were thrown out for discussion, and out of the resulting deliberations came the basic outline of the Skins. We must have been pretty smart back then, for there's been little or no change to the concept in the intervening years.

The format rests on four basic foundation points. First, there is money to be won on every end of the game; any money not won in one end is carried over and added to the next end's money. Secondly, money is the deciding factor in declaring a winner; the team with the most money wins. Thirdly, the team with last-rock advantage can win the money only by scoring two or more points; the team without the hammer can win the money by "stealing" the end. Number four: In the case of a tie, each team has one shot—a draw to the button (sweeping by the shooting team only)— to decide the winner. And finally, the teams are put under intense pressure by having to play the game within a prescribed time limit.

I had begun my research on time clocks in 1983 and was sufficiently satisfied with the theory to suggest it for the initial Skins series in 1986. And when it worked there, it was easy to suggest it for the 1989 world championships in Milwaukee. (But you've already read all about time clocks in Chapter 26.)

There were three main elements that made the Skins hugely popular. First of all, as mentioned, it was a made-for-television event, and the combination of outstanding commentators Vic Rauter, Linda Moore and Ray Turnbull, together with the "star" appeal of four world-calibre teams, created excitement and instant credibility. In 1986, with $30,000 in prize money, and with the aforementioned Al Hackner, Ed Lukowich, Rick Folk and Ed Werenich on tap, we knew we had a winner. For the record, Werenich came away with $22,000 that year. It was the first of his nine Skins appearances.

Secondly, there was the appeal of big money. Thanks to McCain, the prize money jumped from $30,000 to $50,000 in McCain's debut year of 1989. The prize money then escalated each year, until in the 16th (and final) year of the food firm's sponsorship, the prize money was a whopping $150,000. Okay, so it's nowhere near the millions in the

Wayne Middaugh (front) and Kevin Martin (rear) were two of the all-time money winners at the annual McCain TSN Skins Game. McCain Foods (Canada) photo by Errol McGihon

televised Skins Game of golf in the United States, but for curling it was huge. And if you want my opinion, the Skins Game in curling was, and is, much more exciting, more fan-friendly than golf's version. Harrumph.

An aside here: I should add that both McCain and TSN insisted I become a part of the annual ritual, as chief score-keeper, timekeeper, tub thumper, statistician, umpire and historian-cum-record keeper. Mind you, I only did the triple-threat job for a year or two. It became more of a juggling feat than I wanted, so we recruited local timekeepers and statisticians to keep me company on an often chillingly cold perch near centre ice.

The third element of success was the Skins' journey around the country. Where the Brier, Hearts and Worlds all command the attention of larger communities (a diminishing list of potential sites), the Skins was able to visit some of the smaller curling areas of the country. Over the years we visited every province and the Yukon Territory. Most of the curling centres we selected would never have been able to attract top international curling to their community had it not been for the Skins. And although some of those towns suggested we use the local arena, we said no, we'd stick to the local curling club, thank you. It was cosier, and with spectator seating erected on the adjacent sheet of ice, there was an intimacy that appealed to fans and curlers alike. On more than one occasion, a skip facing a particularly dicey situation turned to the audience and asked "what do you think I should do?"

That intimate competitive area also created one or two "oops" moments. I remember the time Archie McLean had just returned from an overseas business trip and even though suffering from jet lag, came out and sat in the bleachers. When the producers in the truck heard he was present, they asked if I could spot him, and I was able to indicate where he was seated. Then just as the camera zeroed in on him so he could be identified, the jet lag produced one of the most prodigious yawns you have ever seen. Exciting stuff, eh, Archie?

If you were one of the 16 Skins curlers, you were a winner before you ever arrived at the club. There was no entry fee; your transportation and hotel rooms were provided; you were given a per diem allowance (as if you needed it), there was plenty of sponsor product available in the lounge; there were fans present who wanted to buy you a drink; and, if you performed well on the ice you could walk away with a big bundle of booty. No wonder the curlers told the local media, year after year, that of all the events they played, the Skins was their favourite.

The success of the McCain sponsorship attracted a second sponsor—JVC—to bankroll a Women's Skins Game, which began in Thunder Bay in 1996, but only lasted half as long as the McCain Skins. Having the top women's teams take part added another dimension to the already popular event. It also provided me with one particularly memorable moment, in 1998. That was the third straight year Sandra Schmirler's Olympic-bound team came to the Skins (still in Thunder Bay).

Now everybody who knew her has a "Sandra" story. Here's mine. By now, the Free Guard Zone was in play and on this occasion there was a lead stone in front of the rings...or was it biting the rings? If it was in front, it couldn't be removed; if it was a biter, it could be removed. Sandra signalled she wanted the chief umpire—me—to make the "in or out" decision. I approached the situation with foreboding. If it was that close, my decision could make a major difference to play in that end. But as I peered down at the stone, it was obvious that it was outside the rings by a good centimetre (or half-inch to my non-metric eyeballs), and I told Sandra so. "Yeah, I know that too," she told me, "I just wanted to get you on camera!"

Chapter Forty
COMPLETING THE CIRCLE

THE ROOKIE CURLER COULD HARDLY BELIEVE HIS GOOD FORTUNE. AS the youngest member of the club, he had been invited by the top-ranked skip to play lead in a major Montreal-wide bonspiel. And in one of their games, they had scored curling's ultimate reward: a perfect 8-end.

Some curlers never ever see an 8-end in their entire curling career, and here the rookie not only had been a witness to one, but had also been involved in one. Surely a Brier triumph, since there was no world championship at the time, was the next logical step! The Brier appearance, however, turned out to be ephemeral, at least a Brier appearance as competitor. Nine years later, however, the rookie did get to the Brier, his first, and still a memorable, experience.

But if the Brier turned out to be a fantasy, the 8-ender was real, and every time the rookie looks at the sterling silver jigger, handed out by a liquor company back there in 1951, it opens a floodgate of memories, and the rookie remembers it as if it was yesterday. Not only had his foursome put all eight of their stones into the rings, but it turned out they had stolen the end; that is, their opponents had last rock and thought they could get out of the end by putting that final rock right on the button to score a single point, or at the most, give up only one or two points. But, *quel horreur*, the opposition skip *hogged his final shot*—after which there were handshakes all around.

The rookie vowed, then and there, that if he ever became a skip, and if ever an opponent had eight stones counting against him, he wouldn't try to snuggle up to the button; he'd throw a high hard one at the biggest clump of

In the last year of the Silver Broom, the gathering of the PPP took place in Glasgow, where 1985 president, Robin Brechin (front row, second from right), entertained a number of previous Silver Broom presidents. As an honourary member of the PPP (rear left) I joined the four in the rear row: Art Cobb (Utica 1970), Laurie Artiss (Regina 1973, 1983), Harvey Marshall (Duluth 1984) and Chuck Hay (Perth 1975). From left to right, front row, were Lennart Hemmingson (Karlstad 1977), Hans Thaut (Garmisch-Partenkirchen 1972, 1982), Brechin (Glasgow) and Hans Maeder (Bern 1979). Photo by Michael Burns

granite in the rings. Give up one or two points, three, four, maybe even seven, but not, *definitely* not, eight.

In particular, the rookie remembered all this, and so much more, on April 6, 2006, in Lowell, Massachusetts, some 55 years later, when he was invited to speak at the 35th anniversary of the founding of the Pond Hoppers Club, and was given free reign to reminisce about the years between that 8-end jigger and the current state of the game.

So, why do I still find curling a part of my life that continues to bubble with excitement? Shouldn't I be just a bit blasé, bemused by it all, perhaps even infected with a smidgen of ennui, 55 years after that dream count, the 1951 8-end?

To say that curling has been good to me is self-evident, if you've managed to get this far in the book. Good to me? Listen up—it's been fantastic, amazing, wonderful, and I hope you will understand when I say I hope that I have been good for curling.

Curling has given me a wealth of wonderful friends in all parts of Canada, Scotland and the United States, as well as in other parts of the world I thought I'd never see, when I was a kid growing up in Toronto.

Throughout the Silver Broom years (1968–1985) the various presidents of the world championship organizing committees became close friends. They also became—at the close of "their event"—a part of an exclusive fraternity known as the PPP, or Passé Past Presidents. The PPP logo and pin (designed by Laurie Artiss) showed a tombstone, with flowers around the base, for the irrefutable reason that "there is no one as dead as a past president!" Somehow, during the hectic week of each Silver Broom, the current president was required to find time to entertain the other PPP members present and, of course, it was impossible to plead any number of excuses or contingencies to get out of the hosting job, since all of them had been through the presidential exercise themselves. As might be imagined, the stories always flew thick and fast.

I journeyed to Lowell for three reasons. First reason, of course, was for the games. From my very first days with the Brier, and later the Silver Broom, I was firm in my conviction that the most important element of any championship is the game, and by extension, the players. If the competitors—and I don't care what event it is—are treated shabbily, then that event will soon fold. I was fortunate that, at the world level, I was able to work with some very talented people at Air Canada, and that they agreed it was essential we look after the players well.

There are other important people at any event who should be cosseted too, and I know some of you will find it hard to agree with my next nomination. But humour me for a moment. Since I have spent a lifetime in the media, it's no surprise that I think of my media brethren—and sistren (if there isn't such a word, there should be)—as being vital to any championship. An event that is played in secret can never succeed. So I would argue that the media are essential to the success of any major competition. In earlier days, when spectators would complain about the choice location of the media bench, I used to reply that one person on the media bench might be writing, or voicing a report, for anywhere from 10,000 listeners to a half-million readers, easily 20, 50, or 100 times as many as paid to sit in the stands. So as an organizer and promoter, I wanted to be sure the media mavens were able to do their job as easily as possible...comfortably too.

Don't forget, a spectator can take the day off, if he or she wishes to do so. But as a writer or broadcaster paid to do a job, my employer expected me to be at the games the entire day if I was to report the news accurately. Not only that, but at the end of the day's competition, when the fans were partying, I and my media friends were slaving over a hot typewriter, or laptop, or we were editing audio tape or putting a voice track on a TV report. So later, when I exited the media bench for the organizer's perch, I vowed to ensure the media reps had proper working facilities. And then, after providing for their work needs, I tried to make sure they had a good time. So whether it was a late night party, after all the deadlines had been met, or an early morning visit to a nearby curling club for The Brass Whisk, I wanted it to be an occasion to remember.

I wanted to be in Lowell for a second reason. Every two years the World Curling Federation holds an election of officers, and for the most part, they are ho-hum affairs. But there is a three-term constitutional limit for members of the three-person management committee (president, vice-president, director of finance) or for one of the four member-at-large positions, so the sixth-year elections are vital. Lowell would see such an election. More than that, 2006 would mark a major changing of the guard, and I wanted to see who would be the new WCF leaders. I wanted to see if I could discern any change in direction for the world of curling I had come to know over the past 40-plus years. I knew, since nominations had closed a month or so before Lowell, that Les Harrison of Canada (Moncton, New Brunswick) would be acclaimed as the new WCF president, only the third Canadian to be so honoured. I also wanted to know who the other key players at the world level would be.

Since Gunther Hummelt of Austria became WCF president in 1990 (and after him Roy Sinclair of Scotland), the major focus of the federation had been to get curling recognized as a medal sport in the Olympics. It was a lengthy effort that saw the membership of the WCF expand from 10 nations in the early seventies to some 46 countries by 2006.

In 2006, with curling's participation in the Winter Olympics looking solid, what would be the new thrust of the federation? What would a world body under a Canadian leader look like? How might curling change in the 21st century?

It took a total of 17 ballots in the antiquated, confusing, cumbersome election before the new seven-member WCF executive was determined. In addition to Harrison as president and a second acclamation, Warren Lowe (United States) as director of finance, Kate Caithness (Scotland) was elected vice-president, with the following four members-at-large: Patrick Hürlimann (Switzerland), Hiro Saito (Japan), Leif Öhman (Sweden) and Niels Larson (Denmark). Where will their leadership take the curling world over the next six years, including the 2010 Winter Olympics in Vancouver/Whistler?

The third reason was pure vanity. I had been invited to speak at the annual Pond Hopper party, and since 2006 would mark the 35th such party, and since I had been instrumental in establishing the Pond Hoppers, I wanted to be there. Many of my best friends from around the curling world would be present. How many more times would I get the chance to be with them?

The Pond Hoppers was one of those ideas that had seemed rather silly when it started, but somehow it had caught on, and here I was, in Lowell, reminding some of the original members of the ACSBPHAICBJS, and some later members of the NARPHAICBJS of their role at the world championship. Okay, okay, I know you want to know about those

Through all the Silver Broom years, and more, Connie Partridge was an indispensable member of the administration team. In 1984 she was honoured in the opening parade at the world championship in Duluth. Photo by Michael Burns

initials, so let me just say that the original group was called the *Air Canada Silver Broom Pond Hoppers And International Curling Buff Jet Set*. Once Air Canada had bowed out of its sponsorship role, the Pond Hoppers elected to continue, and all that was needed was a slight change in name. To become a member you still had to cross an ocean to attend a world championship, but all that was necessary, for the organization, was to remove the ACSB part of the title and replace it with NAR—*New and Revised Pond Hoppers* etc. It didn't take long before it was shortened to the Pond Hoppers Club.

There was a simple reason behind its formation. By 1971 a growing number of curling fans were attending the Silver Broom, and many of them were using the services of Air Canada to get there. We wanted to change the orientation of those fans from that of a casual spectator to that of participant. To those who qualified for membership (cross an ocean, remember?) we gave a pin, a scroll and an invitation to an annual party. Connie Partridge, who worked alongside me in Toronto, became "Keeper of the Rolls," and was a favourite of all Pond Hoppers. Later, when it appeared the Pond Hoppers might fall apart, Jan Schneeberger and Sheila Longie from the United States volunteered to look after the club, and now the army of Pond Hoppers, if they were ever to attend a championship en masse, would number over 10,000. You could say it had become a significant success, and I was happy to be a part of that 35th occasion.

I titled this chapter "Completing the Circle." Here's why. In Chapter 1, I imagined a conversation between Baron Pierre de Coubertin and Vince Lombardi. Now that I have passed my biblical "three score and ten," I have finally accepted the fact I will never fulfill Lombardi's injunction by winning the Brier or the World. I do think, however, that I might qualify for a pat on the back from the Baron.

I think I have stayed the course, taken part. I have, perhaps, triumphed in some things, and I know I have been a part of the struggle. I may not have conquered too often, but I allow as how I have fought well.

I began my curling journey by covering the first Schoolboy Curling Championship in 1950. By attending the 2006 World Men's Curling Championship, I think I have completed the circle.

BIBLIOGRAPHY

Bittle, Dallas S., George Karrys, and Gerry Geurts, eds. *Black Book of Curling*. Calgary: Top Floor Media Inc., 2005.

Bryson, Bill. *A Short History of Nearly Everything*. Toronto: Doubleday Canada, a division of Random House Inc., 2003.

Chaput, John. *Saskatchewan Sports Legends: One Hundred Years of Athletic Distinction*. Calgary: Johnson Gorman Publishers, 2005.

Herman, Arthur. *How the Scots Invented the Modern World: The True Story of How Western Europe's Poorest Nation Created Our World & Everything in It*. New York: Three Rivers Press, a division of Random House Inc., 2001.

Jennings, Andrew. *The Great Olympic Swindle: When the World Wanted Its Games Back*. New York: Simon and Schuster, 2000.

———. *The New Lords of the Rings: Olympic Corruption & How to Buy Gold Medals*. New York: Pocket Books, an Imprint of Simon & Schuster Ltd., 1996.

Lefko, Perry. *Sandra Schmirler: The Queen of Curling*. Toronto: Stoddart Publishing Company Ltd., 2000.

Maxwell, Doug. *Canada Curls: The Illustrated History of Curling in Canada.* Vancouver: Whitecap Books Ltd., 2002.

Pezer, Vera. *The Stone Age: A Social History of Curling on the Prairies.* Calgary: Fifth House Publishers, a Fitzhenry & Whiteside Company, 2003.

Scholz, Guy. *Gold on Ice: The Story of the Sandra Schmirler Curling Team.* Regina: Coteau Books, 1999.

Simson, Vyv, and Andrew Jennings. *The Lords of the Rings: Power, Money and Drugs in the Modern Olympics.* Toronto: Stoddart Publishing Company Ltd., 1992.

Tiefenbach, Arnie. *Say It Again, Sam!: Life in and beyond the Richardson curling dynasty.* Regina: The House That Sam Built and Future Marketing Inc., 1999.

Weeks, Bob. *The Brier: The History of Canada's Most Celebrated Curling Championship.* Toronto: Macmillan Canada, 1995.

INDEX

Page numbers in italics refer to photographs.